Slow Train to Guantanamo
'The book gives an insight into Cuban daily life, Caribbean
communism, the food, the beer, the colours, the smells
(good and bad) and the realities of an artificial economy
that the package deal tourists will never even glimpse. If
you have ever been to Varadero and Havana (the standard
package), read this book, then go back and see the real Cuba
whilst you still can. If you have never been to Cuba, read this
book, and if you then don't want to go to Cuba, you have
no soul, and they wouldn't want you there anyway. Go to
Cuba, but take your own toilet seat, and paper, the locals will
understand' – J. P. Hayward

1989 The Berlin Wall
'The best read is the irreverent and engaging account by
Peter Millar, who writes for the *Sunday Times* among other
papers. Fastidious readers who expect reporters to be a mere
lens on events will be shocked at the amount of personal
detail, including the sexual antics and drinking habits of his
colleagues in what now seems a Juvenalian age of dissolute
British journalism. He mentions his long-suffering wife and
children rather too often, but the result is full of insights and
on occasion delightfully funny. The author has a knack for
befriending interesting people and tracking down important
ones. He weaves their words with his clear-eyed reporting of
events into a compelling narrative about the end of the cruel
but bungling East German regime' – *The Economist*

'The most entertaining read is Peter Millar's *1989 The Berlin
Wall: My Part in its Downfall*, a witty, wry, elegiac account
of his time as a Reuters and *Sunday Times* correspondent in
Berlin throughout most of the 1980s' – *Spectator*

D0921981

'*1989 The Berlin Wall* is part autobiography, part history primer and part Fleet Street gossip column ... Millar cast aside the old chestnuts and set about reporting on the reality of life under communism. In bare Stalinist apartments, at hollow party events ... Volker the gravedigger-cum-hippie, the Stasi seductress "Helga the Honeypot", Kurtl the accordion player whose father had been killed at Stalingrad, and the petty smuggler Manne who has been separated from his parents by the Wall ... Energetic and passionate ...' – *Sunday Times*

All Gone to Look for America
'Succeeds in capturing the wonder of America that the iron horse made accessible to the world' – *The Times*

'Witty yet observant ... this book smells of train travel and will appeal to wanderlusts as well as armchair train buffs' – *Time Out*

'Fills a hole for those who love trains, microbrewery beer and the promise of big skies and wide-open spaces' – *Daily Telegraph*

The Black Madonna
'With a journalist's keen eye and ear, and a born storyteller's soul, author Millar has written a truly compelling, globe-trotting thriller. Rich in history and cultural detail, *The Black Madonna* is a page-turner of a novel that flings us into the heart of the essential conflicts of our times. Look out, Dan Brown, make way for Millar' – Jeffery Deaver

Stealing Thunder
'An intelligent thriller ... fast-paced and convincing' – Robert Harris

PETER MILLAR is an award-winning British journalist, author and translator, and has been a correspondent for Reuters, *Sunday Times* and *Sunday Telegraph*. He was named Foreign Correspondent of the Year for his reporting on the dying stages of the Cold War, his account of which – *1989: The Berlin Wall, My Part in its Downfall* – was named best read by *The Economist*.

An inveterate wanderer since his youth, Peter Millar grew up in Northern Ireland and studied at Magdalen College, Oxford. Before and during his university years, he hitchhiked and travelled by train throughout most of Europe, including behind the Iron Curtain to Moscow and Leningrad, as well as hitchhiking barefoot from Dubrovnik to Belfast after being robbed in the former Yugoslavia.

He has had his eyelashes frozen in the coldest inhabited place on Earth – Oymyakon, eastern Siberia, where temperatures reach minus 71°C, was fried at 48°C in Turkmenistan, dipped his toes in the Mississippi, the Mekong and the Nile, the Dniepr and the Danube, the Rhine and the Rhone, the Seine and the Spree. He crisscrossed the USA by rail for his book *All Gone to Look for America* and rattled down the spine of Cuba for *Slow Train to Guantanamo*.

He has lived and worked in Paris, Brussels, Berlin, Warsaw and Moscow, attended the funerals of two Soviet leaders, been blessed six times by Pope John Paul II (which would have his staunch Protestant ancestors spinning in their graves), and he has survived multiple visits to the Munich *Oktoberfest* and the enduring agony of supporting Charlton Athletic.

Peter speaks French, German, Russian and Spanish, and is married with two grown-up sons. He splits his time between Oxfordshire and London, and anywhere else that will have him.

Marrakech Express

(On and Off the Rails in the Sultans' Kingdom)

PETER MILLAR

Arcadia Books Ltd
139 Highlever Road
London W10 6PH

www.arcadiabooks.co.uk

First published by Arcadia Books 2014

A catalogue record for this book is available from the British Library.

ISBN 978-1-909807-59-4

Typeset in Minion by MacGuru Ltd
Printed and bound by CPI Group (UK) Ltd., Croydon CR0 4YY

Arcadia Books supports English PEN www.englishpen.org and
The Book Trade Charity http://btbs.org

Arcadia Books distributors are as follows:

in the UK and elsewhere in Europe:
Macmillan Distribution Ltd
Brunel Road
Houndmills
Basingstoke
Hants RG21 6XS

in the USA and Canada:
Dufour Editions
PO Box 7
Chester Springs
PA 19425

in Australia/New Zealand:
NewSouth Books
University of New South Wales
Sydney NSW 2052

Contents

Prologue

IT WAS ONE OF THOSE MOMENTS when you think the TV remote might have gone into interstellar overdrive, switching randomly at high speed between news, soap opera and light entertainment. Only in real time. In real life.

A few minutes ago my friend Abdel had poured a liberal measure of vodka and Coke into a red-and-white spotted mug and handed it to me, with the whispered afterthought, 'We can nip round the corner for a toke of *kif* in a minute.'

But right now I am standing on a street corner, wreathed in acrid smoke, a youth in a sweaty singlet next to me holding an axe and machete above my head while a 12-year-old boy on my right brandishes his fists aggressively, and in my hands is a bloodied skull, recently stripped of its flesh.

From a nearby rooftop Abdel's pretty young nieces are looking down on us, tossing their luxuriant dark hair and waving happily as they prepare to post on Facebook their photos of the ritual slaughter of the lambs.

It could only be Morocco.

I am in Larache, a beautiful, if somewhat neglected, Atlantic coast town in the former Spanish occupation zone – subtly but distinctly different from those that were occupied by the French – as an honoured guest of a local greengrocer's family at the holiest festival of the Muslim year. Toe-deep in freshly spilled goat's blood.

Once upon a time I thought the cover of the Rolling Stones' album *Goats Head Soup* freaky, but it was as nothing compared to the real thing I am now holding in my hands. Yet my reaction is not horror. Maybe just mild shock. But then the vodka helps. As does the *kif* inhaled, deeply, from a long wooden pipe with a little clay bowl, a few minutes later.

The occasion is Eid el-Adha, 'The Feast of the Sacrifice', commonly referred to – for the benefit of non-Islamic foreigners – as the 'Muslim Christmas': the big religious holiday 40 days after the end of Ramadan when families come together, go to prayers in the morning, eat well, then dress up in their finest clothes and parade around town greeting one another in a great celebration of family life. Oh, and slaughter a sheep or two. Each. The slaughtering is left to the men, of course. Specifically to the fathers. Those who do not do their grisly duty are considered in orthodox Islam to be insouciant towards the fate of their children.

Eid el-Adha commemorates one of the most important stories shared by the Jewish, Christian and Muslim religions: the moment when Abraham, ordered by God or Allah aka Yaweh (none of which is actually a name, just a statement of deity) to sacrifice his son, is released from his dreadful promise by an angel who shows him a ram caught in a thorn bush which he may sacrifice instead. The story is essentially identical in all three traditions except for a few details, such as that the Arabic name for Abraham is Ibrahim, and whereas Jews – and therefore Christians – believe that the child to be slaughtered was Isaac, the (more treasured) younger son who would survive to be patriarch of the Jews, Muslims prefer to believe that it was his (more important) first-born, Ismail (Ishmael), who would survive to become patriarch of the Arabs. But then in any story it is only natural that everybody wants their own ancestor to have had the starring role

Such religio-historical hair-splitting, literal or otherwise, is hardly much on my mind. I am in Morocco on a pilgrimage of an altogether different kind: the long-overdue fulfilment of an early-teen aspiration that would eventually lead me on a voyage of exploration through one of the most fascinating, quixotic and exotic countries in the world.

My fascination with Morocco had begun 45 years ago when a magical pop song exploded over the airwaves, which to a generation that for the first time in history could travel widely, other than as soldiers with guns in their hands, summed up a brave new world of excitement and adventure.

It was, oddly enough, written by an Englishman though, given the spirit of the age, it had to be sung by an American band. Not just American, but Californian. It was a song that conjured up an accessible vision of escapism and free love, fuelled by cannabis, a drug dreaded by a hidebound establishment built on class and capital.

Nash's catchy little ditty was a wake-up call for a new generation in a new world, a generation whose fathers had known North Africa, if at all, as drudge foot soldiers, cannon fodder in the wars of outdated empires. Now here was an Englishman, living in California, urging us to take a train from Casablanca going south, blowing smoke rings from the corner of our mouths. It was an irresistible invitation. And we knew only too well that it wasn't tobacco Mr Nash and his friends were smoking.

The magical idea of riding the Marrakech Express extolled the appeal of a city on the edge of a desert, beyond Europe, on the cusp of Africa, a city with a name that exuded exotica, escaped from the world of *One Thousand and One Nights*, a place more unimaginable than the kingdom of the Wizard of Oz, home to mystics, fortune tellers, acrobats and snake charmers. Marrakech was then, as now, the magic talisman that stood for the whole country, credited with giving it its name. For centuries it had been known to foreigners as Morocco city.

Nash said it all with his evocation of brightly coloured cotton, Berber tribesmen charming cobras in the square and buying striped jellabas to wear at home. He had written the anthem of the 'cool in a kaftan, love and peace, man' generation. He conjured up the confusion of adolescence, the optimistic rejection of the previous generation's dour views of reality, and the drug-inspired escapism of the '60s. We too wanted to sweep the cobwebs from our minds, to go out there and see the world as it was, ignoring everything that had been said to us by our elders, who were not necessarily our betters. It was a call to challenge the conventional, to see the world for ourselves.

Okay, so Graham Nash, born in Blackpool, England, in the direst depths of the Second World War, didn't get it quite right. The Moroccan livestock markets, filled with sheep, goats and poultry, might well have seemed like 'animal carpet' but if they did include ducks and chickens, Muslim Marrakech certainly didn't have any pigs. I suspect young Graham's *kif*-clouded mind was recalling some nursery carpet in his Lancashire bedroom.

But the romanticism and escapism expressed through a vision of clear Moroccan skies reflected in someone else's eyes made up for it. To those of us, a half a generation younger, only just waking up to the fact that we were not trapped by history, heredity and a bankrupt social order, it proclaimed one message, loud and clear: 'All aboard the train!'

I am embarrassed to say it took me nearly 40 years to visit Nash's illusory oasis, during which time the shrinking world made it seem suddenly no longer such a distant destination, indeed a standard resort for European tour groups. The first time I visited was with my wife, very much as a tourist, in search of exoticism and sun, and found both in good measure; we had taken in the quixotic delights of Marrakech, seen the sun set over the Atlas and made a trip to the blue-and-white 'windy city' of Essaouira on the Atlantic coast. But had we really even scratched the skin of the real Morocco? In the meantime I had made friends with Moroccans living in London who enthused about their homeland, though not without reservations. You should go elsewhere, they said, get to know the place, travel the way the ordinary people do.

What made me decide that it was time to pack my bags for Marrakech and beyond once again, with a much greater aim in mind than a few days in the sun, was an invitation from Abdel to join his family for one of the greatest festivals of the Islamic year, and the sudden realisation that if I did not go now, it might all, literally, go up in a puff of smoke. And not the sort that Graham Nash could blow smoke rings with.

In 2011 we saw what was almost universally described as the 'Arab Spring', an absurd example of journalists applying a catchphrase from another time and place to a modern event as a form of shorthand to avoid actually having to think about, let alone describe, what is actually going down. The term 'Spring' in this sense goes back to the 1968 'Prague Spring' when Soviet tanks brought a brutal end to the liberalising of communist rule under Alexander Dubcek in what was the capital of the now long-dissolved state of Czechoslovakia. Partly because of the time of year – it actually lasted from January until the end of August – some journo had, in an excess of enthusiasm over Realpolitik, labelled this abortive, would-be 1989, the 'Prague Spring'.

Ever since, any overnight shift in the set social order in a country presumed repressive has been labelled a 'Spring', even if it occurs midsummer or in the depths of winter, and even if, as sadly happened in the original case and in most since, it ends bloodily with little or no improvement. That ended up being what happened in nearly all the Arab countries where the 'Spring' contagion spread, from Tunisia where it began, and has remained the most successful, to Libya where following less than measured Western intervention, dictatorship was replaced with bloody anarchy, to Egypt where the revolution swallowed itself, brutally; twice. From Bahrain where repression was swift and brutal to the Gulf States and Saudi Arabia where little was reported or whatever did happen was suddenly and ruthlessly suppressed to little or no complaint from the rest of the Western world, and eventually to Syria, where 'Spring' became the prelude to a bloody fratricidal civil war.

In Morocco, almost alone, spring never sprung.

As a journalist who has lived under repressive communism in the Soviet Union, Poland and East Germany through the pivotal years leading up to the end of the Cold War, and since travelled extensively in the Cuba of the Castros, I have always wondered what makes a society tip over the edge, or more precisely, what stops it doing so: what makes someone balanced on a clothesline over a chasm become a tightrope-walker rather than an accident waiting to happen?

Amidst the chaos and repression that have been the hallmark of the Arab world over recent years, Morocco appeared to offer a 'third way'. Amidst the so-called 'clash of cultures', which has appeared as if from nowhere to replace the Cold War, to take us back to the Middle Ages when Muslims and Christians were at each other's throats, Morocco, superficially at least, seemed to have kept at least one foot in Graham Nash's idyllic late 1960s. I had to find out if it was true, and if it could last.

My visit to Larache for the festival of Eid introduced me to Morocco up close, at a personal level, and made me hungry to see and hear more of the country that has played a pivotal role in the history of Islam and its cross-cultural influences on Europe from the days when what we now call Spain was a province of the Islamic caliphate, run by Moroccan sultans, up to and beyond the days when Morocco was a colonial possession divided between France and Spain.

All aboard the train!

1

The Not Quite Silent Lambs

SOME MORNINGS you just wake up feeling like an idiot, some mornings you wake up and realise you really are an idiot. Smartphones may have changed the world but they aren't that clever in the hands of stupid people. That's what I felt at 8.30 in the morning when I woke up to realise that my flight to Morocco would be taking off from Heathrow airport in approximately 30 minutes. Never mind check-in time, I can't even get to Heathrow in less than an hour at best (I don't think anybody who doesn't live right next to a runway can, and even then I wouldn't bet on it).

I had set the alarm perfectly for 6.00 on my iPhone, set it to ring again five and then 15 minutes later. But I hadn't noticed I'd set it on silent. There was nothing to do but answer the panicky text message from my friend Abdelillah, which had also arrived silently of course, to tell him to go ahead without me: I would spend the next hour or two trying to find an alternative flight. It is only two days before the highpoint of Eid el-Adha, the most important festival in the Muslim year, the 'greater Eid', coming some 40 days after the 'lesser Eid', known as Eid al-Fitr, which marks the end of the holy, fasting month of Ramadan. For a non-Muslim to be invited into a Moroccan home to share it, is a rare privilege. Abdel was going home to celebrate Eid el-Adha with his family for the first time in years, but unless I found an alternative flight

I would not be with him. And that was an experience I was determined not to miss.

Nearly 14 hours later, I found myself touching down at Casablanca, nearly 300 kilometres south of where I wanted to be, delighted to find Abdelillah, who had borrowed a car and driven like a maniac (which he usually does in any case), waiting to greet me, along with his brother and niece, and all set to turn around and drive back again. As a result it was nearly 2 a.m. when we arrived in Larache – which is a lot easier to get to if you fly to Tangier – to find it unsurprisingly quiet and sleepy, though with still a few cafés open. I suppose if you drink as much tea and coffee as some Moroccans do, it never feels like time to close the shop.

His sister-in-law was not only waiting up for us, she was getting ready to cook. It's not done, Abdel explained, not to feed a guest when he enters your home for the first time. Within minutes I have been given a bowl of water to wash my hands, a cloth to dry them and we are all sitting down ready to tuck into freshly fried fish. Meanwhile, his niece Marwa has nipped upstairs to change out of her street wear and in so doing she has been somewhat transformed: from fashionable but well covered up in quilted jacket, long skirt, headscarf and sunglasses – rather Jackie O, I thought at the time – into a lustrous, dark-haired vision in a diaphanous kaftan, rather more revealing than most European women in their twenties would wear if an unknown friend of their uncle popped in. The other side of the Islamic dress code is that, however much you cover up in the street, to avoid the attention of unfamiliar men, any man admitted into your father's house is automatically part of the family.

Abdel's father, Yusuf, the patriarch of the family and a senior figure in town, now in his late seventies, has wisely retired to bed. He has been out buying a goat and a sheep with Aziz, his other son, a beaming, bespectacled man with a short grey beard that makes him look every bit the university lecturer. Both animals are currently housed, I am some-what surprised to find, on the roof. Yusuf's house is built in the classic Moroccan tradition, one layer above another. The ground floor dates back some 50 years to when he was a young man; he acquired the land and built a simple home for himself and his wife, now long deceased. A black-and-white photograph of her hangs on the wall: a serious, dark-eyed woman in a headscarf, with that straightforward unsmiling pose adopted by people back in the days when it was vital not to move when being photographed.

The first floor was added on for Aziz and his wife and their two daughters, then another floor above that, and finally a terrace area rising to the rooftop where the two animals are now happily munching on straw. Across the city I can hear bleating. There is scarcely a rooftop that does not have a sheep or goat on it, and the remainder will be filled by the end of tomorrow as the frantic last-minute dash to the markets begins. 'People are arriving from all over, there are special trains and buses running,' Abdel tells me. 'You will see.'

✳

I am staying in some comfort in a separate house owned by the family that is being done up for letting or sale, so it is mid-morning when I turn up at the family home. Today's chore is that last-minute shopping for the festival itself, which is tomorrow – idiosyncratically, since it is celebrated today in every other Muslim country in the world. But because the King of Morocco, Commander of the Faithful, rather sensibly, it seems to me, decrees that the new lunar month is decided based on local (Rabat) phases of the moon, rather than those observed in Mecca more than a thousand miles to the East, here the festivals are celebrated one day later. Abdel's sister-in-law is in the kitchen already making *brouates,* little pastry delicacies stuffed with cheese and coated in honey.

I nip up to the flat roof to see the two star participants of the coming festival: a woolly, plump sheep and a nervous, uncertain-looking brown goat. I have no anthropomorphic delusions about the thoughts or emotions of animals, but nor do I believe they are automatons, and if the sheep seems to have got used to the situation and is munching contentedly on the bag of feed laid out for him, the goat is definitely not as happy, possibly because he has never been on a rooftop before, though realistically I doubt either are still aware of that – maybe it's because he just doesn't get on with the sheep. At least I am fairly certain that it is only me who has noticed, and given much thought to the fact that the walls which surround the roof, the floor, and that of the terrace below, where the actual business is to take place, are painted in a water-proof red up to a height of several inches.

On the rooftops all around, the same height or lower, depending on the wealth of the families or the number of generations, sheep or goats wander within the limits of their tether seeking shade from the dry, baking heat, being petted, cuddled or stroked by small children whose fathers, within the next 24 hours, will publicly slit the animal's throat. I can only wonder how much they know. Yet maybe this is the natural way. These animals are not family pets, after all, they have been bought and brought into the home for a purpose, religious and domestic: they are all going to be eaten in the end.

The family is gradually coming to life and I realise that in Larache, at least, the rhythm of the day is more Spanish in style. Breakfast is largely an individual matter for whoever has to be up and out, but there is a standard cold fruits or salad and cold cuts at around 10.30 to 11, while the main meal of the day is taken at around 3 p.m. The evening meal, often little more than a savoury snack, is eaten late, between 10 in the evening and midnight, the family having been sustained in between by a sort of 'high tea' – mint tea and biscuits or sweet pastries – at around 6.30 to 7.

Today is not as relaxed as it might be. Eid el-Adha is officially a four-day festival, but the highlight is tomorrow, when
the 'sacrifice' is made. If you compare it, as Muslims do, to
our 'festive season', then tomorrow is Christmas Day. All
shops will be closed, everyone at home. So whatever we need,
we must buy today.

Larache is a pleasant but unmistakably provincial town,
radically different from Tangier just up the road. Some of
this is due to its Spanish heritage: whereas the French usually
absorbed, or partly blended in with their native fellow citizens in their colonies – many French men took local wives
– the Spanish ruled as conquerors, seeing their colonial territories as 'possessions' (much as the British did in Africa).
The second language here, half a century after the end of
colonialism, is not French but Spanish, even though the latter
has no official status. The main square is officially Place de la
Libération, but the locals still call it Plaza de España. There
is a relaxed, laid-back feel to the place, an everybody-knows-
everybody feel, though in fact it is now a substantial town of
some 110,000 people. The background colours are the same
as those in every Moroccan seaside town, blue and white,
though any pretence at picturesqueness is rather ruined by
the amount of rubbish strewn on the streets. Abdel is embarrassed by it, but shrugs: 'It's the way people are – you have to
educate them.' It is easy to sneer, but I remember the days, 40
years or so ago, when British streets were almost as bad. It has
taken a generation, and a policy of zero tolerance to achieve
the litter-free city centres we have in most parts of Britain
today.

Our shopping list is not as full as some, who have left it to
the last minute to acquire their animal, and are now hastily
– often in near panic – dashing to the impromptu livestock
market set up on the outskirts of town, where farmers have
brought in the last of their offerings. It is a bit like dashing
out for a turkey on Christmas Eve, or it would be if you were

looking only for live turkeys. First we pass by the fish market, an elegant colonnade of Arabesque arches where the produce, straight from the boats, is flapping on the marble surfaces. But the fishermen are not happy. 'The Japanese take too much,' Abdel tells me. 'Nearly 90 per cent of the tuna is flash frozen and flown straight to Tokyo.' We buy a few dozen fresh sardines for just a few dirhams, less than you would pay for a couple at a British fishmonger's.

Abdel, the local boy made good in Europe, has palms to press and anecdotes to swap with old friends of his own and the family. Almost everyone we pass waves to him, and I get a few stories: 'She was a prostitute,' he tells me of one extremely well-to-do looking lady, 'but her best customer was a Spaniard who owned a bar here and left it to her. Now she's worth a fortune. Very nice lady.'

We stop for a coffee just across the road from the fish market and are soon accosted by a toothless, grinning elderly bloke, balding with a beard, who greets Abdel like a long-lost son, and when I am introduced starts talking to me rapidly and enthusiastically. I immediately want to apologise for my lack of Arabic, when it occurs to me that he might be speaking heavily accented Spanish and I pay a bit more attention, until suddenly, like a thunderbolt, I realise what language he is speaking: English. And not bad, Arabic-accented English either, but fluent, perfect English – although perhaps not the variety that would pass in the more traditional language school and certainly not in the boudoirs of Belgravia. He is speaking straight, slang-laden, East End English; what the rest of the world calls 'cockney'. Believe me, when it comes to languages, context can be everything.

Now that the penny has dropped I realise that what he is telling me, one eye glinting conspiratorially, is: 'See, like, I spent a lot o' time in Tower 'Amlets, 'Ackney and down the Mile End Road, an' all. Minicabs and wotnot. Was a grand ol' time that was. Oh yeah, I could tell you some stories.' But then he puts on a more serious face, self-deprecating, and adds, 'Mind you, thing is, I was a bad boy, weren't I, back in them days.' He fingers his beard musingly as if regretting a mis-spent past. 'Got myself deported in the end, di'n I? Can't go back, never, can I? One butcher's at me passport – if I still had one – and I'd be slung out on me ear. Still, grand old days, eh?'

I nod, for the sake of it, and because whatever he was – and I almost dread to think – he seems a harmless enough old boy now. Still, I make a mental note not to get on his wrong side.

We move on, this time to pay a visit to an old friend of Abdel's, an artist who lives in a beautifully renovated old house in the centre of town. You can tell he is an artist because at nearly midday we get him out of bed. Art in an Islamic country is an interesting concept, not least because of the religious ban on depicting any living form, though in the modernist and post-modernist artistic culture, that is less of a problem. I have often wondered whether the imams would have objected to some of Picasso's more abstract cubist portraits: how realistic does a depiction have to be before it breaks the prophets' strictures? I can only imagine what they might think of Tracy Emin's bed.

In any case, the issue has never directly troubled Hamid, whose chosen fields are hardly affected. His passion is min-iature furniture, perfect tiny copies of chairs, couches and tables, all crafted as direct copies of the life-size originals, except reduced to Barbie dimensions. If there was a big market in Morocco for bespoke doll's house accoutrements, he would need a factory. As it is, he sells them individually, as one-offs, to collectors, which is why, now retired from his job in the orange export industry, he needs to supplement his income by giving French lessons. Indeed, he is the one person I have come across in Larache whose second language is French, though even he confesses that there is not much local demand and his is getting rusty.

His other artistic delight is that more traditional one for Muslims: calligraphy. The swirling, flowing form of Arabic writing has always lent itself to elaborate weaving into patterns that look abstract to the uninitiated, but to the Arabist are the perfect merger of artistic licence and the word of God. Except that Hamid is an atheist. He has not the slightest qualms about depicting living beings, it is just that – possessing that more rare quality in an artist; he is also a realist – there is no market for it. But he manifests his beliefs – or lack of faith – in refusing to use excerpts from the Koran, preferring instead the verse of old Arabic poets.

He may well be the only person in Larache – 'Not the only one,' he intervenes, 'but certainly one of very few' – who is completely ignoring Eid el-Adha tomorrow. Nonetheless, we have brought him a present, duty-free from England: a bottle of cask-strength whisky. He licks his lips appreciatively and asks his wife, an elegant woman in her forties who tuts slightly at the demand, primarily because her husband has only just got out of bed, to bring us some whisky tumblers. Abdel does not drink and it is a little early for me, but I hate to see a man drink alone so I join him in a finger's tot. He has two fingers.

The drink turns his attention to the 'Arab Spring' towards which he has an absolute, 'I told you so' attitude. 'Nobody believes in it, at least nobody with any sense. As for this country, we have corruption – look at the mess this city is in, the mayor has let the place go to the dogs – but sometimes you have to tolerate what you have, in case what replaces it is worse.' He shrugs, resignedly, but adds, 'Life in Morocco is okay.' He quietly approves of the regime's tolerant attitude to *kif*: 'There is no money being made in it. It is just something we have always had. It is only when it gets beyond the borders that people make money. Here, at home, everybody turns a blind eye. Sometimes that is for the best.' I ask him what he will do tomorrow when everyone else is rushing to the mosque and then home to perform the sacrifice. 'Stay in,' he says and pats the bottle of whisky.

As we leave, we pass through a square that has, for the run-up to Eid, become an extension of the town's small souk. Like a market-town square in Europe being filled on Christmas Eve with people looking for replacements for the broken Christmas tree lights, buying last-minute presents or looking for turkey-sized oven dishes and silver foil, here are countless knives and hacksaws. There are even refrigerators and freezers being unloaded from a lorry. 'From tomorrow night,' Abdel explains, 'Everyone will have so much meat!'

Down at the impromptu livestock market just north of town by the River Loukos, which meanders into the port, the scene is hectic. Everywhere there are vans, cars with trailers, sheep in woolly clumps almost indistinguishable as separate animals and all over people haggling, bargaining and arguing over prices. 'It is a good day to buy and sell, if you are tough enough,' Abdel laughs. Aziz explains, 'Those who do not already have an animal to slaughter are desperate, afraid that they will not get one and it will bring bad luck on their children, so maybe they will pay more than they would normally, but on the other hand, after tomorrow the price of sheep will slump, because everyone has an entire carcass in the freezer, enough to last them weeks, and the farmers will have nobody to sell to. It is a good day, if you know how to strike a good bargain.'

I can see the challenge, but I can also see how much less stressful it would be to buy a few days ahead. There is also obviously some risk involved, other than financial, in waiting to the last minute. 'This is a scrawny sheep,' Aziz says, 'not good, not much meat,' feeling through the wool of what on first glance had looked to me to be a perfectly acceptable animal. Its owner gestures with a stick for him to go away and leave him alone. It would appear to be the case that today is the best day to sell a substandard animal that would not go down well with a butcher, to someone who is more concerned with fulfilling his religious duties than filling his freezer.

A sudden question occurs to me. 'What do they do in the big cities, in places like Casablanca, where many people live in apartments?' 'Some do not do the sacrifice,' Aziz says. 'Some go home to their families, in small towns or in the country. Some take the sheep up in the lift and kill it in the bath.' Option number three is one I can only boggle at. 'Seriously?' I ask. He shrugs. But of course. What else?

Most of the animals have been brought in on lorries and are displayed in pens. A few of the poorer farmers have only a couple of sheep to sell. The buyers go round them avidly, checking ears and teeth. Two lads in their late teens approach us thinking we are buying, and tell us that theirs are, 'the best, the very best, from our farm on the slopes of Jebel Musa', the great mountain north of here, believed to be, with Gibraltar, one of the Pillars of Hercules.

There is a lot in common with the sort of livestock markets that used to flourish on the outskirts of every English market town, but which, with the ravages of foot and mouth disease and 'economies of scale', have now become a rarity. The main difference here is that the customers are generally looking for a single or at most two animals. There are lots of bright sparks doing the delivery trade too: young men, barely out of their teens, if that, with motorcycle-trucks, a bike with a trailer attached, a makeshift form of transport that these street-wise young Moroccans see the irony in. 'Jaguar', proclaims the logo stencilled, in perfect imitation of the luxury car brand, on the side of one; another says 'Ferrari'; variations include the relatively mundane 'SKYGO', 'Top Magic', or, in an attempt to blend two obsessions, 'Ronaldo Motorcycle'. Into these trailers, bleating sheep are herded – none of them can take more than two at most – while the driver revs up, and prepares to deliver them to the purchaser, a bizarre Wallace and Gromit cavalcade of motorcycle and worried woolly sidecar passengers roaring back and forth to the town.

Driving back, Abdel points out the local pub, unadvertised behind a wooden fence. It occurs to me that with all this bloodshed I am about to witness tomorrow, I might need a drink or two. 'Oh,' he suddenly says, 'that could be a problem.'

'It could?' I query. Surely just a question of nipping in and buying a bottle of something to have on hand?

'Er, the thing is, Eid has officially already started and that means all bars and shops selling alcohol are now closed for four days.'

This is the nearest you can come to giving an Irishman a heart attack: a day of ritual slaughter, and abstemiousness for the next two!

'Wait a minute, I have maybe an idea,' he says.

Ten minutes later we are heading up a track on the outskirts of town that suddenly, unexpectedly, turns into a metalled road, with, at the end of it, what looks like a sentry box and a barrier. It strikes me that a Moroccan army base on the eve of Eid is not going to be the best place to buy a beer or two, but Adel is grinning.

'Give me your press card,' he says.

I hand it over; he summons the guard and gives him a lengthy spiel in Arabic. The guard looks at me, smiles, touches his cap and raises the barrier.

'What was that all about?' I can only ask in puzzlement.

'You'll see,' he replies, accelerating up a gently winding tarmacked road between manicured lawns towards a slick, modern building, which, it finally dawns on me when I notice that the beautifully kept grass has little flags scattered here and there, is a golf course clubhouse.

'This place is brand new, not really opened yet, except for residents.'

'Residents? On a golf course?'

'Sure.' He points to several gleaming white one- and two-storey buildings dotted on the edges of what I now realise is the course.

'They build villas for rich people, from Casa or Rabat. And foreigners. Frenchmen. I told him you were a property journalist and wanted a tour and an interview with the manager.'

'You what?'

'Hey, never mind, it will be nice. I always wanted to see inside one of these things. And maybe the manager, he will get you something to drink for tomorrow!'

There is in the world of foreign correspondents a generic character known as the 'fixer', a local who knows how things work and can cut corners. If the chef lark ever goes belly-up, Abdel has a ready-made profession waiting for him.

By the time we reach the clubhouse, the duty manager is waiting for us, the big boss not being on site today, brushing his hair and adjusting his tie; he greets us in the immaculate, unaccented French that is the language of Morocco's business class.

'It would have been so much better if you had made an appointment,' he gushes. 'We could have given you the grand tour.' Well, yes, but then half an hour ago I had no idea any of this existed, and there is the minor fact that I am not a property journalist. I decide it might be better not to mention any of that, though.

The whole development is much more than just the golf course, he explains. They have taken a whole chunk of coastline with a secluded beach, reached by a private path; we traipse across the greens to a cliff edge to take a look down. A Hyatt Regency hotel is under construction, a Hilton and up to five others are planned and the whole thing is labelled Port Lixus, after an ancient city on the site. He proudly shows us around one of the villas, which is luxuriously appointed indeed, complete with upstairs terrace with stupendous view over the Atlantic and a pool for those too grand to walk down the steps to the private beach.

'Several are already privately owned,' the duty manager tells us. 'And several are available for short rental.'

We return to the clubhouse, where, I am disappointed to note, the bar is closed. 'It is Eid,' the duty manager explains apologetically as if he is not responsible for the customs of the locals.

'Will it be the same when it is all fully opened?' I ask with the sceptical look of an alcoholic atheist on my face.

He does that wonderful 'pouf!' thing that, contrary to what most foreigners think, is not something to do with actually being French, but like the right hand waved limply to indicate a hopeless case, an essential part of the language.

Deciding that there is no point in leaving without at least making an attempt to get what we really came for, I take him to one side, and say, I would really, really like to at least get an idea of what their wine list would be like. He tuts for a moment, then gives me a 'man-of-the-world' nod and opens a drawer and hands me two bottles of Morocco's top Côteaux de l'Atlas, a classic Bordeaux-style red. At least he allows me to pay him for it.

But then it has been a fair transaction all round. Sort of, I think. In the meantime, Abdel, never one to miss a trick, has negotiated a nice price for a rental the following summer to bring his wife and son from England, and invite the family from Larache to experience a bit of European luxury. Job done.

As we drive down the hill I notice a load of old stones and what look like remnants of a couple of ancient columns on the facing slope.

'Oh, that's Lixus,' Abdel enlightens me. 'Never been there.'

'Maybe you should.'

We stop the car and spend the next half hour with a local guide who literally materialised out of nowhere, but for twenty dirhams was good value: we learned that this barely excavated pile of ruins was one of the oldest cities in North Africa, founded around 1200 BC by Phoenician traders from what is now the Lebanon, then conquered by their rivals, the Carthaginians, before becoming part of the Roman Empire after the defeat of Hannibal.

The guide is at pains to point out what are believed to have been fish storage pens, and stone beds where sea salt was dried, just as it is today. He points out that although the site today sits a couple of kilometres inland, the marshes and swamps below (many of which are being drained by the Port Lixus project) are where once the sea came in, making Lixus a major fishing port in antiquity. Barely 20 per cent of the site has been excavated. Our local lad tells us the ancient Greeks believed Lixus to be the site of the Garden of the Hesperides where Hercules collected the famed 'golden apples'. Abdel laughs and says, 'Maybe they were just tangerines?'

He's joking, of course, but it makes me wonder: we think today that all fruits are global, yet we know it's a recent phenomenon. What if indeed some 3,000 years ago some traveller from 'the ends of the earth' brought to Athens or Sparta the small sweet round fruits that grow prolifically in the dark earth around Tangiers?

✳

The morning of Eid itself I have set the alarm on my iPhone for 7.30 a.m. And this time I haven't made the mistake of setting it on 'silent'. I dress quickly, like almost every other adult male in Larache this morning, and head for the mosque. It is a short, brisk walk along the seafront to a charming little mosque at the southern end of town. Already the muezzin's call to prayer is resounding from the loudspeaker at the top of the minaret: *Allahu Akbar,* God is great. In front of me, men in long white kaftans put a spring in their step as he follows up with 'hasten to prayer, hasten to success'. Disconcertingly he is echoed by the bleating of the sheep on a thousand rooftops, and the occasional morning cry of a rooster.

Pale yellow sunlight bounces off the dusty streets as the amplified call comes to a sudden halt and the last few white-clad stragglers shrug off their sandals on the steps of the mosque and dash inside. More are still arriving though and as the communal cry of *Allahu Akbar* goes up inside the mosque there are now believers queuing at the door or simply kneeling on the steps outside. There is another entrance to a separate area for women, and I notice the woman Abdel had pointed out, the former prostitute who now owns half the high street, nip in. Clearly Allah's mercy and goodness know no bounds. And she, indeed, has hastened to success. I hear little of the imam intoning prayers within. It is a short ceremony, Abdel has told me in advance; no sermon, just a few ritual prayers. Everybody wants to get home to get on with the 'business' of the day.

As Hamid had predicted, not everyone in Larache is devout. A lad in his twenties wearing a Nike Dutch football kit, but nonetheless clearly local, strolls past nonchalantly, paying little attention. But already, within five minutes of the first prayer beginning, there is something of an exodus taking place, as the first worshippers begin to stream out, making space for latecomers. There is also, to my surprise, something of a demonstration kicking off on the pavement outside. Not religious or political as such, however, but some dozen or so disabled people, in wheelchairs or on crutches, shouting what one of them translates from Arabic into Spanish for me, 'Step-free access for all'. The rights of the disabled have a long way to go in Morocco, even at the mosque. Firmly a couple of policemen begin to move them along. I step forward to take a photo, but someone in the mainstream crowd shouts at me. It is not good to give an impression of anything but harmony on Eid.

By now, however, a smiling Abdel and his brother and father have come out and grabbed me by the arm to take me back to the house. He is wearing the yellow-trimmed kaftan his father bought in Mecca, a symbol of having performed the haj, the pilgrimage to Mecca that every Muslim is required to make if they can afford it.

'One of these days,' says Abdel, who is something of a 'born-again' Muslim, having been a 'bit of a lad' and a heavy boozer in his youth, 'I got to do it, but nowadays there are so many Muslims in the world, there's a lottery, you have to apply. Not everyone can go. And then it's so expensive. Costs something like £5,000 and that's if you sleep in a tent.' He's not exactly a fan of the super-rich Saudis who control what has become in his eyes a haj industry.

All the way back to the house, we are nodded at and greeted with the words, '*Salaam, eid-mubarak*,' which comes as a surprise to me, the last word being familiar only as the name of the deposed Egyptian dictator. 'It's like in England on Christmas Day,' Abdel says, 'everybody going to church wishing each other "happy Christmas".'

'Er, but what about the "Mubarak" bit?'

He doesn't seem to get it at first, and then laughs, and says, 'Oh, it means "holy", "blessed", something like that, nothing to do with that guy; it's just what people say to one another at Eid.' I later do some research and discover that it is a relatively common name too, though particularly a first name, when is often shortened to just 'Barack'. Now there's something I didn't know.

Back at the house we settle round a traditional breakfast of mint tea, homemade flatbread (*rhgif*) and pancakes called *msemmen* with fig jam and honey, all of us clustered around the television. I am only mildly surprised to find that Moroccan television on the morning of Eid is indeed rather similar to British television on Christmas morning: rubbish.

It is a sofa-based chat-cum-breakfast show from Casablanca, hosted by a group of women festively dressed in spectacular silk and satin kaftans, verdant green, sky blue, sunburst gold. I am making up the epithets; I am sure the designers were more original, but the main thing about them is that they are very, very, very shiny and bright, fairly figure-hugging and while only one of the three is sporting a headscarf, all three are absolutely dripping in bling: necklaces, bangles, bracelets, belts of gold coins, the kaftans themselves embroidered with sequins and glittering multicoloured jewels. Most of the discussion is about fashion: eyelash extension tips, make-up advice, but there is also a short cookery section about making lamb confit (likely to be much imitated over the next few days), a few pop video clips and a long sequence in which our glitzy sofa queens watch and comment on handsome young men in Lycra doing push-ups in the studio. Abdel's sister-in-law tuts and mutes 'Casablanca!'

Meanwhile, the men are already setting to. Abdel and Aziz have pulled their kaftans over their heads to reveal – including what a nifty piece of kit a kaftan can be – that underneath they are wearing shorts and T-shirts. The leather sandals are exchanged for rubber Crocs – Abdel hands me a pair of white ones – and we climb to the roof where the stars of the show are waiting for us. I search their eyes, their body language, to see if there are any signs of apprehension. But they just look like a sheep and a goat. The apprehension is all mine. But then that is because I can see over the wall of the rooftop to those around us, and across the road, one carcass is being skinned.

Old Yusuf has climbed up to the roof now, wearing flip-flops with his trousers only slightly rolled up, still with his woolly hat on, though it must be 28C at least. The goat is led down first, from the upper roof to the terrace below. It struggles a bit initially, not, of course, because it has any idea what is going on, but because it is a goat, and goats don't like going anywhere, least of all down stairs, even though they might be relatively good at them. Eventually it is bundled down and led into the shady corner, where, while it is just getting used to this new, pleasantly cooler place to stand, blissfully unaware that it is facing Mecca, old Yusuf comes over, sits down beside it for a moment and strokes it. Abdel comes over to stand beside him, then abruptly turns the goat upside down, puts one foot on its head to steady it, as his father draws an almost impossibly sharp knife across its throat in the space of a second. There is not a sound from the goat (those who oppose halal practice will tell you this is because its windpipe has been cut), just a mildly startled look on its face, which, to be fair, appeared the moment it was turned upside down, and a strong, fast spurt of blood.

I do not know how long it took. But I am sure – well, almost sure – that it felt longer to me than it did to the goat. Philosophers have long speculated about whether or not all moments last the same length of time to those who experience time, and whether anyone can possible estimate the length of a moment that ends in extinction. But it did not seem like a long time to me. In hindsight, which begins immediately afterwards, it seemed ... I struggle for a word ... momentary. I doubt if 10 seconds expired before the animal was dead, and maybe not even that. But it did not strike me as cruel in any way. Possibly – and I know this is a minefield I am attempting to tiptoe across – even kind. I have never been inside a modern non-halal abattoir, but I am not sure that the process of hanging an animal upside down and stunning it would strike me as any better. There is a moral cost in eating meat, and if you don't want to pay it, you shouldn't take the benefit.

I know one thing for sure, however; there are few adults or children in Morocco who would echo the naivety played up in a British television advert some years ago where a little girl at breakfast says, 'Mummy, where does bacon come from?' and quick as a flash her brother replies, 'It's dead pigs' bottoms. I'll have yours.'

There may be no pigs in Morocco, but as I look over the wall to the roof of the house next door, I see a little girl in a purple kaftan, not much older than the one in that advert, maybe eight or nine, sitting on the wall watching her father skin the sheep that only yesterday she was petting. She knows where her lamb chops come from.

Aziz has now finished the process of severing the head and hanging the carcass upside down from a clothesline, and is using a fine, sharp blade to pierce the skin and begin the process of removing the fleece. Abdel appears at my side with a spotted mug and hands it to me. 'You might need this,' he says.

I glance down questioningly.

'Coke,' he says, with a knowing nod.

'I get the general drift and take a sip, which soon turns into a gulp of half a pint of Coca-Cola, liberally laced with vodka. For the first time, I realise I have been trembling. Not with horror, not with terror, not with disgust, but with pure adrenalin. I have been a foreign correspondent for a quarter of a century, lived through revolutions and counter-revolutions, small wars (at a safe distance), but I have never seen close-up the carnage humans wreak on one another, I am relieved to say. In fact, I am only just realising that I have never seen death so close up that the blood spurted on my feet. And I didn't notice. I look down at the red liquid splashed on my white Crocs and oozing between my toes. Marwa appears, dressed in long tartan shorts and a pink jumper, gives me a curious smile and uses a hose to wash my feet. It is the women's job to 'scrub the decks' as it were, washing the blood down the drains. On the rooftop next door the little nine-year-old is happily doing the same thing.

I take another swig of the 'Coke' to give me Dutch courage and bend down to lift the severed head and 'pose' for a photograph. Mick Jagger would have done the same (wouldn't he?) – on *Goats Head Soup*.

By now, with the speed and efficiency of a professional butcher, Aziz has removed almost the entire fleece, with a little help from the less practised Abdel who gets a word of reproof from his father for leaving a tiny piece of meat attached. Already the animal, that less than half an hour ago was standing on the roof, looks like something you would pay no attention to in an English butcher's shop, unless, of course, you looked hard enough to notice the pendulous oblongs of the testicles. Aziz is about to remove these but only after he has first cut out the offal, the liver, heart and kidneys, which will provide today's meal. Aya is pulling out the tripe, white and glistening in the sun, while removing the colon with its obvious contents (though the fact that there are any contents is an indicator of how little the goat was aware of its fate) into a plastic bag, quickly sealed up for disposal. The rest of the animal must be hung until the muscle texture has relaxed to make it tender enough to eat. They wrap it tightly in cloth, before bringing it into the relative cool of the house.

Then it is the turn of the second animal: one for each father. Abdel is granted exemption because his wife is English and his child is in England (and may or may not be a Muslim, I have no idea and care little), and in any case he has taken part, done his bit in the family's duty. I go up to the roof and see the sheep, backed defensively against the far wall. Islam insists that one animal should never see another animal being killed. Contrary to what many opponents of halal (and kosher) slaughter might say, there is no cruelty intended, quite the contrary. But that said, this sheep definitely knows by now that this is not going to be a good day. It is struggling, trying to break free of its tether. No matter what the awareness of animal species, it is impossible not to notice that the air over Larache reeks of blood and the smoke from barbecues already being erected on the streets.

For a split second – and no more – the ghost of an animal rights activist infests me, and I feel an urge to seize the slaughterer's knife, dash over to the sheep and cut his leash, and send him gambling away, leaping across the rooftops to some grassy meadow in the sky, just as it would happen in a Disney movie (one I fervently hope they never make). But even the realist action movie, where he and I charge downstairs, slashing and butting our way out on to the streets, would actually be a grotesquerie from a black comedy. And in any case, I would happily eat him later. Apprehensive for sure, the sheep is led down to the terrace below, thanks to Marwa, devoid of blood or any visible sign that his erstwhile lodging companion met his end here. A few minutes later and the sheep too is little more than lifeless eyes on a skull on the red floor, a carcass in a butcher's shop and a fleece that would make a nice rug.

Not yet though. The girls, Marwa and Aya, are still taking photographs with their smartphones to post on Facebook. Then Abdel and I take the fleeces upstairs to the rooftop overlooking the street and hurl them over the edge. It is another tradition of Eid, one that includes charity. Down below two young lads in their teens are guiding a donkey cart through the streets, gathering and collecting fleeces in their hundreds. Later they will take them down to the sea and the lads will cast them into the salt water to cure, after which they will be taken home, washed and sold on to the tourist shops in Tangier, or to the export trade. You may own one.

Abdel and I are now down on the street where the teenagers have boiled up water in huge pots and are boiling the sheep's heads to remove the flesh for stewing meat, and lighting barbecues to cook offal. A cheery lad in an Arsenal shirt with a machete and an axe asks me which English football team I support. It's not something I am usually willing to admit to the supporter of another team who happens to have an axe and a machete in his hand, but when I tell him Charlton Athletic, he is not so much relieved as dismissive. He has never heard of them. His younger mate comes up and Abdel sees a photo opportunity, taking the mug of 'Coke' from my hands, which have been clutching it now for nearly half an hour, and replacing it with one of the lads' flesh-stripped skulls. The smoke billows up around us (this is where you came in), and

I find myself with an odd grin on my face. That the camera never lies is a long-discredited maxim, but out of context this would be so easy to misconstrue.

Nor would it be helped by the lad from a rival group of head boilers on the other side of the street who is keen that I should take his photograph too: in a Real Madrid Ronaldo shirt, but with a Palestinian-style keffiyeh wrapped over his head and a pair of fake black Ray-Ban sunglasses covering his eyes, also wielding a machete, though all he has been using it for is to chop wood for the barbecue fire. All of a sudden a competition begins between the two sets of lads as they wave their knives, hacking at the wood and severed skulls and chanting *Allahu Akbar*, almost as if it were rival sets of fans at a football match striving to see who could make the most noise. It is all in good spirit, without the slightest trace of animosity, but for a Western European wimp, all this familiarity with sharp-bladed weapons, skulls, blood and entrails, be they only animal, is a bit much. And it does make me wonder for more than a second whether if a whole society is exposed to this, it makes it easier when the blood is not just animal? How far from this to what we have seen in Syria and Libya? The answer, I know, is a million miles; everything Morocco stands for is opposed to what has happened there. But it has made me think, nonetheless.

Happily Abdel is on hand with a ready remedy for too much thinking. He leads me round the corner to where an 'old school friend' of his is leaning in an alleyway with a traditional long straight wooden two-part pipe in his hand with the equally traditional tiny clay bowl attached to one end. *Kif*, the Moroccan word, so traditional it has become a euphemism for hash, cannabis, the stuff that Moroccans – especially those who took seriously the Koran's strictures against alcohol – have been smoking for centuries. Once it grew wild in the foothills of the Rif Mountains, and still does, though now it is also cultivated. Officially it is probably illegal, though

I doubt there is an official regulation, unless you try to sell it in quantity or export it. For most Moroccans it is part of a way of life, slightly naughty, but no more so than – and depending on your point of view possibly less than – the occasional beer or two.

I have, of course, indulged in my student days, and I have been familiar with it for many years, having an ageing, hippie, American cousin whose life eased so much when he reached retirement age and he got a 'medicinal' prescription for cannabis; he was in seventh heaven when his home state legalised it. However, I have never really been a user, being of the breed that, even in Morocco, would prefer a beer. But then beer is not on offer today. I breathe in, take a long drag – even Bill Clinton would inhale if he had been through the day I just have – and let the mild effects mingle with those of the vodka.

Abdel, who does not indulge in alcohol, takes a deeper drag and stays for longer. He has good reason, he tells me. He went home to drop off my still unfinished mug of 'Coke' only to have his sister-in-law take a sip of it and react in horror. 'I got what for,' he says sheepishly.

'Blame it on me,' I tell him. 'Most people do.'

He smiles reassuringly and says, 'I did.'

＊

In the evening, there was a communal supper of grilled kidneys and liver, none the less tasty for having been living organs just a few hours earlier. There is a paradox in being squeamish about such things when we check in supermarkets that our meat is fresh. I ask Aziz and Abdel to speculate how many animals were slaughtered on the rooftops of Larache today. Abdel has to think for a moment, but Aziz is fairly confident: 'At least 30,000,' he says, 'at least one for each household.' No one has any sense of shock about this (apart from me); it is, after all, a sign of piety, an indication of fathers giving thanks for the blessing of their children, a good bit of business for the local livestock farmers, and an assurance that everybody has meat in plenty over the coming weeks. It is hard to argue.

I feel just a little intrusive as the family prepare for the Eid evening, which involves everyone getting dressed in their finest to go out and promenade the town streets. The men take the women by the arm and greet neighbours, exchanging compliments, remarking on one another's dress, and wishing each other Allah's best blessings; a bit like the population of a small town going to church on Christmas morning, wishing one another 'Compliments of the season, and God Bless'. It will be an opportunity for Abdel to re-establish his local roots, and tell people how well he is doing in England.

I decide that out of basic politeness, and not to get in the way, it is better for me to go out separately and see how Larache celebrates. It is, in its way, a heart-warming but strangely alien and decidedly sobering experience. The Plaza de España (no point in me calling it anything but what the locals do) is packed, with a small funfair of sorts for the children in the middle: there are men selling brightly coloured helium ballons, bags of sweets or popcorn, fizzy drinks; five-to six-year-olds are driving around in little electric cars, both girls and boys, their young siblings being pushed by parents. The adults are dressed in their best, the men in long white or yellow kaftans of cotton or silk, the yellow-striped one indicating the wearer has been on the haj, the women made up to the eyes, literally, with mascara and lipstick and the occasional henna tattoo on their hands. They wear long skirts, to the ankle, and long-sleeved blouses with jackets, but only around half cover their hair with a gaudy silk headscarf that is more a celebration of fashion, and no more a token of modesty that a fascinator at an English society wedding. There is no black on display, no chadors or burkas; this is a celebration of light and colour.

I take one of the few free seats at the terrace of the Hotel Cervantes on the square and watch the world walk by. It is all rather charming, yet at the same time, for me, disconcerting. There is a certain innocence about it, fuelled from a Western point of view by the total absence of alcohol. Abdel comes by with his two nieces, beautifully turned out, one on either arm, he himself in his father's haji kaftan. He is taking them for ice cream. All around me at the Cervantes are seated men, and only men, alone and in groups, drinking lemonade, Coke or tea, playing with their smartphones. Oddly enough, apart from the men-only atmosphere at the cafés, it feels vaguely Midwest American, all the dressing up, gizmos, the exchanged 'praise the Lord' blessings and no booze; a ritual homage to the sanctity of the Coca-Cola company. I feel about as at home as an imam at a beer festival.

Time for an early night and a last glass from that bottle of golf course-supplied Moroccan claret.

Two days later, Abdel and I are on our way home, via Tangier where his cousin Anas works as night porter at the city's smartest hotel. We spend a few hours at the Petit Socco, the elegant little square at the heart of the old city's relatively small medina. From its roué days as a haven for the libertines, poets and those considered sexual deviants in Europe, when it was a so-called 'international city', Tangier has retained just a whiff of worldliness. Its once shady nightlife has been progressively cleaned up since it became part of the Kingdom of Morocco in 1956. Today it is primarily a port city, with the great expanse of Tanger-Med a few miles east one of the largest ports in the Mediterranean, while the old port in the city centre serves as a landing point for ferries to and from Spain, and makes the city an attraction for Costa del Sol tourists being sold an only slightly fraudulent 'taste of Africa'.

We spend the night at his cousin's house in the old town, then at noon on the following day we catch the catamaran to cross the Straits of Gibraltar, from where to catch a cheap flight back to London. As we cross the great rock, subject of so much contention over the years, the other, undisputed Pillar of Hercules, looms before us.

'We could solve the problem,' he says. 'Gibraltar. Its real name is Jebel al-Tariq. You could just give it back. To us.'

He is joking. I think.

2

Blind Alleys and Broad Horizons

IT IS DARK. Very dark. Arriving in Marrakech late at night without a guide is an interesting experience. There is no point in climbing into a taxi, hoping to be left at the door of your hotel. Your hotel's door, like as not, is almost certainly located at the end of a narrow labyrinth of alleyways, inaccessible by hundreds of metres to any form of transport except human feet. Or a donkey. And by now the donkeys have wisely gone to bed.

The nearest a cab, or any form of post-19th century vehicular traffic, can come to the warren of lanes, alleyways and tunnels that forms the intricate heart of Marrakech is one side of the great square, which from dusk on is crammed with snake-charmers, baboon-trainers, snail-sellers and fortune tellers, along with a hundred hassling street-food stalls. Disconcertingly, it is called Jemaa el-Fnaa, the Assembly of the Dead. Unsurprisingly, most tourists, all the way back to Graham Nash, just call it 'the square'.

Nearing midnight, the food stallholders are no longer pestering passers-by so insistently, the pressed-juice stalls are beginning to pack up, and the cobras have been bunged back in their baskets. What activity remains is congregated around the small groups of musicians sitting on upturned plastic buckets, rattling castanets, banging on drums and chanting, or a few of the grizzled storytellers still narrating spellbinding tales of evil jinns and cruel sultans, foolish virgins and wandering merchants, as they have done for centuries in a country with a lamentable level of literacy.

But I have more important things to do right now than breathe in the heady nocturnal atmosphere of Jemaa el-Fnaa: such as finding a place to lay my head for the night. I have not left this to chance, but finding the room I have booked will require more than a little luck. I am following a pen-scratched line on a map, sent to me by Kerstin, the German manager of the riad I have booked. Riads are the grand old merchant's houses, built almost literally one on top of the other, sharing common walls and few windows on the outside world for strangers to peer through. The result is the labyrinth that Marrakech's medina,* the heart of the old city, has evolved into over the centuries.

I feel like Long John Silver squinting at a series of scrawled lines leading to buried treasure, even if in this case the treasure at the end of the trail is no more than a bed for the night. You have to have wandered in Marrakech's medina to understand. But even if you have meandered – or more likely battled your way – through the bustling souks with merchants trying to sell you everything from the inevitable carpet to a painted living tortoise, it is not quite the same as finding your way for the first time to a specific destination amidst the high unwelcoming walls of the residential quarters. In the souks you may get lost, sometimes hopelessly so, but eventually you will come out into some square or open area, even if it is occasionally, dishearteningly, back where you started from.

Down the dark narrow alleyways between the residential riads there is no such guarantee. Even a map resembles at best a maze in a children's magazine: not too many options

---

*Medina just means 'town' in Arabic. The one Mohammed fled Mecca for was originally called Yathrib, but the fame he gave it meant it became known ever after as *the* town.

but no guarantee that you are not following a long track to a dead end. And in the real world, at night, with what passes in Marrakech for street lighting – the occasional bare bulb dangling from a wire strung between two walls – it is only too easy to imagine potential peril suddenly springing out from every angle: front, rear or the dark, barred and lifeless forti-fied doorways, at unpredictable heights and distances. And there is always the risk that after the fifth or sixth improbable, unpredictable, turn down a windowless, high-walled alley-way, you will come across a dead end. With no option but to retrace your steps.

The beginning is easy enough, but then that's before I turn off the relatively brightly lit, still busy rue des Banques, which leads from one corner of Jemaa el-Fnaa. It is some 100 yards along this road, with young boys hauling barrows of stock to or from the shops selling everything from children's clothes eerily displayed on life-size dolls suspended on wires from the shop fronts as if from a gibbet, to second-hand electronic equipment, that I pass under an arch and spot the narrow opening on my right which according to Kerstin's map I am to take.

This is not reassuring because the lighting extends no more than 20 yards before it gives way to pitch darkness. But there isn't an alternative. I pass a door on my right, a high window, with an elaborate wrought-iron grille but no light coming from it, though as my eyes adjust I can just make out a turning to the right a short distance ahead. I turn the corner to face a wall about 10 yards beyond, its flaking plas-terwork illuminated by a light clearly coming from around a corner to the left. I turn in the only direction possible and am in another, much longer alley, the walls tall and forbid-ding and featureless – I could stand in the middle and touch both at once – but at least with two lights, one after the other, casting a pale, yellowy sodium glow on the cobbles below, enough to enable me to avoid the pools of water. It has been raining in Marrakech, something I had not expected. April showers I consider a particularly English phenomenon. The alley goes on seemingly forever, though it is no more than 50 or 60 paces, past another door, set into the wall low on my left. Ahead I can see what appears to be a zigzag as I am forced to do a one-two around a double bend before once again staring down a dark passageway with a light in the middle but darkness before and after. It is eerily silent; the only noise that of my sandalled feet padding on the cobbles. More doors, two on the left, one on the right, so low that it must have been there for centuries, or used only by hobbits. Another door on the left as I pass under the light, in contrast, is high, massive, of dark wood reinforced by iron studs. Just beyond it there is another alleyway branching off to the left, the first time (thankfully?) I have had an option. I glance warily down it only to see an alleyway that could be a carbon copy of the one straight ahead, dark with only a solitary light. I consult Kerstin's scratched lines and continue without turning. Some dozen yards on, the alley I am in also turns to the left, presenting me with an immediate vista of total darkness, with no gradation into yellow light, as if there were twin kingdoms of darkness and light without overlap, no radiance spilling from the one to the other but at the far end a small, wide door set into a wall painted partly in pink. As I walk onwards, increasingly more wary, I realise that the light phenomenon is because I am effectively in a tunnel; the buildings on either side have at some stage in the immeasurable past decided that pedestrian space was wasted above first-floor level. At least the slight curvature of the wall to my left means I can see that the next turn is to the right. Up to now, unless there has been a light shining from one side or the other, that has not been clear until I actually reached the turning. But when I turn it, I am faced with only another dark corridor – or rather another tunnel – running for what seems like miles but again is perhaps no more than 30 or 40 paces in total darkness save for the distant illumination on a wall that is either a dead end or a particularly abrupt turn. I accelerate my pace to reach it. And find doors on either side. Both massive, iron-studded, unwelcoming. Except that one of them has the name of my destination on it. And a great iron knocker, which I lift and rap, feeling like a weary wanderer arriving at Dracula's castle at midnight.

A second later the great door of the Riad Dar Fakir creaks open and I am greeted with a smiling face, and the words, 'M'sieu Millar?' I am invited into a palace of oriental splendour, with marble pillars, a bubbling fountain in a softly lit internal courtyard, open to the starlit heavens with heavy drapes on the walls, fronds of vegetation dangling from the roof and the scent of bougainvillea in flower.

The impeccable, smiling night porter approaches me with welcome words: 'May I show you to your room?'

✳

Early morning on the roof of a Marrakech riad is an almost perfect experience, surrounded by cascading bougainvillea, oleander, radiant hibiscus and leafy potted palms with a view through crystalline air of the mountains that the ancients supposed to support the roof of the world. The snow-capped peaks of the High Atlas stand out blue and white in the bright morning sun, an improbable final barrier between the city and the barren wastes of the Sahara. At this time of day their shaded lower slopes are an only slightly darker version of the pale but deepening blue of the sky above, while the cordillera of peaks above, still capped with white snow in early April, seems little more than a reflection of the horizontal layer of cirrus cloud above.

And yet the desert is never that distant. In fact, gazing out across the anarchic cityscape, you could image all else is a mirage: here and there, sprung from the russet brickwork, bedouin-style tents perch at extravagant angles above the roofs, great swathes of canvas supported on leaning poles with potted palm trees towering above them, and only the vast spiked forest of satellite dishes to acknowledge that this is a 21st-century city and not a nomadic encampment.

It is radically different from last night's ground-level view when all that was visible was closed doorways, with only the level of fortification to give any hint of the grandeur or modesty of the accommodation on the other side. From the rooftop, however, a sort of social status can be inferred, according to whether stone, breeze blocks, brick or corrugated iron are used in the inexorable ascent of each building until it reaches what is the generally agreed limit of four – or maybe five – stories. Yet all of this paraphernalia is blissfully redeemed by that breathtaking, surreal backdrop of the Atlas rising in the surprisingly near distance, and, seemingly so close you could touch it, the red brick minaret of the magnificent 12th-century Koutoubia mosque which dominates the city.

For all their antiquity, the survival of the greatest riads of Marrakech is primarily a 21st-century phenomenon. For decades after Moroccan independence from France in 1956, the new country in its drive for modernisation neglected the ancient houses that had once belonged to rich merchants who, over the centuries, had based their trans-Saharan trade caravans in Marrakech. These magnificent old buildings, too big for most locals to buy or run, were falling into disrepair, until gradually a few entrepreneurs, many of them Europeans, began to spot their potential as the ultimate in boutique hotels.

The riads are based on a plan with roots in ancient Roman domestic architecture, when Morocco was the province of Mauretania (the name survives in the modern nation of Mauritania, further south than Roman rule ever extended and to this day involved in border disputes with its northern neighbour). Other than a few villas in the Italian countryside, there are no better functioning examples of ancient Roman upper-class housing than these. Like their classical predecessors they look inwards, not outwards, arranged around a courtyard that served as a lightwell providing the best benefits of shade and sunshine, with a little garden and possibly a fountain in the middle, while the rooms for both sleeping and dining were arranged around the sides. It was a format that in the Roman world allowed a dignified, maybe even stolid image to be shown to the world while in reality modesty in every form could be left at the door.

This inward, private lifestyle presented itself admirably to Islamic values, too, when the Arab invaders arrived in the 7th century. But whereas the Romans set their villas a discreet distance apart, in cities such as Marrakech, a walled enclave of souks, as the houses grew upwards and multiplied, they grew together, tightening and complicating the labyrinthine structure of alleyways. Instead of private but inviting villas, these are thick-walled fortresses among countless others down narrow winding alleyways that may or may not be dead ends, each with just one massive wooden door reinforced with heavy brass bolts, opening on to an inner world of unknown dimensions.

The Dar Fakir is a splendid example, for those who can find it, with its open courtyard surrounded by an array of reception rooms for dining or drinking or just chilling out, though in the current climate I am glad to note the luxurious divan-equipped corner room boasts a great log fire built into the walls. The eight rooms on the first floor are arranged around the central court, which allows guests to choose their levels of privacy. Over breakfast Kerstin tells me the previous week she had a group of Swedish 50-somethings on a second-wedding hen party who had taken the whole place and could be seen gleefully running naked through the ground-floor fountain. I try – hard – not to imagine it.

Just entering a riad is like delving into another dimension in time and space; distances become warped, the rooftop of a building that is a 15-minute walk away through the twisting ground-level alleyways, is seen to be a mere few hundred metres away at rooftop level, from the point of view of the sparrows chirping as they peck at the crumbs of your breakfast. From the roof of the Dar Fakir, I spot the reassuring top floor of Salaama, in the rue des Banques; reassuring, because on my first fleeting visit to Morocco, it played a pivotal role in acclimatising me, literally.

I had assumed, wrongly, that despite being a Muslim country, Morocco's attitude to alcohol would be like Turkey's: that it would be mildly tutted about by the devoutly religious, but other than that, openly available. The Moroccan attitude to the demon drink, however, is much more complicated, and perhaps a tad more hypocritical. Alcohol is allowed; vast numbers of Moroccans, in particular the middle classes, drink, mostly wine, and more often than not from the many excellent Moroccan vineyards, while beer is also brewed, both under licence and by domestic breweries, and is widely consumed, particularly by working-class men, and tourists. But it is not openly on show in most places; this being Morocco there is almost always a parenthesis. The idea is that alcohol should be drunk (if you wish) but not seen. In most towns or cities restaurants will serve wine but not outside on street-level terraces. They may not even advertise it on the menu outside, but will have it available inside. Or on the roof.

Most bars – and nightclubs – are located in the *villes nouvelles,* the new towns built by the French and in which their own rules were paramount while in the medinas, the traditional hearts of the oldest cities, the locals were left more or less to their own devices. But even then the bars are not as public as you might think (or hope). Bars flourish – on a relatively small scale – but are expected to be 'modest', in other words, their windows are often opaque, rather in the way that in Victorian Britain pub windows had frosted or mottled glass so that the delights available inside should not be on open display to upstanding Christian gentlefolk who might find their values corrupted or their morality offended.

But the point I am coming to is that on day one of our first trip to Marrakech, I found myself so worn to a frazzle by the heat and confusion that by midday I was gasping – literally – for a cold pint. And no, a glass of mint tea, or even a freshly squeezed orange juice wasn't going to do the trick. There are times when only a cold beer will do. And when you're hot, dusty and sweaty in a city where you are suddenly afraid you might not be able to get one, that sentiment is magnified a hundred times over. So when a dusty street urchin grabbed my trousers, thrusting a leaflet into my hand, my natural instinct to brush him away was immediately mollified when he said possibly the only few words of English he knew: 'Mister, mister, cold beer.' Lead me to it, Aladdin, was my automatic response, and within minutes we were seated on the rooftop terrace of Salaama, staring out at that magical view across the Atlas Mountains, with an icy Flag Spéciale, Morocco's most widely drunk beer, in front of me. Two in fact; Salaama runs a happy hour most days.

✳

As you will have gathered, it is not hard to get lost in Marrakech. All you have to do is take the wrong direction. Once. Which is what I immediately do on emerging from my one-direction mousetrap maze, now, in daylight, awake with kids playing football and old ladies squatting on the steps by those impenetrable doors. I'm not sure why I turned right, knowing that Jemaa el-Fnaa is to the left, but I did. The idea, lurking in my subconscious, had been to wander a bit, absorb the atmosphere, avoid the obvious sights in favour of the accidental ones, to traipse aimlessly along streets where the sounds are not those of foreign tongues, but those of the local populace, the domestic environment. That is proving in this case to be a serious mistake.

The chief misapprehension that many visitors to Morocco frequently labour under is to think that the souks are merely colourful marketplaces selling carpets and leather pouffes to tourists. They are, but they are much, much more than that: they are the soul of the city, but also its hands and feet, the places where life is lived to the full, and that means not just fun and food and drink, but also noise and dirt and excrement. Here, within seconds, I have found myself in the back-streets, streets where the ramshackle shops sell lots of plastic, much of it – as anywhere these days – made in China, as well as spades and shovels, pick axes and what might pass for gardening, or mining, tools. There are also a lot of clothes shops: not the sort that sell exquisite Moroccan leather jackets, but the sort that sell Y-fronts, outsize bras and heavy wool jellabas, and largely inhabited by men wearing jellabas, sensibly enough as the weather is unseasonably chilly and there are rain clouds overhead.

This is all very atmospheric in its way but it reminds me of one afternoon a year or two ago when I took the wrong turn out of Hammersmith Tube in London and ended up in Shepherd's Bush market, looking like my vision of Kandahar in a cold climate. And Shepherd's Bush doesn't have mopeds. Mopeds are the curse of Marrakech. In streets too narrow for any four-wheeled vehicular transport – except a few very narrow hand carts – where once there were donkeys, now there are mopeds. Noisy, smelly mopeds ridden often by several people at the same time, and when not, then carrying unrealistic loads, and in any case going far too fast. The attitude of Marrakchi moped-owners is akin to that of drivers in the Zil lanes of the old Soviet Union: I have transport, you have not, therefore I am more important than you. In other words: your life is in your hands and it is not my problem.

Coughing and spluttering, and generally feeling as fed up with a city that right at this moment seemed to have all the charm of Shepherd's Bush in a heat wave, with no pubs, I am struggling to find my way back towards the more amenable heart of the city – where the tourists and the bars are – when I realise from the five-pointed star and inscription on a wall that I have wandered into the Jewish quarter, known here, as in all Moroccan cities, as the *mellah,* which correlates with an Italian word we are more familiar with – *ghetto* – only without the negative connotations. There are no negative connotations, or at least the atmosphere created by the Palestinian-Israeli conflict has created fewer problems with Morocco's Arabs, because for much of history, the two lived side by side, and were even subject to the same vicissitudes of fate. Marrakech's *mellah,* like most, dates from the early 16th century, which is when the country saw a mass influx of Jews. Far from arousing hostility, they were welcomed as fellow sufferers, because the reason for the influx was that the 'Christian Monarchs' Ferdinand and Isabella had just celebrated the completion of their *reconquista,* the end of over 700 years of Moorish rule in Spain, by expelling from their lands not just all the Moors, who were sent back home to Morocco, but also all the Jews, who for years had lived in their midst under tolerant Islamic rule. They were resettled together – the Jews admittedly given their own area in which to build their own places of worship and practise their own customs – and things remained pretty much like that until the 1950s, when most of the population emigrated to Israel, leaving many of the *mellahs* either to crumble or be taken over. Marrakech's *mellah* has done both: it has been resettled largely by Arabs while crumbling at the same time.

By now I was crumbling fast too, and needed to get some refreshment. Luckily, identifying the *mellah* had enabled me to get some sort of a handle on where I might be in the vast sprawl of the medina. By a process of hopeful elimination, trying as hard as I could to keep the *mellah* behind me, within a mere 10 minutes of panting and plodding, I finally emerge from the rabbit warren on to the eastern side of the Jemaa el-Fnaa, tired, hungry and thirsty.

It is really only at night that Marrakech's great square becomes a mass eatery. But in the middle of the day, there are scores of little 'cafés' in the alleyways leading into the souks proper where you can get an excellent meal, and in particular that most delicious of Moroccan specialities: lamb *méchoui,* slow-cooked lamb leg or shoulder, marinated for hours if not days in *ras-el-hanout,* that near mystical blend of up to 35 spices, proudly blended by each individual merchant – the literal translation is 'top of the shop' – that is to Moroccan cuisine what salt and vinegar are to fish and chips. I am ushered up to an open rooftop table with a magnificent tiled floor, only slightly cracked in places, with a piece of linen stretched between two wooden poles for shade, and a magnificent view of the soaring minaret of the El Koutubia mosque, Marrakech's architectural marvel. The only downside comes when I, half-expecting the answer, ask about the possibility of a cold beer. The young lad, younger than my own sons, gives me a look as if I were a naughty schoolboy, nods towards the minaret, then shrugs with a knowing smile and offers me some iced water or a mint tea.

I opt for the iced water. Mint tea is one of Morocco's specialities – the national drink, consumed in vast quantities throughout the day – and at first taste it is an absolute delight. It's pretty good second time around too, as long as it's not being offered by some chubby bearded bloke trying to sell you a carpet who insists on calling it, with a patronising grin, 'Berber brandy'. Somebody needs to tell the carpet sellers that if they really want to offload a rug at anywhere near the prices they start off at, they would be well advised to serve French brandy instead. It might work wonders for their profits. The other reason you can quickly grow tired of Moroccan mint tea is the amount of sugar they pile into it. Set against our current sugar paranoia in European and America, the average Moroccan consumes about six months' maximum permitted allowance on an average afternoon. I kid you not. Morocco has one of the highest rates of diabetes in the world. And the worst thing is that they don't seem to take it seriously. There is even a series of black humour rom-com movies entitled *She is Diabetic and Hypertensive, and She Still Refuses to Die*. Honest! They are now on the third instalment. I bet the plot's a killer.

The other view from my lofty lunchtime perch is as interesting as the towering minaret, if rather more down to earth, literally. If I glance over the side of the wall behind me, I am looking down on the 'roof' of the souk. This is a very rough use of the word 'roof'. Wandering through the souks you have an impression of being in some giant, almost organic building, grateful to be indoors rather than under the glare of the Moroccan sun. Today it is not that hot, though thankfully the grey skies have gone, but the labyrinth I am looking down on is a 'covered market' only in the same way that a Masai warrior's cow-dung hut is a desirable residence. The covering over the maze of alleyways, that from within give the appearance of being a building, is in reality a remarkable agglomeration of junk: the main covering comprises sheets of plastic, occasionally supplemented by black bin bags, laid across the alley from one side to the other, held in place on the roofs of the shops either side by old wooden planks, bit of corrugated iron, red roofing tiles and shards of pottery. You might call it a jigsaw puzzle, but only in the sense of piling all the pieces over a given area of the table and hitting them with a hammer until they more or less fit. If they ever had a serious thunderstorm here, the roof would cave in, in a big way.

The *méchoui,* when it arrives – you can't rush slow cooking even though it has been in the wood-fired oven since dawn – is delicious; fragrant and juicy and falling off the bone. All it really needs is a nice claret, or even a cold beer.

Time for the Salaama, which is just across the square, and where I have agreed to meet Kerstin. It has to be explained here that this is no accident: it was when I was dragged by the street urchin to Salaama that we came across Kerstin, a bright 20-something German from Wuppertal in the Rhineland who spent her school years in England and then moved to Sweden, and is comfortably trilingual, struggling still with her Arabic, but getting by in French. She fell in love with Marrakech and Morocco on first sight, lives with a Moroccan boyfriend and manages both Salaama and Dar Fakir for a wealthy local businessman.

At the bottom of the precipitous stairs as I leave, I notice that the entrance to the souk, just to the left, would appear to be the cobblers' quarter. Not that they are actually selling shoes here: wonderful soft leather *babouches* that serve as either slippers or sandals or both are available just about everywhere in Morocco, though I have often been amused to see that when it comes to it the majority of Moroccan men prefer naff Adidas or Nike trainers. The guys here are shoe repairers. And that is fortunate because, despite a fondness for *babouches* I am wearing my favourite pair of Birkenstocks and the heels are worn down. Time to test the local market. Before I can even suggest what I might want done I am facing a barrage from either side, a virtual onslaught of cobbler services. Purely at random, I choose one and ask what it would cost to have my shoes re-heeled. 'Eighty dirhams, sir, good job, last a lifetime.' Seven pounds is probably rather less than I would pay in London but it seems a bit steep for Marrakech; however, as it's the first price he suggested, it's unlikely to be the best. 'Hmm,' I mutter, 'sounds a bit expensive.' Immediately the cobbler next to him offers the same job for 60. I offer 20, and they guffaw, but immediately the one on the left comes down to 40.

I nod in agreement, and in a flash he has laid out a piece of cloth on the ground for me to stand on. I take off one shoe and

hand it to him, but by the time I offer the second, his neighbour snatches it from my hand. This is a tussle I don't want to
be involved in, except that I would like both shoes back and
with the same heels. For a few minutes I fear they are about to
come to blows amid a machine-gun torrent of Arabic invec-
tive, but then they shake hands. It would appear they both
have the same stock of heels and will split the job 50–50. Fine
by me. After that, it is all about the performance. Normally
getting a pair of shoes re-heeled is, if you'll pardon the expression, a fairly pedestrian experience, done while-you-wait only
if you have brought them in and are wearing another pair, and
even then you're told not to walk on them until the glue dries.
Not so in Morocco. Over the next four minutes, I am treated,
as if watching a race, to two high-speed demonstrations of
slicing hard rubber with razor-sharp knives, sizing and
cutting replacement heels and then two spectacular bursts of
flame as each in turn spreads a substantial dollop of glue on
both shoe and heel, produces a cigarette lighter and sets fire to
both, and rams them together. Not so much Timpson as Billy
Smart. I can only imagine what British 'health and safety'
officials would say. Thirty seconds later I am good to go. I
hand them 50 dirhams, 25 apiece, just for the performance.

As I cross the square heading to Salaama, where I have
agreed to meet Kerstin in search of some local advice, I discover yet another side to the great Moroccan belief in recy-
cling: a man selling used false teeth, and not just sets, but
individual ones. I make a note to keep going to the dentist
regularly.

Kerstin arrives late, having had problems with a British
couple just arrived at the riad, who are in the midst of 'a
domestic', apparently as a result of having consumed too
many gin and tonics on their early morning charter flight
from Stansted. They are also in shock at not having a row
of bars in the nearest street, though Kerstin has in mind for
them a few places in the *ville nouvelle*, including one where

you can actually have alcohol outside because the bar-cum-restaurant has cleverly erected a row of portable high hedges around its terrace area. It is only the medina, she adds, that is quite so strict on alcohol, though the rule of thumb is that it should not be sold within sight of a mosque, which explains the meaningful nod from my lunchtime waiter. Salaama, it turns out, is just sufficiently tucked away round the corner from Jemaa el-Fnaa to be out of the direct sight line of the Koutoubia mosque.

By late afternoon, trade is brisk, with punters happily making the best of the seemingly never-ending 'happy hour'; mostly foreign tourists are relishing the view of the Atlas, which, since their resplendent curtain call in the morning, have faded into the sky as if they were indeed a mirage, and are only now reappearing miraculously as the setting sun paints them with a glowing pink. Kerstin is trying to suggest eating places, mostly, I soon discover, owned by the man she works for – funny how quickly people can go native in Marrakech – but I reject them all, not least because those in the *ville nouvelle* offer food that is too European in orientation, but also because I know from my last visit that it is impossible to enjoy or at least experience to the full Jemaa el-Fnaa without eating there, and I have already got my own plans for that.

But I do ask her help in finding one meal I am determined to eat in Marrakech, the dish that throughout the rest of Morocco the city is famed for, but which in reality is remarkably hard to find, other than at family feasts. *Tanjia* is not to be confused with *tagine,* the everyday, everywhere dish of meat and couscous that is Morocco's staple. In fact *tanjia* is not the dish but the pot it is cooked in: a basic fired-clay urn with a capacity of a litre or two, fully glazed on the interior but still rough on the exterior. Some time back in the mists of time, unmarried Marrakech working men thought of a great wheeze for having a delicious meal ready for them at the end of the day with the minimum of effort and expense, and without needing a woman to cook it. The idea was that they would fill up their *tanjia* with meat and veg and drop it off at the town hammam or communal bath house, where they could come back and clean up after a hard sweaty day, then pick up their dinner and take it home. It remains to this day an essentially male dish, although the womenfolk are occasionally prevailed upon to rustle one up for a family occasion, except that the long, slow cooking process makes it hardly a spontaneous supper and not an easy dish for restaurants to put on their menu without it being pre-ordered.

In fact, asking around local restaurateurs as to where I might find the real thing produces a blank, although most promise me they can provide 'very same thing' – any Moroccan restaurateur will promise you almost anything – but are obliged to admit that unless you are prepared to wait for four hours, it will not actually be the genuine article. Even the ever-resilient Kerstin is stumped at first until she suddenly has a brainwave: 'Café Clock,' she exclaims, makes a phone call, and all is set. 'Tomorrow at midday,' she pronounces.

✳

By now dusk is well and truly upon us, and 'the square' is coming into its own. It is hard not to be overwhelmed by the sheer sensuousness of the experience that is Jemaa el-Fnaa. It is unlike anywhere else you have ever been and are likely to be, a blend of the oriental, the *One Thousand and One Nights* vision of the Arab world, with the sounds, rhythms and colours of sub-Saharan Africa mutated into something quintessentially Moroccan, a fusion of cuisines, cultures, con-men and cupidity. Marrakech is a fusion of the transplanted cultures of Arabia with those of sub-Saharan black Africa, overlaid on that of the oldest indigenous inhabitants of North Africa, the Berbers. It was the ancient Greeks who gave them that name, based on the fact that the supposed inventors of democracy and champions of equality considered anyone who didn't speak classical Greek to be just saying 'bebebebebe'. The Berbers call themselves *Amazigh* (confusingly, the plural is *Imazighen*), which roughly means 'the people' in the same way as the name of the Cheyenne tribe in North America, and that of the Allemani German tribe meant 'all men'. Having adopted Christianity, Judaism and Islam as they passed through, they still retain their distinctive identity as well as three linked languages.

Today, it is hard to imagine that something as individual as Jemaa el-Fnaa, which so reeks of the mediaeval world with its acrobats, snake charmers, fire eaters, musicians and monkey tamers, which seems as if it has survived unchanged down the centuries, was briefly, in the heady, would-be modernising years of the late 1950s, a bus station, with lines of buses where the market stalls now stand. It didn't work, partly because the traditions of the place refused to make way, but also because the city and the country realised they were killing something the world would come to see. They gave up the bus station idea just in time for the '60s to take it over, for the world of foot-loose hippies, Esther Freud's *Hideous Kinky* and yes, Crosby, Stills and Nash. Half a century on, the hippies now come back as pensioners on nostalgia trips, but Jemaa el-Fnaa remains a feast for all the senses.

It is also a feast for the body. In particular the row upon row of restaurateurs, all with their ingredients laid out on barrows beneath bright electric lights: fish, squid, octopus, crab, chicken and lamb kebabs, mountains of couscous, fresh vegetables, almost everything edible you can imagine, except – and Mr Nash, you really should have done your homework – pork chops.

Trying just to walk between them is a travail as tourists are considered fair game and every white-coated tout will cluster around you at once, with the usual multilingual cacophony of 'Where you from, *de donde vienes, d'où tu viens, wo kommen*

Sie her, otkuda vy?' Yield to a conversation and before you've explained you're from a little town on the outskirts of Milwaukee (why is it that Americans in particular, many of whom have never left the country before, seem to think that everybody in the world will know, or want to know about Pitchfork, Missouri or Potatoville, Idaho?). Not that it really matters where you come from – although if you say Paris or London, you will invariably discover that the tout has an uncle/cousin/sister living there – because before you've got anywhere or ordered anything specific, he will already have piled high a plate with more food than you can eat, or possibly even pay for – it usually includes the most expensive fish or lobster he can find, and prices are nowhere near as cheap as you might think for an open-air market stall grill. The experience is worth it, just about, but tonight I am heading directly to the stall which has no touts trying to drag in the tourists, partly because it is always packed, and in contrast to almost all the others, you actually have to queue for a place, but primarily because the only tourists who come anywhere near it are those with their cameras out. The menu, you see, is simple: sheep's heads.

Not whole sheep's heads, you understand. It is perfectly reasonable to order a half. Or just the brains. They sit there in a little row of their own, like white rubber-veined jellyfish the size of an orange. I have eaten brains only once before, bizarrely enough at Dracula's birth house in Transylvania back in the pre-1989 days of communism when they were the only thing on the menu, with Bull's Blood Hungarian wine to wash them down. Tonight, however, I am being less ambitious: '*Demi-tête et une langue, s'il vous plaît, chef,*' I order. Half a head and a tongue. Yum!

Okay, some straight talking here: I am the first to admit that often, when I see something on a menu and have no idea what it might be, I commit the adventurer's folly: I order it. To find out. But this is not quite like that. I love tongue. It is one of those cuts of meat that either immediately estranges or entices people, like a lot of offal. Jellied veal, for example. Whatever happened to that? In my childhood, tongue was something poor people ate. More recently, it was declared taboo because of the BSE 'mad cow' disease scare, as was oxtail, which I also love. You either like gelatinous food or you don't. When tongue was declared legal again, I even had a go at buying and pressing my own (not my own tongue, you understand, but one bought from a local farmer), turning that giant version of a familiar organ into the rolled, pressed deli speciality. It worked well enough, but everyone I offered it to complained that it looked too much like ... well, a tongue.

The lamb's tongue I am served up here is tiny in relation to beef tongue, barely a tenth of the size, a long fat sliver, much longer than a human tongue but not as wide. If you are throwing up by now, get over it. We are animals and most of us eat other animals. Get over it, or stop; those are the only alternatives. Unlike the stuff you might buy at a butcher's or, heaven forfend, supermarket, the tongue here comes not in wafer-thin slices, but in cuboid chunks. It is still quite moist too, not dried from any packaging process. That makes it just that little bit more challenging, even for aficionados, but then tongue is always a texture thing: a combination of gelatinousness and grainy soft meatiness. I'm not proselytising here; you either like it or you don't. I do, and the guy serving it to me nods approvingly as I wolf it down.

Unfortunately I am not quite so successful with the *demi-tête*. Normally I am not flustered about consuming animal body parts – I have shared the pre-dawn bullfighters' breakfast of *cojones de toro* (literally bulls' balls) prior to the early morning 'run' at Pamplona, Spain. They are supposed to give those who consume them courage. There are no testicles on the table here, just the grizzled, roasted head of a sheep (Larache is still a long way ahead of me), laid out with dozens of others in parallel lines at the back of the stall; it would take an eagle's eye to notice that most have already been cleft and reassembled for show. My half is severed from the other (uncannily like that scene in *Breaking Bad*; don't ask, you've either seen it or you haven't), then whacked several more times to break it into bite-sized pieces before being handed to me on a paper plate. Happily, against all popular mythology, the eyes are missing. But what remains is undeniably a semi-skull, the comparisons with most other mammalian anatomy, including our own, awkward to ignore. As someone plagued with sinus problems, I find it somehow simultaneously revolting and empowering: I take the fork with gusto to root out slivers of meat from inside the cheekbones and nasal cavity. Yum. Really!

Like Solomon with his sword, the Moroccan market cooks mean what they say; it's a skull cleft down the middle, so I have the bonus of an extra half tongue, but also half a little orange-sized rubbery brain, which I fear I cannot bring myself to attempt. Call me a wimp, if you will, but sometimes the *cojones* let you down.

I still have another course to get through on my walk on the wild side of Marrakech cuisine: boiled snails in gravy. This is another one of those Jemaa el-Fnaa stalls that never needs to employ touts, is rarely visited by tourists, and is always filled by locals. There is a reason for this: Marrakech snails are nutritious, tasty and cheap. Obviously, famously, the French have been eating snails for centuries, but then so have the English, in one way or another, at least before the Victorians, with all the wealth of a global empire, eschewed the poor folk's food their descendants had been brought up on. Not that snails were always – or even are now – poor people's nosh. They were brought into England by the Romans, who I can only imagine took a brief summer or two before thinking to themselves: what Italian delicacy could make the most of a cold dank climate where it rains most of the time?

In the meantime we forgot how to eat them – as a substantial part of the population also did with that other great culinary Roman import, bunnies – and only rediscovered them in the

20th century as an 'I dare you', supposedly exotic French food, of which the main attraction was the herb and garlic butter, and the snails, labelled *escargots* to appease the English desire not to know which animal they might be eating, often bought separately to the shells and stuffed into them after cooking. The Moroccan experience is, as ever, totally different.

The snails here are smaller, which can be a relief to the squeamish. In fact the shells are so small, that when we refer to the average edible European snail as 'carrying his home on his back', it is like referring to a four-bed detached compared with a one-bed inner-city flat. These are small flat-pack snails, their shells barely more than a centimetre across, delicate in colour with light swirls, and above all, they don't come smothered in large dollops of garlic butter. Of course, I realise that that in itself might be an immediate turn-off for those people whose prime reason for indulging in *escargots* in the first place was an excuse to consume large dollops of garlic butter without feeling guilty.

Instead Moroccan snails, rather than being big, black, obese Italo-French imports are runty, skinny jobs cooked in a large pot of what I can only describe as a sort of diluted peppery Bovril with a dash of Marmite and served up in small bowls that hold a dozen or so. To say they are delicious might be overdoing it – I confess to being a garlic butter fan myself – but they are nutritious, and as I am also a Marmite fan, though I doubt very much the archetypal English yeast paste has played any role in the broth, there is a certain strange kudos-earning satisfaction in slurping it down. In fact, it is probably better than the snails. Snails are cheap – two dirhams a portion – and that is why most Moroccans eat them. In fact, it is probably the only reason. Pulling one of the long – and it is surprising how long some of them can be, given the small size of their shells – black molluscs out and watching it wiggle on the end of a cocktail stick (despite being boiled and definitely dead, they do somehow still seem to wiggle), takes quite some effort to actually swallow the thing. Next time – if there is a next time – I shall bring my own garlic butter.

I finish my meal by moving to another stall for a *canelle* – thin slices of orange sprinkled with sugar and cinnamon – and a glass of grapefruit juice, twice as expensive as orange juice, but because they rarely have it pre-prepared you at least get the benefit of seeing them squeeze it before your eyes; there is a reason why those stalls of oranges are all packed to above eye level, and I regret to say that, despite the ludicrously low price of oranges in Morocco, there are still more than a few traders in Jemaa el-Fnaa prepared to serve a 'here's one I made earlier' diluted drink as supposedly freshly squeezed juice. Morocco is a country where honesty is paramount but it is as well not to take anything on trust unless you have either seen it, or been told, hand on heart – an endearing custom that also survives from Roman times when it symbolised allegiance to Caesar – that it is what the vendor says it is.

It is, of course, not just those who have something to sell on the Jemaa el-Fnaa who want your money. The jugglers and acrobats are not performing free, nor the musicians. There is a surreal dream-like character to the square as the evening wears on. For only a few dirhams it is worth taking a seat or just joining the standing circle around the musicians, many of them experts in, or at least heavily influenced by, the *gnaoua* tradition, sub-Saharan in origin, with its compulsive, repetitive, hypnotic rhythms from the drums and heavy iron castanets, the swirling chants of the singers and the twanging of their strange, idiosyncratic stringed instruments, somewhere between the mediaeval lute and the modern banjo. I find myself standing there spellbound for more than 20 minutes (though it only took two for one of the band's gang of hangers-on to bring the hat round, he is happy with a few dirham coins), in trance to what seems to be one endless song.

When I finally tear myself away it is for the sake of spending a few more dirhams to watch that other spectacle that

Jemaa el-Fnaa is famed for: snake charming, which is every bit as weird as anything I have ever witnessed at close hand, possibly closer than is comfortable. Whether the cobras are, as I have heard, de-fanged, or at least de-venomed (if that is possible) I have no idea. A zoologist friend once took some of the magic out of it all by telling me that snakes can't actually hear and are just following the motion of the pipe because they suspect it might be an enemy. I have no idea but it certainly looks to me like the things are moving in time to the music. Watching the cobra's fabled hooded head emerging from a basket, rising sinuously and swaying to and fro in time to the eerie, exotically melodic music from the long pipe, is hypnotic. He could probably get me dancing if he tried. In any case I am keeping my distance. I also bottle out when his assistant – the man who makes sure the audience pay up for the show – presents me with a large python to put round my neck and offers to photograph me. I tell myself it's only because I'm afraid he will do a runner with my iPhone that I decline, but I'm not kidding anyone, least of all myself.

Nonetheless, before I can protest too much I have a large lump of snake laid across my shoulders that he is – inevitably I fear – calling 'Monty' with a knowing toothless grin. Too much sugar, mate, I want to tell him, except that I am trying my best not to show my extreme discomfort at having a sinuous reptile weighing several kilos slowly, almost soporifically – I hope – curling around the back of my neck. This thing is large – easily more than a metre long – heavy, and all too palpably alive. The idiot who put it there is grinning insanely, chanting 'photo, photo'. I wave the idea away and indicate to him with a ten-dirham coin that what I really, really want him to do for his dosh is to get this monster off me, before it decides to settle down for the night. Eventually he gets the message. And I make a run for it, before anybody tries to get me on kissing terms with the cobra.

3

Hot Pots and Hot Spots

BEFORE MEETING MOHAMMED the chef to learn how to make a *tanjia,* I decide to make the best of the district by visiting the famed Saadian tombs, widely regarded as Marrakech's greatest monumental treasure

First, though, I have to walk there, a fair trek through the winding streets that lead down to the 'royal quarter', worsened by the fact that just as I am about to set out, the heavens open. Equipped with the riad's token umbrella I set off through a torrential downpour that all of a sudden turns the usually sunsoaked or blissfully shady alleys of the medina into a monochrome snapshot of mediaeval chaos, as the excess rainwater floods out of rather than into the drains, turning the cobbles into an ice rink with mogul fields, exacerbated by sheets of cardboard packaging tossed on to the street and reduced to a slushy mire. Down by the Badi palace there is almost disaster as an unstable horse-drawn *calèche* lurches out of an alleyway. This is the sort of 'romantic' buggy used for taking tourists with too much money on sight-seeing tours, complete with golden stand-up headlights and driven by an Obi Wan Kenobi lookalike in a thick woollen jellaba, hood pulled up so far over his head that only his grizzled grey beard is visible and clearly the road ahead is invisible to him. The buggy is barely wide enough to pass through and all but collides with a motorised ice-cream seller coming in the opposite direction and a group of confused and clearly terrified Japanese tourists with brollies pulled down over their heads so they can't see anything either. By some magic nobody is hurt, which doesn't stop a lorry laden with sodden fruit trying to barge its way past the scene of the near accident. I decide to hire a guide to enhance the experience. She is a portly, head-scarfed woman in her mid-forties who was educated in France, where she also studied English.

The Saadians were the late 16th-century Moroccan dynasty, roughly contemporary with England's Tudors, and Sultan Ahmed al-Mansour, a sort of combination of Henry VIII and Elizabeth I. He took over from his brother when the latter died at a stupendous battle against the Portuguese in 1578, known as the Battle of the Three Kings, because not only he but also his deposed predecessor and the Portuguese monarch all died. Al-Mansour is buried here, dead of the plague in 1603. The dynasty ended with the takeover by the Alaouite brothers Moulay Rachid and Moulay Ismail in the mid 17th century, and their descendants have – with the interlude of colonial occupation – ruled ever since. So determined was the ferocious Moulay Ismail to wipe out the memory of his predecessors that he pillaged and all but demolished their great El Badi palace, of which little more than a few massive walls survive. He bricked up the doorway to the tombs with the result that they were completely forgotten about – he also moved the capital to Fez – and only rediscovered in 1917 by the French, who commissioned their *Beaux Arts* department to restore them.

My guide turns out to be a bit of a waste of time. She has clearly seen all this so many times that she rattles off an obviously learned-by-heart spiel and then leaves me to look at them on my own while she stands in a corner smoking, and definitely not earning herself a tip. The tombs themselves are magnificently decorated with Arabic calligraphy within the ornate funereal chamber, but there is something bleak about the line of angled slabs that contain the mortal remains. As well as those of the sultan and his wives, there is a long row of tiny tombs, one for each of his children who did not make it to adulthood, most of them, like Al-Mansour himself, victims of plague.

I have a question or two for the guide, but, bizarrely, she is much more insistent on telling me how much the Moroccan Arabs liked the Jews, were really nice to them and regretted it when most of them upped sticks and move to Israel in the 1950s. This is interesting and I can see that she might want me to understand that the derelict state of the Marrakech *mellah* today is not the result of some purge, but simply the product of mass emigration. 'I will take you to see the *mellah*,' she says, 'because you are Jewish.'

This is clearly not a question, in either case. 'Er, no thanks, and not really,' I find myself replying awkwardly.

But she is smiling reassuringly, 'We like the Jews very much in Morocco.'

Jolly nice, I think to myself, glad to hear it and all that, but as there are only a couple of thousand at most and that does not in any way include this Northern Irish-born 'proddy'...

'So we go there now, yes? Because you are Jewish people.'

This is getting difficult. Not because I don't want to see the *mellah* but because I walked round it too long by accident yesterday, and very dull it was too.

'Well, not really...' I start, meaning to say, I've already seen it, but adding, 'and I'm not Jewish.'

This only gets me a suspicious eye, and another reassuring smile, as if I am somehow deliberately trying to conceal my Jewishness, which is a puzzle, because I don't really look very Jewish. At least, I think not. Racial stereotypes can be dangerous as well as silly, especially when confused with religious ones. I should know; I grew up in a community in Northern Ireland where a substantial proportion of the population believed having your eyes too close together meant you were a

Roman Catholic. But sometimes – tall blonde Germans, neat, thin Japanese – there are general rules of thumb that have token validity. I would not for a moment presume to try and define those of a historic diaspora community like the Jews (not least because I try to avoid walking through minefields), but as far as I know none of them apply to short, pale-skinned, mildly-freckled, fair-hair-going-to-grey Irishmen. I mean, no offence, but Adolf Hitler looked more Jewish than I do. Just where, I wonder, is she getting this from?

'But you speak English?' she ventures.

'Ye … s … ss,' I reply, wondering where there this is going.

'You are American!'

'No!' I answer, very definitively.

'So you are not Jewish?'

'Er, no.'

And that, it would seem, is that: a quick lesson in how global political attitudes can warp people's perceptions. For some reason that I can only take to be Washington's adamant support for the state of Israel, based, it is true, on the large Jewish community in the USA, this relatively well-educated Moroccan woman has developed her own false syllogism famously summed up by, 'All cats have pink ears, Socrates has pink ears, therefore Socrates is a cat,' except that in her case it is, 'Americans speak English and are mostly Jewish, you speak English, therefore you must be a Jewish American.' The world works in weird ways.

Foolishly, instead of the *mellah* and because I have half an hour or so to spare, I let myself be coaxed into making a short detour to see a 'friend of hers' who actually makes carpets and will be working at her loom right now. This is a classic error, which I should have spotted, having once been lured by an Egyptian offering to show me a shortcut to the antiquities museum in Cairo into an imitation perfume shop owned by his cousin. Inevitably, the 'friend with a loom' turns out to be a vast carpet-selling emporium, which just happens to put on a 'weaving demonstration' by the door to coax people in. Within moments a large bearded man is trying to force some of the inescapable 'Berber brandy' into me as he unrolls carpet after carpet. I spend the minimum time possible admiring them and lie that I will come back, leaving him disgruntled and her without a tip, and take my leave, not even daring to ask directions to the rue de la Kasbah.

By some miracle, soaked and slightly stunned, I make it to the far end of rue de la Kasbah, unmistakable for the oversized stork's nest balancing apparently precariously on a tall pillar above an ancient city gate. Café Clock is tucked inconspicuously through a door on the left, through a crumbling gateway that leads into a series of rooms that could be a Chelsea art gallery with a kitchen. Café Clock is an anomalous institution, but an institution nonetheless, born in Fez as the brainchild of a Yorkshireman. Mike Richardson's gastronomic roots go back to his days as maître d'hôtel at London's Wolseley and The Ivy restaurants, but he has since relocated to Morocco as a lifestyle choice and dedicated himself to providing authentic local food for foreigners, not as a restaurant as such, but as a cross-cultural exchange, with displays of local art and poetry readings. Café Clock will put on an evening of Moroccan traditional storytelling, with English translation, but might counter that with English folk or fairy stories translated into Arabic. You are as likely to encounter Morris dancing as belly dancing. The success of the original venture in Fez has now been followed up in Marrakech. And although they too rarely conjure up a *tanjia* – other than for their hugely popular cooking courses – Mohammed has volunteered to walk me through the process.

I could do with a drink first, but not quite true to all of its cross-cultural ambitions, Café Clock has no alcohol licence. But the waiting Mohammed, a genial grinning guy in the house trademark blue sweatshirt, is only too willing to rustle me up a magnificent drink of squeezed limes, mint and sparkling water, while he gets together the basics for our cooking expedition: a two-litre-size *tanjia* pot into which he has already put some crushed garlic and a few basil leaves.

'I had them here,' he explains, as we head out into the rain, now mercifully reduced to a drizzle. 'The spice merchant will do the rest.'

Indeed he does, but first it is the turn of the butcher. We make our way into the food souk halfway up the street, where a grinning butcher with a dark beard is only too happy to haul down with a meat hook a hunk of lamb shoulder and, wielding a machete like some medieval warrior, hack it into bite-sized chunks.

'One kilo okay?' Mohammed asks, and I nod, wondering how big an appetite he thinks I have, but it turns out that a kilo is considered the minimum size necessary for a proper *tanjia*. Then it is off to the spice man, here, in a more local market far from the tourist-swamped souks, without the usual fascinating but mostly phoney cones (most are just plastic shapes with a thin layer of spices applied by glues). Mohammed rattles off to him in Arabic what he needs, but the merchant knows his stuff. To the basil leaves and 100 grams of crushed garlic, now lying beneath the chopped lamb, he adds three teaspoons of *ras-el-hanout*. Then we have a good grating of nutmeg, a dash of cumin, a dash of powdered ginger, two cardamom pods, a big pinch of saffron, a spray of olive oil, a couple of chunks of salted butter from a big plastic tub in which it is protected from the air by a coating of olive oil, and finished off with a preserved lemon (dried with salt to remove the moisture but keep the flavour) and a cupful of water. This has all been done for us by the spice merchant. He wraps it up, metaphorically and literally, by producing some greaseproof paper that he folds over the top of the urn and ties tightly with a piece of string. Effectively he and the butcher have done the culinary part of dinner, all for the price of their ingredients. All that remains for me to do – and I am getting to see the attraction of this one-pot meal to the single bloke back in the day – is the cooking, and even that is going to involve minimal effort on my part.

From the souk it is a short walk up the street to a little low building with three doors. In a cleverly economical use of facilities, practised here for more than a millennium, the one building serves both as bathhouse, bakery and communal oven. It is not much to look at from our side as we approach, nor in fact from any other side, although there is an appealing smell of baking bread emerging from the doorway on the left. On the right there is the hammam entrance leading into different bathing rooms for men and women. A hammam is on my list of Moroccan musts, and maybe, had I thought about it, today would have been the day to give it a go, but my focus for the moment is on matters culinary – and in any case I have been assured the hammams of Fez are the best in Morocco.

The door in the middle is the one Mohammed gently knocks on, and it is opened by the gatekeeper to hell who smiles and ushers us in. At least that is what it looks like and feels like, though this is probably the one day of the year in Marrakech when it is 14C outside, the sky is grey and there is a persistent English drizzle in the air, so I am actually happy to walk down steps into what is effectively the boiler room of a furnace. It is like the interior of some ancient hermit's cave, the sort of place in which the Dead Sea scrolls might have been concealed: grey, dark and dusty, except that the one source of light is the fiery red glow from behind the metal hatch that Ali, the guardian of the furnace, opens to reveal to us as he shovels in more wood. This inferno serves two purposes, Mohammed explains: behind the wall to the left are the baker's ovens, behind the wall to the right is the hammam. The one furnace heats both. He hands the *tanjia* to the stoker, who takes it and places it almost reverently next to what, as my eyes become accustomed to the eerie, red-blue light, is a little line of four or five other *tanjia* pots next to the baker's wall, and gently banks up still-glowing ashes around it. I hand him, on Mohammed's instructions, 14 dirhams (£1) and he indicates that, as the furnace is at full blast, cooking time will be a little shorter and I should come back to collect it in three and a half hours or so.

And that's that! I now have a bun in the oven, so to speak. And there's nothing for me to do for the next three and a half hours except find somewhere to stay out of the rain – the one thing I really hadn't been counting on in Marrakech – and maybe have a beer.

I'm well aware, of course, that the latter isn't going to be all that easy; it's just that on a dreary wet afternoon in London it would be my default option and even though I am more than well aware that I am not in London, the weather seems determined to convince me otherwise. My first option is a couple of cafés I recall from an earlier visit, one of them memorably named Le Nid de Cigogne (the Stork's Nest), for the very good reason that there is a huge stork's nest on the tower of the mediaeval gateway next to it. Storks are a feature of Marrakech, their huge ungainly nests of sticks and straw woven into the structure of any sufficiently lofty building, from mediaeval minaret to modern communications mast.

I make my way up the rickety stairs to the room with a view that serves as the main service area, only to find out that not only is there no view, because the shutters are down to stop the rain coming in, but also that this hasn't been quite effective enough and the seating is damp. The waitress, sitting glumly in one corner with her headscarf wrapped around her and ear glued to her phone, seems less than overly anxious to give me a menu and when she does I realise that in any case this isn't the bar that serves beer; it's the one next door. I make my excuses, lamely, and she goes back to her phone call.

Not that there is a lot more joy to be had next door. The Café du Kasbah is indeed the place where I remember sitting on the roof terrace with an ice-cold glass of Casablanca in

32-degree heat under a straw parasol, enjoying the view of the aforesaid storks' nests and the bustle of the street below. But I had clearly forgotten that the beer was an option only upstairs on the terrace, so that the gaze of passers-by in the street might not be affronted by the sight of alcohol being consumed, and today, for obvious reasons, not least of which is the fact that the straw parasols look more like used floor mops, the roof terrace is closed. I could just have settled for a coffee or mint tea – though it's extraordinary how quickly the initial exotic appeal of the ubiquitous 'Berber brandy' soon degenerates to the level of a cup of sugary Nescafé – but the moment has passed.

Right now, with the rain getting heavier by the second, the more appealing option, for reasons that will become clear, is the strange and wondrous emporium of the Complexe Artisanal next door. In Morocco the concept of the *ensemble artisanal* is a government-backed label for craft emporia where tourists can browse and purchase the products of local traders without the hassle and haggling of the souks. You are never going to get the deal in an *ensemble artisanal* that you might – just might – in a souk, but on the other hand you are also not going to get ripped off in the way you might – in fact very probably will – in the souk. And it won't take half a day.

Many of the government-sponsored *ensembles artisanaux* feel like country craft fairs. The Complexe Artisanal in Rue de la Kasbah more closely resembles the ground-floor entrance hall to Harrods, at least in the days when it was owned by the Egyptian Mohammed Al-Fayed, and laid out in a gold-and-jade kitsch parody of a pharaoh's treasure chamber. The main difference, though somehow it only makes it worse, is that this is all upstairs, reached by an escalator that takes you up like an ascension to heaven past the marble cherubim and seraphim (Muslims do angels too) to a riot of opulence where no piece of furniture can be too bulky, and certainly none too engraved or insufficiently inlaid with gold!

For obvious reasons, therefore, I have never been sure if this particular Complexe Artisanal has the same degree of government – fair price – backing, or is just an easy one-stop shop for busloads of Americans and Russians (the two nationalities deemed most likely to be big spenders and averse to haggling) to be dumped off to have their wallets lightened. But *prix fixe* is definitely the rule. Not that this is in any case the place for a bit of casual impulse shopping unless you have the kind of home and extra baggage allowance than can comfortably accommodate life-size marble statues of Romanesque soldiery, angels and cherubs.

Those items alone are probably enough to convince you that the *complexe* in Rue de la Kasbah is not just your average everyday emporium of Moroccan crafts. This is a place for not just artisans, but *artistes* (the 'e' is deliberate), as witness some of the more remarkable interpretations of patio and dining furniture available in the adjoining salon. Fancy some little bar tables and stools made out of glazed-in bicycle wheels, with twisted crossbars as legs, with seating to match, the wheels here serving as chair backs? Or how about some pop-art industrial sculpture with human-size 'Transformers', those iconic kids' toys where cars and lorries can be twisted through contortions to change them into giant weapon-wielding robots, except that in this case the various engine blocks, radiator grilles, spark plugs and 'big ends' are unlikely ever to be feasibly re-engineered into even an approximation of a working vehicle, which of course they never were?

But the *pièces de résistance* have to be the full indoor dining set of table and six chairs, the latter made using motorcycle mudguards, suspension springs and various other engineering debris to form each in the shape of Ridley Scott's human-sized, man-eating, lizard-like Alien. Just the thing to give you an appetite. If you happen to have a few hundred thousand dirhams to spare.

Visually sated, and with the rain still hammering down outside, transforming the cobbled streets around the kasbah from their normal vivid hues into a monochrome grey, I decide to make my way to the one spot where I know I can pass the dreary afternoon in best male Moroccan fashion, with a beer and a snack while watching football: the extraordinary Grand Hotel de la Tazi. All I have to do is find it.

The main obstacle to doing so, given that I know roughly how to get there from here, turns out to be His Majesty King Mohammed VI himself. A remarkable family of survivors, the current dynasty of Moroccan rulers has survived for over 300 years, through wars, invasions, occupation, dismissal by colonial powers, political upheaval, military coups and attempted assassination; first as sultans, the ancient Arab rulers' title, then, after mid-20th century independence from the colonial powers, adopting instead the more European title of 'king'. It is a story of adaptation, improvisation and innovation that will emerge as appropriate in these pages, but what had an immediate impact on me in Marrakech at this time was the habit, akin to that of Europe's mediaeval kings in the days before mass-media when first-hand sight and word of mouth were what mattered, of reinforcing his presence to his people by travelling the country. And at this particular moment he was arriving in Marrakech, as was evident from the sudden activity around the gates in the high red-brick wall that seals off the Royal Palace, a vast area of the city next to the Kasbah, of which the impenetrable, featureless wall is the only public face. Right now the gates were flanked not just with the usual police guard but with khaki-clad soldiers and the Royal Guard themselves, unmistakable in their splendid ceremonial red uniforms with white capes and green-and-white *képis*.

But it would appear nobody is quite certain exactly when His Majesty is about to appear. Just as I approach the palace, on the other side of the road, aiming to cross at right angles in the direction that I am fairly certain leads to Le Grand Tazi, the police suddenly stop traffic in all directions. And that very definitely includes pedestrian traffic, as is made abundantly clear to me by two heavy-set blokes in plain clothes but with telltale spiral cords running from earpieces. For a moment everything screeches to a stop and for five minutes or so we remain like that as if frozen in motion, until gradually the cacophony of car horns, primarily coming from those to the rear of the queue unaware of the cause for the hold-up, builds to a crescendo. Marrakech traffic is chaotic enough on an everyday basis that occasional hold-ups are taken for granted and it is assumed that the only way to remedy them is to parp loudly enough for someone up front to break the logjam, however perilously.

The police look at the plainclothes guys, who in turn glance at the Royal Guards, who are no longer as stiffly at attention as they were a few minutes ago, but more particularly at a man standing next to them in a dark suit, white shirt and expensive-looking sunglasses, holding a walkie-talkie to his ear. He nods in their direction, they nod to the police and the pandemonium that is normal urban traffic in Marrakech resumes with a vengeance. And that also includes pedestrians, who are brusquely hurried on their way. I cross the road, but go no further, intrigued by the possibility of getting a glimpse of His Maj. This is clearly not to the liking of the burly bloke in a brown suit who had gestured for me to be about my business; he frowns and in a trice another man on my side of the road, the sort of type in frayed jeans, a worn jumper and a baseball cap that I would normally have taken as a member of the urban underclass, has grabbed me by the arm. He smiles and says first in French, then in English, that I should move along.

For a minute or two, I play the 'Englishman abroad' part, saying how much I'd like to see the king and adding, for good measure, 'We love our queen too'. This flummoxes him for a moment, but only a moment. Then we are all at attention again, the traffic stopped, pedestrians allowed to proceed in one direction only – away from the palace – and police out in the middle of the road, and the man in the baseball cap scanning the crowd with one eye, the other fixed firmly on me. The only movement and sound, apart from the inevitable, still distant, but slowly building cacophony of horns being parped, is the sudden loud clattering of iron-rimmed wheels and the whinny of a horse, as a black-and-gold decorated *calèche*, a much grander version of the vintage horse-drawn carriages usually seen taking tourists around Jemaa el-Fnaa, rattles across the wet cobbles up to the palace gate, and is waved inside. All of a sudden I am reminded of the bizarre scene I witnessed at the funeral of the former Empress Zita of Austro-Hungary, in Vienna a quarter century ago, when thousands of nostalgic fans of the deposed Habsburg monarchy in period re-enactment uniforms lined the similarly rain-soaked cobbled streets to watch her ornate horse-drawn hearse pass by.

Then the customary pandemonium resumes. Clearly His Majesty has been yet again delayed. The man in the baseball cap nods at me, then shakes his head, making it clear that, monarchy-fan or not, the idea of me hanging out on this particular street corner any longer is not going to be appreciated. And as it is still raining, this time I am not about to argue: one convoy of black limousines, after all, looks much like another. The trouble is that the one direction I want to go in remains out of bounds, leaving me no choice but to take a detour, which, given the warren of streets that constitutes what might laughingly be called town-planning in most of Marrakech, even outside the labyrinth of the medina, is always a risk.

Before long I realise I've taken a wrong turn and am back in the souks, except this time it is a souk with a difference. Moroccans may believe in a mixed economy but not in a mixed high street. Where one merchant sets up shop, another in the same line of business will surely follow. And another. And another. So, amidst what might generally be known as the souk district of any town, we have the fruit and veg souk, the leatherware souk, the haberdashery souk, the carpet souk, the clothing souk, etc. Right now, it would seem, I have wandered into the middle of the second-hand car parts souk, including relevant repair shops. The wet pavements are piled high with tyres, new and used, outside dark and dingy rooms that open on to the street and would be a treasure trove for any old-fashioned mechanic, from genuine grease monkeys to the Trevs and Garys of the world whose idea of a fun Saturday is taking apart the big ends on the Hillman, in the days when men were men and cars could be souped up or stripped down with spanners and socket wrenches rather than laptops running software analytics. Here there are a plethora of spark plugs and sumps, maybe even big ends themselves for all I know, the sort of stuff that if you still find it at all in Britain, is likely to be in ancient workshops tucked under railway arches.

Meanwhile the adjacent alleyway is a specialist emporium in its own right: the used white-goods souk, with battered washing machines and fridges with broken doors stacked on top of one another, none of them looking remotely usable. It reminds me of a part of Streatham in South London where a sizeable Algerian community has gathered and seems to make a living selling used catering equipment to each other. It is all oddly reassuring, surprisingly 'green' in an oil-stained sort of way: equipment being used and recycled rather than just thrown away and replaced. But as a district to walk around on a cold damp afternoon in a city not a stone's throw from the Sahara desert, it is still rather depressing. A piece of 21st-century kit comes to my rescue, albeit oddly allied with a living survival from the distant past.

I turn to my iPhone, on which the GPS system – thanks to the fact that I zeroed in on Marrakech when I had access to Wi-Fi – seamlessly locates me down said back street on the wrong side of the royal palace. Not that satellite maps are as much use as they might be elsewhere in a city centre that is, for the most part, a warren of mediaeval alleyways. But there is one advantage to Marrakech in that respect: it has a main central square, the Jemaa el-Fnaa itself, which turns out to be simultaneously all but invisible and incredibly easy to locate. Marrakech's famed market place has defeated the satellite imagery, by virtue of its most predominant feature: the huge array of food stalls sending clouds of smoke into the air. Whenever the eyes of the sky, be they Google's, Apple's or more probably those of the US Department of Defence, have tried to focus on the Jemaa el-Fnaa, all that was visible was smoke signals. But at least I can work out the right direction to walk in.

Eventually I see the longed-for, but less than promising, peeling pink-painted plasterwork of the corner building that proclaims on the rather grimy sign above the door, 'Grand Hotel Tazi' and below, rather improbably, 'Restaurant, *Piscine*'. The restaurant I know exists, although few visitors of any sense consume much of its food, but the *piscine* seems optimistic, to say the least. I push the dented, silver-coloured metal door between the cracked faux-marble entrance pillars, only to have it fly open unexpectedly, almost flattening the doorman-cum-security guard on the other side, who nonetheless beams broadly: he knows why I am here.

Until relatively recently – a decade or so ago – the Grand Hotel Tazi was the only place inside Marrakech's medina licensed to serve alcohol. From the days when Graham Nash visited with his girlfriend and the events described by Esther Freud in *Hideous Kinky* were played out, until close to the end of the last century, everyone from hairy hippies seeking an alternative high to *kif* to high-end travellers desperate for a gin and tonic to Moroccan men who fancied a beer and some footie on the telly, flocked to the Tazi. The hippies and the high-enders are gone, but a motley crew of Western tourists and local beer and football fans remain the core of its clientele.

The Tazi still has an atmosphere all its own, though: somewhere between the stage set for *Casablanca* and a 1950s New York hotel lobby. In reality, its furnishings are rather more modern, but create such a dated atmosphere that it is almost impossible not to place it further back in time than it really belongs. The main lobby itself is dark, particularly compared to what is normally blinding sunshine outside, though on a drippy day like today, there is little real difference. No sooner have I burst through the door than the familiar sight of the plump, genial lobby porter in his smart suit has bustled over to see to my needs, which he has of course already anticipated. I glance around the lobby, taking in, as ever, all its particular glory: the walls and ceiling painted to look like marble; the dusty unlit chandeliers; the bizarre, semi-idyllic, almost certainly 1950s fresco of a young woman with some agricultural produce on her back – reminiscent of the sort of paintings they used to hang in the foyers of hotels in Albania; and of course, next to the door, the obligatory photograph of His Majesty, Mohammed VI, black and white in smart suit and shades, to all extents and purposes the fashion role model for the doorman standing directly next to it.

The lobby seating consists of vast leather armchairs, big enough to swallow you whole, arranged as if they still belong to some 1960s first-class airport departure lounge. In contrast to this post-luxurious gloom, the room beyond, effectively the hotel bar, has not a lot to recommend it with its hard flooring, 1970s sofas with fraying upholstery and some spartan rattan-backed chairs. On the other hand, the light is actually on, which is a plus, considering that bars selling alcohol are, as a rule, signally lacking in translucent windows. There are also – no doubt thanks to the atrocious weather conditions outside – more than a few customers, including some middle-aged, obviously French couples sitting together over a couple of bottles of the inevitable Flag Spéciale, chain-smoking and chatting in desultory fashion to one another.

But by far the great majority of the customers at this time of day are solitary Moroccan men, beer in hand and cigarette in mouth. Right at the front, in pole position for the wall-mounted flatscreen television (not everything about the Tazi is stuck in a time warp) is yet another Obi Wan Kenobi, the hood of his thick woollen jellaba pulled up over his head, staring straight ahead through thick lenses. I glance up to see what is so deserving of his unbridled attention: Stoke City leading Hull 1–0 in the closing stages of the 2013–2014 Barclay's Premiership.

By and large, apart from a few exotic details, mostly sartorial, the scene could be any British working-class pub on a wet midweek afternoon. Alongside the door to the empty restaurant (its tables laid optimistically with paper napkins for dinner), a middle-aged bloke in a long brown overcoat, with a rumpled porkpie hat on his head and a long blue cotton scarf slung over his shoulder – on his fourth Flag judging by the bottle count on the table in front of him – is deep in conversation with a younger man in an olive corduroy jacket, beige Argyle-pattern jumper and straight-leg jeans. If they were in an English bar I would wager they were discussing horses, the odds on the 3.10 at Cheltenham, or football, whether Stoke could hold on to that 1–0 lead. Behind me a man in his thirties is dressed in a distinctive red-and-silver puffa jacket, jeans and Nike trainers, pretending to watch the football but in fact talking quietly the whole time on his mobile phone. He could be a drug dealer. In contrast, the man next to him has sunglasses pushed back on his head over a thick mop of long curly grey hair with jeans and a well-worn chequered jacket that looks like it has come straight from Oxfam; he could be a French artist down on his luck or an eccentric Oxford don. What he actually is – as well or apart from anything else – is a Barcelona fan, and he grimaces when they miss a chance to score against Atlético Madrid, a game which has clearly taken precedence over Stoke v Hull on the TV channel.

A tall, elegant, balding man in a brown pinstripe suit that Al Capone might have approved of, although the fact that it is of a more modern vintage is clearly attested to by the flared trousers, and a rather remarkable striped yellow tie, enters, glances at the television, shrugs and slumps into a chair with an air of resignation. Spotting him, the chubby, cheery porter dances up behind him to bestow a matey – and yes, in Morocco that is the word for it; there are still some differences from English working-class pubs – kiss on the top of his bald pate. The newcomer looks up in surprise, then gets up to embrace the porter, who immediately bustles off to fetch him a beer. With it he brings a couple of little plates for me, in honour of the fact that I have already finished my second Flag: a saucer of fresh, hot, salty, buttered popcorn, and a saucer of spiced olives. All in all, on a wet afternoon in a city on the edge of a desert, the Grand Hotel Tazi serves its purpose admirably: a sort of secular purgatory as comfy as a pair of old *babouches* for those whose preference is for the easy-going life. In its very own way, it is an incomparable element in the make-up of Marrakech.

But before long it is time for me to go and pick up my dinner, which I rescue from the ashes, glad that the spice merchant thought to make the rest of the string he used to tie on the paper covering into a handle: the pot is far too hot to touch. I take it back to Café Clock to show to and share with Mohammed. A kilo of lamb is more than enough for two. It turns out that the legendary local dish is so rare that more or less all five of the kitchen staff want a taste. They rustle up some couscous and a spiced yoghurt side dish and Mohammed cuts through the paper cover on the *tanjia,* to release a rich savoury scent of spiced lamb. There is general agreement that the dish is delicious, the soft melting meat delicately spiced.

It has also attracted the inevitable cluster of Marrakech's endemic feral cats to crouch around us, sharp-eyed, glaring up at us with obvious rabid hunger. I have never really been much of a cat lover, always considering them to be something of a baby substitute – you know, mewling, crying, always needing to be fed or patted or shown how to go to the toilet and, all too often, cleaned up after. But I have to confess to getting improbably fond of – or to put it more correctly, acquiring a respect for the plucky little feral felines of Morocco, forever skulking under cars as if to examine the exhaust pipe, or chilling out in a patch of shade while clawing whimsically at some fatty piece of offal accidentally dropped from one of the outdoor butcher's blocks.

There's a sort of defiant independence to them, a sort of ballsy 'what's it to you, mate?' attitude that tells you they would scratch your eyes out if you tried to stroke them – 'getting a bit fresh, are we, sunshine?' – that comes over as admirably self-reliant when compared with the slack-eyed, wanton, legs-in-the-air prostitution of our overfed, domestic eunuchs. Top Cat would have hung out with these guys. But Mohammed is insistent they do not get any scraps from the table. 'If you encourage them, they will never leave.'

*

But Marrakech is not just the medina. Most Moroccans who come to Marrakech come not for the Jemaa el-Fnaa, to have their fortune told or watch a snake charmer; they come for the drink and discos. Rock'n'Kech is an aspirational place all but hidden away high on a rooftop not quite as far as it should be from the Koutoubia mosque. I end up in there only because of a street tout who hands me a leaflet as I head out of the medina to sample the joys of the *ville nouvelle* and find myself, not for the first time in this city, walking in a circle. At first I am not so sure: the doorway leads down a narrow corridor, which turns into a tight staircase with a black or purple painted wall. Not exactly welcoming until it opens out into an airy rooftop bar, open to the elements, a high wall along one side performing the necessary role of preventing any sight line to the minaret of the mosque. A few drinkers stand chatting happily at the bar while one of those, now commonplace, imitation-flame, pyramid space heaters flickers up and down. There is a thumping disco beat going down, but the barman tells me it is too cold, even though the morning rain has long gone and the temperature was rising throughout the afternoons. 'This time of year,' he says glumly, 'it should be 28C in Marrakech, not 18C.'

I ask him for some further recommendations and he shrugs, unwilling to lose custom, then reluctantly admits that I might try Café L'Escale, where they often have live music, or maybe, he says a bit hesitantly, African Chic, which I have heard touted as a celebrity-spotting venue, both of them bars situated further out in Guéliz, which is what the locals call the *ville nouvelle*. How far to walk? He shrugs. 'Maybe a taxi?'

Thanks to the compact structure of the medina, I have as yet had little experience with Marrakech taxi drivers, but there are enough of them standing in an unruly clump around the trees on the edge of the square, the nearest they are allowed into the medina. At the sight of a potential fare, they brighten up and at least three of them start hurrying towards me. There obviously isn't a hierarchical cab rank structure going on here. I mention L'Escale to the first one to get up to me, and he virtually bundles me into his cab, beige like all the others that serve as *petits taxis* in Marrakech – conveniently, I am to discover, each city has its colour code – as opposed to the *grands taxis* which offer longer-distance trips between towns, effectively functioning as buses. He insists he knows the place and will take me there for just 50 dirhams. I suggest he might have a taximeter but he insists it is broken and fifty is 'very good price, cheap'. This obviously suggests I am paying over the odds, but it is late at night, and as far as I can make out from the map this place is at least 20 minutes walk away, so I briefly propose 30 then settle on 40, which is about £3.50, as much as a London cabbie would charge to take you to the other side of the road.

We are halfway there, hurtling up Avenue Mohammed VI at a right rate, when I ask if he might know what time the place closes. He hesitates for a moment, says '10.30' and then adds, cheerfully: 'But no matter, it is not open today anyway.' What? I say he might have mentioned this earlier but all I get is a shrug. There is no point in pursuing the argument so I suggest instead he take me to African Chic, the Rock'n'Kech bartender's other suggestion. It is, in any case, closer, except that it requires him to carry on a hundred yards or so until he can make a U-turn, which he does, then pulls in to the side of the road and says, 'It is just down there, not far, but it's a one-way street.' I glance up and can't see a no-entry sign but the road does seem narrow enough and all the cars parked on it are facing towards us. Seems fair enough, until he adds, '80 dirhams, please.'

'Wait a minute, we agreed 40.'

'That was to different place.'

Yes, I want to point out, and this is actually closer, but have the sinking feeling it isn't going to do any good. On the other hand, I'm the customer and I'm already out of his car, but there again the last thing I want is to be reported to Moroccan police for doing a runner.

'Forty,' I insist.

'Sixty, absolute minimum,' he insists.

I snarl and hand him a 50-dirham note, which is the smallest I have anyhow without scrabbling through my loose change. He snarls, snatches it and speeds off, leaving both of us in a bad mood, it would appear, though when I learn the truth about Moroccan taxi fares, I realise he was probably laughing his head off. We have, of course, only been arguing about a relatively small sum of money, and more for him than for me, but there is a principle at stake here. And 'thieving cabbie' is not a trade attribute anybody should be proud of. Even those licensed to charge the fares they do!

African Chic is also not exactly 'just there'. He was right about the road; although it is one way for its entire length there are some drivers who do not know about it. In any case I walk at least a half a mile before I reach the said establishment, which has a DJ-wearing bouncer on the door. But trade can't be booming because he hardly gives me a second look. Inside I can see why. For all the guff about 'Keanu Reeves once dropped in for a night out', the current clientele are mainly middle-aged and older French men with expansively endowed sub-Saharan African ladies in hot pants and little else on their arms or, more frequently, laps. There is live music promised for later, the barman tells me as I take a place in the ultraviolet glow that passes for lighting in these sorts of places, and order the only Moroccan beer in the house, the elegantly malty Casablanca which comes in at a chunky 65 dirhams – and advertises itself as the one beer from Morocco exported to the USA – but then I am in a club of sorts, and there was no entrance fee at the door. Over the next half hour or so, I sink two of them, tasting mainly the chill, and watch the scene.

It isn't much of a scene. A couple of young Dutch women come in and 'ooh' and 'aah' a bit, primarily because they have identified a pic of Keanu, I suspect, amidst the various 'so-and-so celebrity was here' snapshots on the walls. One of the advantages of being on the upper edge of the middle-aged cohort, is that you develop a remarkably well-honed immunity to the cult of celebrity, partly of course because you no longer recognise those who are the new famous. Once, a decade or so ago, I spent an evening drinking next to Noel Gallagher at the bar of the Groucho Club in London, and left thinking he was just some loud-mouthed Mancunian. Mind you, for all I know it could have been Liam.

One or two of the large African ladies glance in my direction occasionally but soon lose interest when I occupy myself with the peanuts. Even if I were in the market, they're definitely not my type. Nor is the whole African Chic experience, I quickly decide. I suspect all nightclubs in the world have a tawdry, underlying naffness, no matter how glitzy the clientele or how high the bar prices. I imagine they all look pretty rough – as do the clientele – in the bare light of morning.

And tomorrow morning I have a train to catch. To Morocco's metropolis: Casablanca.

4

Play It Again, Hassan

FOR A CITY THAT OWES most of its fame to a 1942 film shot almost exclusively in an indoor studio in suburban Los Angeles, as far from the location as possible, based on an unstaged play by a writer who, like the cast and director, had never been to Morocco, and is renowned for a song played by a pianist who was in real life a drummer, Casablanca, unsurprisingly, doesn't exactly live up to its global reputation. It is still in the process of establishing its own.

'Casablana is not Morocco,' every wise and weary traveller fan of Marrakech and the other ancient 'royal *cités*' will tell you. But in a very real sense they are wrong. It may not have much of ancient Morocco about it, but it has a hell of a lot of the present and if the current establishment has its way, backed up by the migrating feet of the young in their tens of thousands, it may well herald much of the country's future. It has become par for the course to refer to the country's bustling, populous metropolis as Morocco's New York, but a better parallel in US terms might actually be Los Angeles. In 1907 when French forces first arrived to take advantage of the declining power of the sultanate as the Europeans jostled in what they did not yet know would be the beginning of the end of their eventually self-destructive quest for global empires, Casablanca was a small town of barely 20,000 people.

From its origins as little more than a pirate base, then from time to time foothold in North Africa for Portuguese, Spanish and French in turn, Casablanca has nothing of the exotic feel of Marrakech or the ancient palaces of Meknes and Fez. Its name began as *casa branca,* a Portuguese, lisp-inspired version of its current Spanish-derived name. It has never really been known by anything other than the European name, nowadays almost universally shortened to just Casa.

Today it is by far the country's biggest city, and the one with the greatest gulf between the richest inhabitants and the poorest. There is little doubt that the urban elite of today's sprawling city are embarrassed by their poor neighbours. According to government figures, Casablanca has a population of around three million but when its vast hordes of unregistered slum dwellers, refugees and sundry flotsam and jetsam are taken into account there is nobody who really doubts that the real number of souls seeking a living of some sort in the Moroccan metropolis is over six million. Today, Moroccans routinely refer to it as *la métropole,* much as the British refer to London.

It is a three-hour, relatively comfortable, remarkably restrained journey from the city of snake charmers, story-tellers and souks on the edge of the desert into the city of broad boulevards, financial services, chichi residences and 21st-century slums. Train 608, a clean, smart French diesel maybe 10 or 20 years old, with impeccable seats and armrests, is indistinguishable from any average European train – and certainly better than many in Britain – the only difference being that there are separate male and female toilets. What surprises me most, though, is how quiet is. Not the train but the compartments. I had expected something more like the chatter of Cuban trains, where everybody talks to everybody else. Even in England these days, trains can be an incessant babble, even if half of those nattering away are talking to someone on their phones, and in the supposedly 'quiet coach'. This coach, about two-thirds full, is remarkably quiet, and yet almost nobody is reading. Most passengers sit quietly looking out the window, or close their eyes and lean back for a doze.

As the train glides out of Marrakech station, first the sprawling suburbs of the *ville nouvelle* slide by, sprawling estates that give way, momentarily, illusorily, to an impression of countryside before the real conurbation of Marrakech *extra muros* begins. Barely more than a kilometre outside the northern limits of the city proper its nouveau riche illegitimate child has taken root. Here are block upon block of four- and five-storey sprawling apartment complexes, their only concession to their parentage the russet colour of the concrete and the intricate wrought-iron frames around their windows, whereas the true badge of their allegiance can be found in the regimented rows of dishes that line the rooftops; for these are satellite cities in every sense.

Yet the urban infestation is not yet complete; here by the rail side a peasant farmer busies himself with his horse and cart, while his wife bustles around a few chickens outside the door of a house that seems to have grown out of the ground, its dirt-coloured breeze blocks like a natural scabby outcrop of the earth amid the palm trees.

Just when it seems we have finally left behind us the furthest flung outpost of Marrakech, crossing over a wide, fast-flowing (given the rains of the past few days) russet river, more red than brown, a folly fantasy emerges from nowhere: a Disneyland cross between Taj Mahal and carnival, all blue and green and red and golden domes, with fanciful details in contrasting colours, like some Las Vegas casino designer's nightmarish vision of an Islamic fun version of Moscow's St Basil's cathedral.

Happily – hysterically – it is there and gone in little more than the blink of an eye, an outtake from an acid-trip flashback, and the long sinuous train is winding at last beyond the trappings of tawdry tourism into a barren landscape where the High Atlas with their rugged grandeur finally decline into a series of rocky pimples that melt into the greening plains on which small herds of goats wander, grazing on whatever they can find between the stones, scrub and occasional incomplete cacti hedges.

Sidi Bouthmane, one of those types of halt familiar to railways in wilder parts of the world, is not so much a station as a passing place where we wait 20 minutes for the sister train coming in the opposite direction. There's little more to feast the eyes on than a small power transformer station, a few semi-derelict structures and a couple of women in full veil poking sticks at their flocks of sheep wandering among the olive groves and looking increasingly soggy as the rain sets in again.

For most of the journey between Morocco's most popular tourist resort and its biggest, most aggressively bustling and Westernised city, train 608 winds through remarkably underdeveloped countryside that is for the most part little more than a stony desert covered with barely enough topsoil for scrub grass and herbs to just about flourish and provide pasturage for the lonely goatherds to ply their solitary trade, donned in hooded jellabas. Above the level of the scrub only the occasional grove of windswept olive trees or clump of vicious-looking cacti sprout from the landscape.

Eventually as we wind down towards the coast, the largish town of Settat is the first real indication of a more urban presence, followed by Berrechid, the outskirts of which are marked by six-storey blocks of flats eerily reminiscent of Soviet-era Russia. As we pull out of town, paralleling the now dual-carriageway road for the last 20 kilometres or so into Casablanca, I notice two older men standing in a field of growing vegetables, wearing white hats and leaning on sticks. I'm tempted to snatch a picture of their rustic content alongside the pace of modernity, when suddenly, with no obvious warning, the pair of them almost simultaneously raise their sticks and begin brutally laying into one another with such apparent violence it is both hilarious and worrying at the same time. But then they are gone and I can only hope in the abstract that it is no more serious than the other night in Marrakech when I saw the elderly doorman at the restaurant Marrakchi, clad in red fez and thick white woolly jellaba, suddenly turn on a man of a similar age with whom he had only seconds before been apparently conducting an amiable conversation, and rain blows on him before receiving a few back, and in a matter of a minute both putting their arms round one another.

A new pair of passengers joins at Berrechid and settles down opposite me, deep in conversation, possibly father and daughter; he with a craggy, handsome, weather-lined face, and swept back hair à la Michael Douglas, in a smart blue zipper jacket and jeans, she in fashionably wrinkled tight designer jeans and a tight black upholstered leather top with matching upholstered leather handbag, over a pink top and with a stylish tube-thingy scarf and suede boots, her dark hair not only uncovered but stylishly swept back to reveal diamanté bow earrings. She would not be out of place in Paris or London, or even necessarily in Marrakech, except that there I would have put her down as a tourist and here she is obviously local.

They are only on board for a few minutes, deep in conversation all the while, before disembarking at Casa-Oasis, a salubrious-looking suburb. But it is not much longer before we are crawling through the outskirts of Casablanca: grimy concrete walls above the railway cutting, wrought-iron windows covered with hanging clothing, industrial and household debris along the tracks. Before entering the *ville nouvelle* proper, the train first has to crawl through the modern underside of Morocco's metropolis: its *bidonvilles*. The term dates from the early 20th century as a native French expression to equate with the English shanty towns or slums, which in turn originally designated the outskirts of Dublin. It has its roots in the old Norman French for a bucket or tin can, which by extrapolation has come to mean something embarrassing or rubbish.

Walls just over two metres high surround most of the *bidonvilles,* which might easily be taken, certainly from the train tracks, for remarkably evenly-distributed rubbish tips, topped out with sheets of plastic or bits of corrugated iron, were it not for the forest of satellite dishes above them. The poor of Casablanca may not be able to afford a roof over their heads, but even the most impoverished can shell out for a concave link to the heavens to shelter beneath. But then that's 'Casa' for you, an intriguing, contradictory clash of culture within one nation. Casablanca is Morocco's laboratory, its cultural nuclear reactor, and whether the result is fusion or fission could yet decide whether this country continues on its route to becoming one of the most modern, tolerant countries in Africa and Islam, or the cauldron of catastrophe.

Old and new Casablanca are immediately evident the moment I climb off the train. Quixotically the station that might be considered the more central is Casa Port, obviously down by the sea front, but that is not the terminus for most passenger trains. The end of the line is more commonly Casa Voyageurs, set on the suburban edge of the city centre, an ageing early 20th-century building, elegant in the French colonial style, spruced up on the outside but a little scruffy around the tracks.

But by the time I have crossed the road outside, after first fighting my way through the usual army of unofficial would-be taxi drivers, I come across the newest and possibly most splendid example of what Moroccan modernisers, who importantly include His Majesty, think their country should aspire to: a state of the art, 21st-century, urban tram system, complete with automatic ticket machines and touchscreen barriers. The rails are laid into the road, often with grass between and on either side, just like the system that transformed Bordeaux's riverfront from a dirty, traffic-clogged road alongside a series of rusting warehouses into a post-industrial elegant boulevard, and won the splendid 18th-century frontages along it the accolade of joining UNESCO's World Heritage Site list. The colonists may have gone but the French influence in infrastructure and manufacturing is still strongly in evidence, particularly as the bullet-nosed, glistening, red tram glides at an almost silent whisper to a stop.

I have pre-booked rented accommodation online, but all I have is an address with little real idea how to find it. I had been counting on a taxi-driver, even if my experience in Marrakech had warned me that jumping into a cab in Morocco and asking to be taken to a location I didn't know was likely to be a fraught and probably expensive adventure. It was not – which is not to say that it was any the less frustrating, just not in any way I imagined as I headed up the street from Place des Nations Unies to the *petit taxi* rank.

To get a brief idea of how far I might be going – and therefore just what sort of price I might be arguing about – I stop at a café where a waiter is clearing an outside table and ask him if knows how far it is to Ibn Rochd. He glances at a colleague for a second, then they both nod and point up the road, though whether he is suggesting it's walking distance or pointing at the taxis I am initially unsure until he makes clear: '*C'est pas loin, m'sieu, dix dirhams,*' and he makes a gesture of a man holding out a ten-dirham coin, indicating I should poke it at the taxi driver. I smile thankfully for this almost literally priceless piece of information and head off. Behind me the waiter calls out in emphasis, '*Dix dirhams, m'sieu, pas plus!*' It would appear that if taxi drivers are hoods, then the good folk of Casablanca are not happy to see tourists ripped off.

To my surprise, nor are the taxi drivers. The first *petit taxi* I come across – here in Casa they are red – is happy to take me to Ibn Rochd. He seems happy with 10 dirhams too, when I do as suggested, and simply nods as if it were the most obvious thing in the world. I am impressed. All the more so when it seems that, far from walking distance of the city centre, even without a backpack which I had very much hoped would be the case, getting to Ibn Rochd is quite a drive, at the very least a couple of kilometres and most of it up and down steep hills. But the real problem is when we finally get there, or where the driver thinks is there, and he stops and points to what appears to be a hospital. With good reason, as the large sign in front of me declares Centre Hospitalier Universitaire Ibn Rochd. 'Non, Non,' I insist and tell him once again I want the rue Ibn Rochd. He shrugs, gestures at the road we have just driven up and makes it clear that he expects both his 10 dirhams and me to get out of the car.

This is not entirely satisfactory but as 10 dirhams is about 80 British pence or €1, it seems cheap at the price, and it does indeed sound fairly reasonable that the road leading to Ibn Rochd hospital might indeed be rue Ibn Rochd. All I need to do is find number 9. Except that there isn't one. As my *petit taxi* heads back downhill to the *grande ville* I am left staring at a street that on one side is lined with hospital outbuildings, largely behind a fence, and on the other with various commercial premises by and large dedicated to the hospital and healthcare worlds, such as pharmacies, general drug stores and places to buy soft drinks and snacks. Not one of them looks remotely like an apartment block offering accommodation to travellers. I try one of the pharmacies, asking for number 9, but get only a blank stare. Not 100 per cent sure whether this is because the assistant has a poor command of French – unlikely but not impossible in a pharmacy – I try another question: is this indeed the rue Ibn Rochd?

'C'est l'hôpital Ibn Rochd,' she says, gesturing up the road.

I smile, patiently I hope, and say, 'Non, est-ce que c'est la RUE Ibn Rochd.'

This gets just a funny look and the equally deliberately patient reply: 'Non, m'sieu, c'est la rue des Hôpitaux,' which, from her point of view ought to be obvious. Obviously.

Feeling rather stupid at this point, I ask if she knows where around here rue Ibn Rochd might be. She doesn't. This is not looking good. I am not feeling smart. I am also no longer quite so impressed by my honest taxi driver. The best idea I have at this point, and it is not exactly a brainwave, is to wander around the surrounding streets in search of one that might be called Ibn Rochd and see if it has a number 9. You might be wondering why, after having proved so successful around the car-tyre and used white-goods souks of Marrakech, modern technology in the form of either Apple or Google maps has not by now saved my – if you'll pardon the word in an Islamic context – bacon. The answer is a simple one: no data connection, no Wi-Fi, no pre-loaded map of Casablanca. My phone is showing a little arrow that marks exactly where on the surface of the planet I am, but with only a blank grid background rather than a street map it is not exactly much of a help.

Not that it necessarily would be a help even if I had the data. I have come to learn that street names in Morocco are an ill-defined concept. Not all streets have them; those that do have often been changed, particularly since independence; those that might not have been changed are also locally known as something quite different; and of those that do have names, not all are given in both French and Arabic, and even if they are, as I am to find out repeatedly, not all the transliterations from vowel-less Arabic into Latin characters are identical. Indeed, it is not even necessarily the case that they should, particularly given that Moroccan Arabic, although written identically to classical Arabic, is pronounced quite differently, and vowel sounds present in one spoken form of the language may sound different, or be missing altogether, in another. This is even true within Morocco. Ibn Rochd, for example, is also written in French as Ibnou Rochd.

Just to make some of this a bit clearer – or not – it turns out that Ibn Rochd was a real historical character, a Muslim polymath who was born in the 12th century in Córdoba, in what we today call Spain but was then the Moorish (virtually synonymous with Moroccan) province of *Al-Andaluz* (or Al-Andalus, hence Andalusia; this is not just an Arabic problem). He was quite the 12th-century whizz kid, being an expert in astronomy, geography, maths, physics, Andalusian classical music, and not just Islamic philosophy but also Aristotelian philosophy. In fact it was translations of his work into Latin that reintroduced Aristotle, who had been banished in the Dark Ages as 'too pagan' for the Christian fundamentalists of the time, to Western Europe. His writings were deemed controversial by Muslims at the time but subsequently led to him being considered the 'founding father of secular thought' by many Europeans, not least for suggesting that reason and religion ought to be considered separate.

Beyond his philosophy, though, the main reason he is remembered in the way he most frequently is in the Arab world, is for a book called *Kitaba Kulliyat fi al-Tibb,* which was translated into Latin as *Colliget,* but is best rendered in English (and easiest understood) as 'General Medicine'. His work was a million miles from bloodlettings and leeches too: he made major contributions to early neurology, first suggesting the existence of Parkinson's disease, and was one of the first to work out the function of the retina in the human eye. He might well be considered the Arabic equivalent of Hippocrates. Hardly surprising that there are hospitals named after him.

Except for the problem of the actual name. His actual full name was Abu i-Walid bin Ahamad bin Rusd (أبو الوليد محمد بن احمد بن رشد to you purists), which was a bit of a mouthful even for fellow Arabic speakers who routinely shortened it to Ibn Rochd or Ibnou Rochd (ابن رشد) or even, depending on your accent I suppose, as Ibn Rushd. But even that was a bit of a stretch for his European translators who just wrote down a garbled version of what they heard which came out (fairly improbably) as Averroës, or occasionally Averrhoes. He was buried in 1198 in his family tomb. I'm tempted to go and see it one day, just for old times' sake, if I ever make it to Córdoba or Cordova or Qurtuba (قرطبة), or whatever! (If you think this is an unusual problem in transliterating from Arabic, consider that over the years the founder of the Islamic faith has been referred to by Europeans as Mohammed, Muhammad, Mahomet and his followers as Moslems, Muslims and Mahometans.)

Meanwhile, back on the streets of Casablanca's hospital quarter I'm losing the will to live, or at least to waste any more time trying to find an apartment which may or may not exist and which I've only booked but not paid for, and in any case if it is around here somewhere it's too far to walk into the city centre and back on a regular basis. An offer to help by a middle-class-looking woman – dressed in Western fashion with knee-length skirt, no headscarf and opulent string of pearls – probably more concerned with why a middle-aged bloke in jeans with a rucksack might be staring at the door of her house (looking in vain for its number), also comes to nothing. It's time for a taxi. Which means, of course, that there are none available. Even the couple outside the hospital aren't interested: both have been pre-booked.

Eventually, down on the main drag back into town, a *petit taxi* slows down and parps next to me, a sure indication he is looking for a fare. I jump in, and ask for Place des Nations Unies, which is where I started my quest for Ibn Rochd and seems to be the nearest thing to the city centre, and so I'm puzzled when the driver looks puzzled at the name. I add *près de la medina* and he smiles in recognition and says. 'Ah,' followed by something that may or not have been, 'Anfa!' but turns the car thankfully in the right direction.

This turns out to be the oldest name for Casablanca itself, dating back to Berber days in the eight century, which is way before any of the current medina existed. Its market place was the spot chosen by French architect Henri Prost to be the focal point of his *ville nouvelle* but seems to have retained its place in the popular tongue even after the new name of Place des Nations Unies was bestowed, probably in honour of the 1943 Casablanca Conference when the Second World War allies, who had already given themselves that title, met, as it happened, in the Hotel Anfa.

To my delighted and diminishing surprise, the cab driver immediately switches on his meter, showing a colossal starting price of 1.20 dirhams, at which rate it may barely hit 10 dirhams by the time we get back to the city centre. A few metres further, as we stop at a traffic light, a large lady in bright print dress and headscarf with a weighty shopping bag gestures for us to stop, which we do, and she climbs in the front seat. She is going in the same direction. But after a few moments' conversation, all in local Arabic dialect, which means I have understood nothing, there would seem to be a problem. The driver stops by the kerb, orders her out, then sits waiting for her to come back; I am confused, but happily not in a hurry. After about five minutes, she returns, starts to climb in but after a brief exchange with the driver, he reaches over, pulls the door closed, leaving her fuming on the pavement, and drives off.

Glancing in the rear-view mirror, he sees my puzzlement, laughs and explains in French: 'She says she had no money, so I say why did you get into the taxi? She says she means she has no change, and asks if I can change a 200-dirham note. I don't have that change so I send her to a shop to get some. She says the shopkeeper won't give her any, but that is because she doesn't buy anything: some little thing, anything. She thinks because I have a European in the car, you will pay. So I threw her out.'

I am bemused by both his honesty and sense of fair play. I ask him if he has always been a taxi driver. He laughs again, and says, no, tells me his name is Ahmed and he used to work in an office in Paris, but they paid him off, and after the Schengen accord came in he suddenly found he had to get a work permit. Schengen not only gave complete freedom to cross frontiers in nearly all of Europe (including non-EU Switzerland, Norway and Iceland) with the exception of the paranoid UK (and Ireland, reluctantly tied to the same regime because of the border with the British north); it also meant that citizens from the former colonies lost some of their rights. Ahmed found – and still finds – it outrageous that a Dutchman can work in France without a permit but he cannot. He came back to Morocco, got a job with a local firm, but in the end they too paid him off. Cab-driving was a last resort. 'But at least I am honest,' he says, 'unlike some.' I nod in agreement though so far it has been my experience that Casablanca cabbies make their Marrakchi cousins look like highway robbers. He drops me at '*Anfa*', and I ask if he can recommend hotels. He says there are all sorts: big, modern, expensive on one side, and old, rather run-down on the other. I clamber out, offering him 20 dirhams, the smallest coin I have, only for him to reinforce his claim to honesty by not just offering, but insisting I accept 10 dirhams in change.

On the other side of the square is the vast white bulk of the Hyatt Regency, looking imposing, expensive and just about identical to every other Hyatt Regency on the planet. Right in front of me is the Hotel Excelsior, looking like it might once have been every bit as impressive as befits its name, but probably only 90 years ago. It has a grand French colonial façade, with peeling paint, and steps up to a dark lobby with aged wood panelling, an intricate carpet that in places still has some remaining fibres and a tall, elegant-looking man in a brown suit who might well have been a bellboy when it opened. I ask if they have a room for a couple of nights and he glances to one side, at an open door in the lobby, then explains that they do, that it is a room for three but *I* can have it at a single price, if I do not mind that the lift is broken and it is on the third floor. At 270 dirhams a night (about £22) I decide I have wasted enough time looking for a place to lay my head for the night and accept. Fifteen minutes later, having climbed up what turns out to be four floors – he wasn't counting the empty mezzanine floor – and watched the state of the decor in the hallways deteriorate from faded flowery wallpaper to flaking paintwork, I reach the end of a corridor, with a hardwood door that leads into a room with peeling paper, a double bed and a single bed, all made up with heavy blankets, and lace curtains over a shuttered window that doesn't seem to be closed properly judging from the clanking, parping and general commotion outside. I walk across to it and gaze on to what must once have been the finest panorama of central Casablanca: the square below and the great tower over the medina. Yes, it is noisy and dirty – though the whisper-quiet tram gliding into the stop hints at a very different potential future – but hey, it's Casablanca, that's what I've come to experience, and at least there is a basic but clean en suite with working toilet, so I decided to cut my losses and stay.

So what else, halfway through the afternoon, but to head for the one thing that more than anything else is the globally recognised symbol of the city visited as practically the first stop on their itineraries by almost every tourist looking for the most famous (and mythical) 'of all the gin joints in all the world': Rick's Bar. Except, of course, that there never was a 'Rick' in Casablanca, any more than there was a bar in Casablanca that remotely resembled the one in the movie.

That was until a gang of financially flush Americans – known predictably from Claude Rains' most famous line as 'The Usual Suspects' – under the aegis of an enterprising woman who just happened to have been US consul in Casa, and knew what her fellow countrymen came to seek and failed to find, bought a building in the old colonial style by the waterfront on the edge of the medina and renamed it.

It is a long time since I last – admittedly for the third or fourth time – saw the movie, but when I get to the white stucco building glinting in the sunshine with the seagulls circling overhead, it looks nothing like the bar I remember being swathed in smoke or fog with vintage French automobiles outside. In front of this place is a huge tour bus whose Japanese passengers are all inside the foyer buying 'souvenirs' of a Disney-style mock-up of a fictional bar, the inspiration for which wasn't even in this country.

The stage play, which never found a producer, was written by Murray Burnett and Joan Alison and originally entitled *Everybody Comes to Rick's*. The ambiance in the movie was really more akin to Tangier (where Caid's bar in the Hotel al-Minzah, which we will get to eventually, also claims to be 'the original').

But Tangier, being an 'international city' at the time – where Germans, British, Americans and French could and did dine together at the Café de Paris – didn't suit the plot, which required a conflict of interest between a policeman of the Vichy France regime (which nominally ruled Casablanca) and German overlords.

The real-life prototype for Rick's was probably a bar in Marseille visited by Burnett with his wife in 1938, when the flood of wartime exiles and refugees was just beginning. Ironically, there are not many cities in Europe that resemble Casablanca more than Marseille, with its huge North African population.

Because it's here, and so am I – like Hillary and Everest – I go inside, take a seat at the bar, alongside a couple of American couples who clearly believe they are visiting the 'real thing' and order a cocktail. There is none of the faded elegance, conspiratorial hush, or – remarkably in Morocco and probably because there are no Moroccans here except for the staff – cloud of cigarette smoke. Just some wealthy Americans off a cruise liner talking loudly over peanuts and wine.

I suppose my cocktail should have been gin-based even in a replica of the most famous 'gin joint in all the world', but instead I opt for my all-time favourite: a Brazilian caipirinha, which turns out to be a mistake as they don't have the *cachaça* spirit it requires. I opt for Bacardi instead; they don't have Havana Club either. It's okay, but literally nothing to write home about, or come back for. It also turns out that tonight is the one night a week when there isn't a piano player churning out a stereotypical run of 1940s classics and the inevitable *As Time Goes By* at least once an hour. I count my blessings and head for the door.

The medina too, as I amble back through it towards the city centre, has a slightly Disney feel – all *babouches* and pouffes, stuff bought by tourists rather than Moroccans. However, there is no sign of what my friend in Rabat will later tell me is the real indication of a genuine souk for the locals: a stall selling men's underwear. There is, however, a bit of a commotion halfway through, with thickset men in sunglasses on every corner, and I can just glimpse through a narrow gateway several dark Mercedes on the coast road beyond: it turns out that the King is visiting today, not at the vast mosque on the seafront built by and named for his father – which is on my list of things to visit – but at a smaller one in the medina. I'm beginning to suspect he is following me.

At the far end of the medina, however, where the main road cuts in from the coast towards the city centre, I come across La Taverne du Dauphin, just back from the street and it is an absolute goldmine of a find in Casa. It is not initially obvious, because what in France would be a prime sitting-out and people-watching terrace is sadly isolated from public view – and view of the public – by a fabric screen, to keep the eyes of those who might object from the sight of alcohol consumption. On the other side of it, however, the consumption is going ahead just fine. In early evening this is an after-work hotspot. The clientele is mixed, though mostly male, not unlike a heaving City of London pub at the end of the working day, if slightly more refined: there is a television at either end of the bar, neither loud, one showing the inevitable football game, in this case Réal Madrid beating Dortmund 3–0 in the Champions' League, the other a wildlife programme with images of African crocodiles bringing down wildebeest, an atmosphere not uncharged with testosterone. But only a few customers are quaffing bottles of Flag at the bar; there are more clad in smart suits, clearly just finished a day at the office, each with their own individual half-bottles of wine. It's hard to imagine any of them in an Obi Wan Kenobi jellaba.

I've seen enough to convince me that this is at least as good a place as any for dinner, except that there is a problem: the main restaurant area, to the rear of the bar, is already full. The waiter looks disconsolate until he asks, 'Maybe no smoking?' It turns out that there is an upstairs dining room, more or less identical and half-empty, but it has the dire requisite that smoking is not allowed, which for most Moroccan men makes it out of the question. I couldn't be happier. Especially when the food arrives. The waiter's recommended fish carpaccio is a delight: wafer-thin slices of pale raw whiting with the merest tint of pink, though that is probably from the drizzle of wine vinegar which with a sprinkling of dill adorns the dish. I can't imagine why the place isn't packed out with Japanese. Not that they haven't already done enough to damage Morocco's fishermen by scooping North Atlantic tuna out of the ocean by the ton and flying it to the Tokyo fish market. I follow it up with a lamb tagine that is soft, succulent and served with chickpeas and apricots. Delicious.

By this time even the non-smoking section has filled up and the waiters are apportioning arriving diners to share tables. Already I have acquired as dining companions a young Frenchman of Tunisian origin, an elderly American lady who says she has escaped from the monotony of her cruise ship companions who have all gone to bed early, and a bright

Canadian woman in her thirties. The French-Tunisian orders in Arabic, though he says he has a little trouble with the local dialect, which provokes a gasp of amazement from the Canadian woman: 'A little!!! I can't understand a word.'

'You speak Arabic?' I ask her, impressed.

'Yes, of course,' she replies with a smile. 'I was born in Egypt.' She explains she is on a study course in Morocco but is stunned by how little of the language she understands.

'The most annoying thing,' she is at pains to point out, 'is that they all understand me perfectly, but when they reply I'm left there with my mouth hanging open. I can hardly understand a word.'

'Is it just the accent?' I ask.

'No! Not at all. There are lots of words I don't understand. The thing is they all watch Egyptian soap operas on television and so they understand perfectly but they can't actually speak it.'

As a bit of a linguist myself (but with no more than a few basic 'hello, goodbye, thank you' type words in Arabic) I have long known that Arabic is basically a written language, and that (like Chinese) different nations from different parts of the Arab world can all read each other's newspapers and books, starting with the Koran, which is defined – fairly obviously – as the ultimate in correct Arabic. But (similar to the Chinese) they all have different pronunciations for a word written the same way. But that was about the height of my knowledge.

Between them Fatima, the Canadian woman, and Aziz, the Tunisian-French bloke, do their bit to enlighten me, in a conversation which in itself takes a bit of following, given that Aziz has only a little English, about the same level as Fatima's French; I have both but no Arabic. The American lady sits quietly and smiles.

'They call the language here *darja*, which really just means "dialect",' Fatima says.

'It is the same in Tunisia,' Aziz chips in. 'We also call what we speak to one another *darja*, though of course it is not the same *darja*. Here they have lots of words borrowed from the Berber, but also some from the Spanish and the French,' he adds. 'For example, here they call a cigarette lighter – *briquet* in French – a *brika*, whereas in Tunis they would say *brikija*. Also here they say *bartma* when they mean an apartment.' They also, he adds, have loan words from Spanish, especially in the north. A classic example, he quotes, is what we used to call a *baguette* in English but thanks to supermarket-led dumbing-down now call a 'French stick'. 'Many people say *parisiana* down here in Casa, but up north in places like Larache they call it a *komera*,' which apparently comes from the Spanish *comer*, 'to eat'. Understandably enough, he has not much idea about the words derived from Berber.

But not one of us – even the relatively silent American lady, who only gradually lightens up as a bit more of the conversation switches for her benefit to English – has a bad word to say, in any language, about the quality of the food, from the whiting carpaccio to delicious grilled calamari with garlic and parsley to piri-piri king prawns to a medium-rare steak. Or the wine. I have managed to get a glass of the relatively rare Moroccan pale rosé wine, Volubilia Gris, which I first tasted in the seaside resort of Essaouira.

To my surprise, the older American lady is the only taker when I suggest 'going on' to visit a few of Casablanca's bars, not the noisy nightclubs along the corniche but a few of the genuine local 'pubs' in the city centre. But on the way there, she bottles out, saying she needs to be up early for their visit to the 'big mosque' before the cruise ship sets out again in the afternoon. I bid her good night, doubting she would have enjoyed a typical Moroccan 'pub' in any case.

I was right about that. It is easy enough to spot a bar in Casa, easier in fact than in most other Moroccan cities save Tangier. Most of them cluster together in the city centre along the rue Allal ben Abdallah, all within a few yards of each other, with names like Rallye or Regent, windows dark but not opaque, doors open to the street. I choose at random one on a corner which appears to be called Scillant, not least because it has an old familiar neon sign outside – okay, the neon isn't working any more but it's still a big sign – advertising Mützig lager, once upon a time a well-known, if unremarkable Alsace French brand, bought up by Heineken and moved to Africa where, apart, I think from Congo and Rwanda, it has become extinct, replaced by the dreaded Dutch giant brewer's global trademark cat's piss. They don't actually have Mützig on sale here, just the usual Moroccan brands, but's still a pretty good indication that, with its darkened glass and Dickensian small windows, this is actually an alcohol-serving bar, and has been for some time.

Not only that, it's as much a bar as any I have seen anywhere: a place with a long, wooden counter, blokes swaying just a little unsteadily and a buxom barmaid in her late twenties wearing a push-up bra. Tourist guides to Morocco tend to say places like these are 'male-dominated and not necessarily female friendly'; in reality these are as female-friendly as any city-centre, old-fashioned bar in Birmingham, Manchester or Milwaukee. 'Metrosexual' they are not, upscale cocktail bars they are not, but if you want to down a few beers, relax, have a smoke (try that in Manchester or Milwaukee) and chat about anything and nothing to the bloke next to you at the bar, they are as fine as anywhere on the planet. And just to make me feel at home, they even have a genuine English tradition: the clocks are five minutes fast, so they can throw you out earlier. I nudge my way to the bar, where the waitress gives me a high five and hands me a bottle of Stork lager with a 'yes or no' expression on her face. I smile back and take the bottle.

The old Mützig has been replaced by Moroccan-brewed Heineken. Everybody is drinking the two native beers: Flag

Spéciale and Stork (Casablanca is too expensive for all but the showiest Moroccans). Flag is light in colour and taste and comes in 25cl bottles, Stork maltier and stronger and comes in 33cl bottles. And in here, it costs just 18 dirhams (about £1.50) a bottle, well below the prices in most tourist resorts but still only just affordable for the average Moroccan.

I'm doing the economics here, because the bloke I've got talking to at the bar is an accountant from Rabat but working for a big company here in Casa, a reminder that Rabat is to Casa what Washington DC is to New York, the political but not the commercial or population capital. His name is Taoufik and he is a 'Casa' fan, in a big way. 'In a few years, you wait and see, this will become the New York of Africa,' he says proudly.

'Really?' I ask.

He takes the question more seriously than I had intended, buys another Stork, then turns to me and says, 'Yes, I think so,' before adding: 'Or maybe Dubai. Which is not so good.'

'Why Dubai?' I ask.

'Because of what they are doing to the old port.'

Shocked by my ignorance Taoufik, like the good account-ant he no doubt is, explains to me that, with the backing of His Majesty the King (may God be with him) there is a grand plan, set up back in 2011, to create a whole new cityscape covering 12 hectares of luxury flats, new hotels, shopping malls and a 200-mooring marina as well as a terminal for international cruise liners. The whole enterprise has the backing of a $5 billion grant from the Gulf States, primarily Qatar, Kuwait and the United Arab Emirates, plus separate funding from Saudi Arabia, His Majesty's own pocket and Moroccan state money (which some sceptics would mutter quietly amount to pretty much the same thing) as well as grants from the World Bank and European Bank for Reconstruction and Development.

This is all a bit more than I had expected to discover in what looked like a working-class pub, but Taoufik indicates discreetly that the 30 or so customers nattering at the bar or the stand-up tables include at least a couple of top lawyers and bankers, though most of the rest are probably working men, artisans, butchers, barbers. 'Some people in this country frown upon alcohol,' Taoufik says, looking serious, but adds with a smile: 'We are equal in the pub.'

5

Reach for the Sky

MORE THAN ANYTHING ELSE, one structure dominates Casablanca's skyline from any aspect. In most Moroccan cities, you might expect it to be a mosque. In Casablanca there is a sneaking suspicion that it might turn out to be the sky-scraper home of some bank or business consortium, or just possibly some international hotel. It is therefore a little bit disappointing to find out – if you are told in advance – that it is, actually, a mosque. But that is only until you see the thing.

This is not just any mosque. It is the largest in Morocco, the largest in Africa, the sixth largest in the world, and pos-sibly the only one with a roof that can be opened or closed like the Centre Court at Wimbledon. It was completed on the Prophet Mohammed's birthday in the year 1414, which in the Christian calendar was 30 August 1993 (which explains the sliding roof).

This colossal towering structure, with its minaret at 210 metres high, visible from all over the city, is built right on the shoreline, between the port and the Hank lighthouse, part of it on reclaimed land and part even extending out over the ocean itself, deliberately in reference to the Koranic reference to 'God's throne is upon the water'. It was completed by an army of men working day and night (1,400 in the day, 1,100 at night), using the finest Moroccan materials and craftmanship, with a further 10,000 artisans working for five years on the mosaics and carvings. The locals claim St Peter's in Rome would fit inside. I do not have the volumetric expertise to check that one out, but I slightly doubt it, though at 200 × 100 metres and with a capacity for 25,000 worshippers at once, it is one big building!

Its 1993 opening was, to the annoyance of the man who commissioned and oversaw it, a disappointing four years late, and the prophet's birthday was not his first choice of date. He had intended it to be opened on his own 60th birthday. Begun in honour of Mohammed V, the king who had led the country to independence, it was conveniently dedicated to 'the Sovereign of Morocco, Commander of the Faithful', which at the time just happened to be the man who had kicked off the project, to date Morocco's most controversial monarch, Hassan II, of whom (much) more later, and it has ever since (even since the succession passed to his son, the current Mohammed VI) been known as the Hassan II Mosque; like the pyramid of Cheops, a monument to a man who was sure of his place on Earth and wanted others to be sure of it too, even after he had departed.

I was determined to pay my homage, not least because it is the only mosque in Morocco open to non-Muslims. There were, I knew, normally several guided tours a day. I had only one problem, but I thought it was a big one: I had neglected to notice that today was Friday, the Muslim day of prayer, the least likely day of the week to get into a holy building. I asked the guy behind the desk of the hotel if he thought there was any chance, but he glanced up as if I had stunned him out of his hangover, which I probably had, shrugged his shoulders and redirected his attention to the fine grain of the wood on his desk. I left him to it. There seemed nothing for it but to go to the mosque and find out in person. After all, the American lady at dinner the night before had suggested her tour party would be visiting it today.

I trundled down to the seafront road, grabbed a *petit taxi* (getting to be quite an expert at this now) and, after stopping to pick up a fellow rider who was going a bit further, handed my cabbie the now customary 10-dirham coin and jumped out in front of what has to be one of the most jaw-dropping constructions on planet Earth, particularly one completed in the last 30 years but looking like it has stood on the same spot for centuries. It is not just the massive bulk of the mosque itself, with its soaring, pink, carved marble walls culminating in the mammoth tower of the minaret, but the setting, the brilliant blue sky beyond, the white crests of the Atlantic waves crashing on the rocks around it and the seagulls wheeling in the sun.

Straining my neck to look up at the façade, I made my way in something like awe across the vast granite-clad square embraced by a colonnade to the front, like St Peter's in Rome, and I would later be told that on the grandest days this provided space for an additional 80,000 worshippers in addition to the lucky 25,000 inside. Well before I reached the door, however, I was – unnecessarily – halted by a turbaned imam, who quickly pointed out that this entrance was for Muslims only. Apologising profusely for something I'd had no intention of doing, I asked him as politely as I could if there might be a possibility – even on this holy day – to be allowed inside the mosque. He looked back at me gravely, as if I had suggested spitting on the grave of the prophet, then broke into a big smile and said, 'Sure, there's a big cruise liner in town today, and after the lunchtime prayers are over they'll be running tours in the afternoon. Check the times over there.' He had indicated a small group of men standing in a cluster next to an underground entrance to the mosque who, it turned out were indeed, official tour guides waiting for the afternoon rush. 'Come back at 4 p.m,' I was told.

＊

That left me with several hours to kill, an excellent opportunity to nip out for a stroll along the 'corniche', once envisaged by the French colonialists as Casa's answer to Nice, St Tropez and Cannes, a long beach washed by the blue Atlantic and studded with bars, restaurants and hotels. To get there I can see no better option than the swift, clean and reliable ultra-modern tram, one line of which ends up at Ain Doub, a salubrious suburb marked on the map at the far end of the city beach. The ride in itself turns out to be an enlightening vision of Casa's vision of itself, past, present and future, quickly winding out of the city centre into Maarif, the well-to-do area of Casa, with smart apartment blocks and high-rise offices, then beyond past a couple of the high walls built around the *bidonvilles* to protect the affluent middle class from the sight of their impoverished fellow citizens (or perhaps to prevent the conservative and recently rural slum dwellers from catching sight of their urban fellow citizens in decidedly un-Islamic short skirts with their heads uncovered, and only their eyes concealed – behind Oakley sunglasses).

Casablanca is a classic example of the ancient Moroccan enthusiasm for new building over renovation. Some of the finest structures from the French colonial period, particularly around the Place Mohammed V, where architect Henri Prost laid out his vision of a grand French city square lined with public buildings, are gradually dropping into disrepair. But none so fast as the post-independence 'modern' buildings thrown up in the 1960s and 1970s. Be they blocks of flats or offices, most are gradually disintegrating. Perhaps it is all part of the spin-off from the grand new plan for Casablanca that Taourik was telling me about the night before. But too often grand plans remain just that.

They are in evidence, for example, as the tram makes its way towards the affluent Ain Diab beachfront district, looping out from the inner city and *bidonvilles* for the easier construction option of building a smart new public transport system over land that isn't actually in use, which means we come to a halt regularly at newly built stops, complete with electronic ticket dispensers and terminals, in the middle of wasteland. The tram does its best to stay as far as possible from any of the grimy shanty towns that can be glimpsed from within its spotlessly clean air-conditioned interior. I wonder if the Oakley glasses can be pre-programmed not to see the poor people. That there are great plans for this area, there can be no doubt. We glide to the usual silent stop at the halt named Cité Financière, which you could be pardoned for thinking might be the Wall Street of Morocco's financial hub, were it not for the fact that the only inhabitants at present are dandelions. The Cité de l'Air stop, which conjures up visions of luxurious high-rise apartment blocks – or at least the social housing this city so badly needs – currently rises no higher than one floor, if that, given that the only buildings on the site are a few semi-derelict houses and a pile of rubble or two.

Just who the Abdullah ben Cherif stop is named for I have no idea, and perhaps nor did the engineers who laid the track, for the tram doesn't even break speed, let alone halt at this wasteland. It is only at the penultimate stop on the line, along the route de Sidi Abderrahman, that we come across housing again, and by now we are very much into sub-Saint Tropez littoral mode. The tram comes to the end of the line at Ain Diab, and we stop outside a Harley Davidson dealership, at the end of a row of two-storey villas on a long avenue of tall palms frequented by elegant young women toting designer handbags and sporting elegant ponytails. If there is a headscarf in sight, it is worn loosely wrapped around the neck – heaven forfend it should cover up that coiffure.

Ain Diab beach is nice. Just nice. It has sand. Lots of sand. Natural sand, ground down by the waves of the Atlantic pounding on it for millennia. Cannes has sandy beaches too, but then Cannes spends €650,000 every year to reclaim its sand from the sea. The Med has stony beaches, which is what you get if you don't really have tides. But the Med also has people on them, far too many people, most of them wearing very little. Ain Diab also gets crowded, so they say, in summer, but mostly with blokes playing football. Bikinis aren't big in Morocco, even on the Casa corniche, and I mean that in the worst possible way. Right now, in later April, even though it's 24C, warm by most European standards – 'Phew, what a scorcher!' by British tabloid newspaper standards – there is next to nobody on the beach, and the few keen souls are well-wrapped up. Even the few women who have gone down to the sand are actually wearing headscarves, not to cover up their hair but to keep them warm. Most of those who go out to the corniche actually go for the beach clubs, little patches of walled-off beachfront with cafés or restaurants, though you can't get a beer or glass of wine anywhere visible from the street, which is a rather drastic difference to Cannes.

As my afternoon agenda is dominated by the biggest religious building in Morocco, it seems only fit that while out at the corniche I take a look at the biggest monument to the most popular modern Western religion: the Morocco Mall, Africa's biggest indoor shopping centre. Unfortunately it is beyond the far end of Ain Diab, and although it is clearly too cold for the locals to be chilling on the beach, it is far too hot for me to walk that far. But then, now that I know the secret of taking cabs in Casa, no sweat!

There isn't a rank around, but as opposed to London where you often have to risk life and limb by jumping into the middle of the road to hail a cab, in Morocco, if they see someone walking less than totally enthusiastically, a *petit taxi* will slow down and parp as he passes, even if he already has a fare: the more the merrier and the more the 10-dirham coins add up. Sure thing, within a few minutes a little red Fiat parps his horn at me; I nod and jump in holding out my coin and saying '*Mall du Maroc, s'il vous plaît.*' He looks askance and tells me that it's a five-euro fare to the mall. I guffaw at this, but realise he's probably got me down as a French tourist. So I try the bluff – I know, I know, it's only 5 euros for a two-mile trip, but as I've said before, it's the principle of the thing. I offer him 20 dirhams, tops – it probably is a little farther than the average ride I've taken, though I'm not sure about the Ibn Rochd marathon. He's a bit bemused by my sticking to dirhams, though, and ventures, '*Vous habitez içi?*' Lots of Frenchmen do, these days, you see. I pull my best Parisian accent and tell him I have an apartment in Maarif, which is the part of town most French expats (and posher Moroccans) prefer.

'*Eh ben,*' he replies, as you do to Parisians, and we agree on 40 dirhams. Return. Payable in advance.

It sounds like a mug's deal and I'm not wholly convinced he'll be there when I come out, not that I'm planning a major shopping spree, but by the time we zoom down the dual carriageway along the coast, it doesn't seem an unfair price even if he isn't.

The mall at first glance doesn't seem as monstrous as I'd imagined when told it was the biggest in Africa. Africa is a huge continent; the Hassan II mosque is a huge mosque; but I'd forgotten that as continents go, Africa isn't a huge consumer market. But that's because I'm only looking at one end of it. The thing goes on forever. The Mall du Maroc is big – a huge multi-storey white blob like a beached Moby Dick. It's more than half as big again as London's Westfield Centre, bigger than all but two in the US, and contains a one million-litre aquarium. I am unsurprised to learn that it is owned by Marjane Holdings, which just happens to be owned by His Majesty, King Mohammed VI (may God be with him).

Happily, thanks to the internal display map, I realise this before I've wasted too much time wandering around in an environment that basically looks like any other mall almost anywhere, including the number of women in full-face veils and burqas, virtually the first I've seen in Morocco; but that's almost certainly because they're from the Gulf, and probably here while their husbands are doing the deal that's going to turn Casa port into Dubai-Atlantis!

Outside, to my surprise, my cabbie is still waiting for me, after all, exactly where he said he would be, although that might be because the alternative would be joining a long rank at the tail end. There again, it might just be because he's honest, and on that assumption I tip him another ten dirhams when he drops me back again at the Boulevard de la Corniche from where I intend to walk the coast route back into town just in time for my appointment at the mosque.

✳

When the Hassan II mosque was being built, there were a few brave souls who dared to suggest it was a vanity project for a monarch whose idea of his own importance had outstripped reality, and was draining money that could have been better used for social services in what was at the time – and to a lesser extent still is – a poor country. The demolition of a shanty town in the vicinity aroused local wrath and there was not exactly a warm greeting for the king's decree that every household in the country would pay at least a token sum – enforced by the police – towards the mosque's construction. The total cost, according to latest estimates, was just under €600m (£540m) with a further €50m (£42m) since spent in repair work, particularly to the concrete pillars supporting the area 'upon the water', from the erosive nature of salt and waves. On the other hand, on a day like today, with a liner in town, Morocco's greatest religious building would appear to be Casablanca's biggest tourist attraction and with each and every one of us paying 120 dirhams (€12, £10) for the 40-minute tour, I reckon they have taken a minimum of €3,600 (£3,200), and this on a day when it has been partially closed to the infidels. It may well be that in the end it is the infidels (a word whose usage has always troubled me, given that a Latin term was obviously originally applied by Christians to Muslims and not vice versa) who end up paying for most of it.

After sorting out the groups of the faithless into linguistic subsections – French, German, Spanish or English, and it must be a big cruise ship for there are multiples of all four – visits begin with a trip downstairs to the ablution chambers, where worshippers clean their feet by paddling for a bit in warm water in a low hall of marble pillars with subdued lighting, a bit like the sort of relaxing room you might find in the antechamber to the 'wellness' centre in a Shangri-la 'six star' hotel.

But it is only when you actually enter the prayer hall itself – shoes off and in a bag – that the vast proportions and decorative splendour of the Hassan II mosque strike home, not least because the whole central section is flooded with bright sunlight pouring in through the open roof and illuminating the beautiful elaborate paintwork on the carved cedar wood. Only in Morocco, I think; it's hard to imagine a congregation at St Paul's being happy on a wet Sunday in November to discover that they haven't got a roof over their heads.

Even so, my recent experience in Marrakech has made it quite clear that the sun doesn't always shine, even on the fringes of the Saharan desert, and just when I was wondering if they let in worshippers with brollies, our guide points out that in this most modern of great religious temples, the roof is electrically retractable. Within five minutes of a rain shower starting, the hand of Allah – or at least his earthly servant – can cover the heads of the faithful. It was the old king's wish, the guide explains, that, 'The faithful who come here to pray can do so on firm ground while contemplating God's sky and ocean.'

And he isn't joking. Further out to the edge of the great hall there are transparent tiles in the floor supposed to give a vista of the ocean beneath. Today they aren't; it just looks a bit murky down there, and the guide is keen to usher us away. I wonder if the repair works over the past decade may have obscured the faithful's view of God's ocean in their well-meant effort to prevent God's ocean from showing who is boss around here.

Our guide, meanwhile, is eager to expand upon the mosque's extraordinary fusion of traditional Islamic – and Moroccan in particular – artisanship with modern technology. For example, there is a high-speed lift within the minaret to take the imam up to his vantage point over the city to give the evening call to prayer. Not surprising really, given that the tower has 60 floors and I can imagine that otherwise he would be a bit out of breath. And, also, the top of the minaret itself boasts a laser beam focused permanently in the direction of Mecca. Then there is the fact that the main door, opened only when the sovereign visits on ceremonial occasions, is made of titanium and raised vertically by hydraulic lifts. And, perhaps what might seem the greatest, most superfluous luxury of all to Church of England flocks shivering in their mediaeval pews, the entire prayer hall has under-floor heating, an experience I can confirm for myself when, having shed our footwear into conveniently provided plastic bags, we proceed barefoot from the temporarily carpeted edges and advance up the centre of the mosque (what in a Christian church would be the aisle) and I feel a cosy warm glow spreading through my tootsies. Nice.

Sadly the ladies do not get the benefit of this as they are required to worship from within the elaborately carved and, I am assured, equally comfortable, though we are not allowed to look, mezzanine floors, which obscure sight of them from the men. Clearly whoever thought that just the sight of a woman, even modestly covered, within a mosque might turn a man into a rampant Lothario, never considered – or didn't care about – any erotic effect on the women gazing down upon several thousand males' arses as they bow towards Mecca. Maybe he was right. What do I know?

What the guide did not tell us was that despite the insistence on almost exclusively Moroccan materials – save for some

Italian marble and chandeliers from Europe's most ancient glass factories in Murano in the Venetian lagoon – and despite the fact that the architecture incorporates not just Moroccan design but elements from the rest of the Islamic world, Hassan II declared he wanted to endow Casablanca with 'a large, fine building of which it can be proud until the end of time'. I guess Allah will decide. But for all those who carped, I can only say that from the beginning of human civilisation, the pyramids, the monuments of Greece and Rome, the palaces of the popes, the follies of the Mughal emperors, the Gothic cathedrals of France and England, have all been built for the gratification, if not deification, of one man, usually a tyrant worse than Hassan II ever was, even in the eyes of his detractors.

✳

Mid-evening takes me back to the Saillant bar on Allal ben-Abdallah, but the atmosphere is somehow subdued compared to the previous night. The reason soon becomes clear. 'It is Friday,' the flirty barmaid tells me. 'We close early. 10.30 p.m.' It is almost that time now. I hadn't really thought about it. Friday is the busiest night of the week in London bars, but here, of course, it is the equivalent of Sunday, in the religious sense, though nearly all of Moroccan society operates in business terms on the Western week, with Sunday as the day shops close. A big barman notices the look of disappointment on my face, and says he knows another place that is open until midnight on a Friday.

I ask for directions and he says it is along the same street. 'But it is a long street. I suggest a taxi.'

This seems like a potential rip-off: no doubt he has a deal with the taxi drivers. But he anticipates my apprehension and holds up a coin: '*Dix dirhams, pas plus.*' The going rate. I shrug. Why not. 'You can always give him a tip,' he adds with a smile.

The taxi drops me at a black-painted bar frontage with blacked-out windows called Peau de Vache, which conjures up a brief vision of the Blues Brothers doing their behind-wire-cage version of 'Rawhide' as drunks throw beer bottles at them. The reality is somewhat different. Inside it more resembles a British city pub circa 1959 (or what I imagine they might have looked like – I'm not quite that old): with black-and-white photos of vintage cars on the walls, alongside a few old bullfight posters, ancient postcard views of the city, a Johnny Walker whisky clock and a stuffed boar's head. There are a few blokes at the glossy veneered bar, obviously regulars, nursing beers and looking like they have been there for hours, and on the other side a blowsy barmaid in a low-cut dress and too much eye make-up, fag in her hands and slippers on her feet. It occurs to me that Nigel Farage might feel quite at home here.

I order the inevitable bottle of Flag and fall into conversation with a shortish bloke (about my height) with thinning hair and a dark suit wearing glasses that make him look disconcertingly like a slightly swarthy-skinned version of French president François Hollande. In particular it's the nondescript suit, though, that makes him seem out of place. Suits are relatively rare among Moroccan men. The only ones I have come across in Marrakech were worn by hotel staff or bouncers – notably those at La Grand Tazi – and although there are substantially more in Casablanca, most were around the bar at the Dauphin: expensive, well-cut and worn by young men who almost certainly work in the city's expanding financial services industry. In other words, the men in suits are what Londoners these days disparagingly call 'suits'.

This man doesn't quite fit in either Moroccan category: bouncer or businessman. There is a reason: he is Algerian. The French colonial experience in Algeria was very different from that in Morocco. Whereas here the French saw themselves largely as 'stewards', in Algeria they attempted to turn the entire country into a part of France, destroying local towns and cities and building new ones while at the same time effectively enforcing European dress and customs. Thus it was that Algeria became a major producer of wine, which was cheaper and of lower quality than French wine, but often shipped over, bottled in France and resold to markets such as Britain that didn't know the difference. Similarly the standard of couture was lower and because the local populace were poorer, Algeria – even after independence – became a country with not a jellaba or burnous in sight, just a nation of men in cheap suits.

His name is Benissa – Algerian names differ hugely from those in Morocco where every second bloke seems to be called Mohammed or some variation thereof – and he says he's a professor of French literature from the coastal city of Oran. It's a bit of a coincidence because although I have never been to Algeria, Oran is a city that has lingered in my imagination from my school-day French literature studies as the setting for Albert Camus's semi-allegorical novel *La Peste*, in which the Nazi occupation of France is construed as a plague.

'It used to be easy to come to Morocco from Oran,' he tells me. 'I could just get in the car and drive across the frontier. Now it has been closed for so long. It is very sad.' I am interested to hear him say this, not least as I am planning to take the train out east to Oujda, on the Algerian frontier, which is the only town in Morocco that – like most of Algeria – was once part of the Ottoman empire, and could easily have ended up in Algeria. The version of Arabic spoken in both countries is similar; it was the bloody Algerian struggle against French occupation that by chance facilitated Morocco's relatively bloodless transition to independence, and at one stage there were grand – unfulfilled – plans for a Union du Maghreb, uniting all the north African countries, including Libya and Tunisia.

But since Algeria collapsed into chaos in the early 1980s and then erupted in bloody civil war – together with Morocco it is the only North African country not to have experienced the badly misnamed 'Arab Spring' having previously had its own exceedingly bloody 'Arab Summer' – the frontier has been closed. The Moroccans insist they want to reopen it and renew ties, but the reality is hard to ascertain and is complicated by Algerian claims on parts of the formerly Spanish South Sahara, seized by Morocco in 1975.* 'To get here I had to fly to Rabat, and catch the train,' he explains. He is here for 'business', he says, reluctant to expand further.

I am no expert in Algerian politics, to say the least, but I know that received opinion in Europe is that Algeria is stuck in a time warp, with democracy effectively suspended. But Benissa is having none of it: 'In my country you can say what you want, the press is free. It is as democratic as France.' He has bitter memories of the civil war: 'We lost 200,000 people. I was a soldier. We were fighting for liberty.' These are questions it is wise to steer carefully around in countries where stability and liberty often conflict with religion and democracy, which includes much of the Islamic world, as the West has found out to its cost in Iraq and Afghanistan. We turned on Saddam Hussein, though he had done the West's bidding for years, and still support a regime in Saudi Arabia that breaks virtually all of our supposedly 'crucial' human rights. Benissa thinks the army in Egypt was right to depose Muslim Brotherhood Mohamed Morsi, a view also held by former British prime minister Tony Blair. 'Morsi is an Islamist; he would have turned the country into a religious dictatorship,' Benissa says. He claims to be a big fan of King Mohammed VI. 'He knows how to run a country like this.'

By now the bar staff are excelling themselves at tapas-style treats. We have had the usual little dish of olives, followed by individual saucers of *harira*, Morocco's traditional spiced lentil soup, anchovies fried in light crispy batter, all just to accompany the endless Flag Spéciales.

---

*For more on Moroccan history, see following chapter on Rabat.

There are other conversations going on around the bar by now. A smartly dressed young lad in his twenties with short, tightly waved and gelled hair who claims to be Italian, though he looks more made-up Moroccan with a pseudo-Italian make-over, is talking music with a fair-skinned bloke in his late thirties, with a goatee and a prominent broken tooth in the front of his mouth. He introduces himself to us as Yani and says he is a Berber (Amazigh) musician, who specialises in bass guitar. This sparks my interest, as on our holiday visit to Essaouira, I met a Berber singer and drummer called Yusuf from Casablanca, who performed an amazing set ahead of the coast city's annual *gnaoua* music festival. He invited me to come see him play in his home city, but I have stupidly lost his contact details. I ask Yani if he might know him: it's a long shot, but musicians can live in tight-knit communities even in big cities.

He says he doesn't know. The 'Italian' smiles sweetly and says he thought Yani knew everything and everybody. We talk music for a while, which Benissa clearly has no interest in. The bar is gradually winding down – the barmaid has even called 'last orders' (Nigel Farage *would* feel at home) – when Yani says he knows a bar down the road that is still serving, and where they often have late-night live music. Maybe I could ask the band if any of them know the elusive Yusuf. This seems improbable, but I suppose it might be worth a try, and in any case the thought of a bit of music and another beer on top of too many already is always hard to resist.

We meander along Allal ben Abdallah until we come to another, black-painted bar. Inside it looks like it's winding down too, even though there is still music going, not live but from big speakers next to a small stage. 'They will play soon,' Yani says, suggesting we take a seat. I go to sit down at a table not too close to the speakers, which are already a little louder than I would like, but still with a decent view of the little stage. 'Not here,' Yani, says, 'over here,' and points to where the waiter is indicating, a small group of sofas behind a pillar.

It seems an odd choice to me with little view of the band, if and when they do appear, but by now the waiter has brought two bottles of Flag and is pouring them into glasses. We can always move if the band materialise.

'So,' Yani says, 'where are you staying in Casa? What is your hotel?'

I laugh with understandable modesty and tell him I am staying in the Excelsior, little more than a fleapit by the standards of central Casablanca. It only takes minutes for me to regret ever having mentioned it. 'Maybe you would like to take me back there,' he says with a wink, putting his hand on my knee.

'Sorry,' I say, removing his hand. 'There has clearly been a misunderstanding.' But he isn't having it, and puts his hand on my arm instead, puckering up and leaning towards me as if for a kiss, the broken tooth more prominent than ever.

I have had this experience before (a long time ago, I am pleased to say), around about 1975, when I was spending a year out from university working as an *assistant* (resident native speaker) at a secondary school in the suburbs of Paris. The Easter holidays seemed like an ideal time to take a break and see a bit more of the country. So I hitchhiked south (my first lift from Paris provided by a British journalist whose advice would change my life) and found myself trekking up a mountain road north of Annecy in the foothills of the Alps, when to my relief a car with a lone male driver stopped to pick me up. More literally than I imagined at the time. I have to admit here that at the age of 19 I was something of a fey youth: trim-waisted (my wife finds this hard to believe) with tight-fitting bell-bottom trousers, long blonde ringlets (à la Roger Daltry in the day) and my shirt tied up above my waist. The driver was a middle-aged bloke of Algerian (or just possibly Moroccan) extraction, and as we wound our way at high speed round the mountain curves, he did his best to make conversation, rather disconcertingly about my private life, including such questions as '*Tu as une petite amie?*' and '*Mais tu bandes déjà, quand même?*' – inquiries intended to determine if I was sufficiently past puberty and whether or not I had a girlfriend.

I responded, as befits a Briton abroad – though, as I fear I always tend to, affecting to be a native to reassure myself that my language skills were up to scratch – with an awkward blend of teen bravado and mortified embarrassment. It was a few seconds later, disconcertingly just as we rounded a curve at some 120kph, that, with barely one eye on the tortuous bends ahead, he reached across and ran his right hand up the length of my thigh in the unmistakable direction of my private parts. This was when I instantly reacted with the one accoutrement that should have immediately marked me out to any true native Frenchman as a Brit: the umbrella resting on my lap (you never know when it's going to rain, do you?). I prodded this into his groin and ordered him to stop the car. Which, on the second attempt, he did, snarling visibly, screeching to a halt and unceremoniously leaving me on the side of the road, a decision I briefly regretted seeing as cars were few and far between and I was a long way from anywhere, until I rapidly realised how much better that was than any alternative. I have never had more sympathy for the victims of Stuart Hall and Jimmy Savile.

But that was nothing as to the ignominy I felt now at accidentally getting myself into a similar situation, except that in this case, not only did my supposed new 'friend' think I might enjoy being buggered, he obviously expected me to be ready to pay for it! Within a microsecond I was on my feet, heading for the door, with broken-tooth, hand on my arm, trying to restrain me, and the waiter, obviously used to his routine, quickly barring my way and insisting I at least pay for our drinks. A bit rich since the would-be lothario with his hand on my other arm had said it was 'his treat', though clearly he had had something else in mind. Happily I had the right change and handed the waiter 25 dirhams, the cost of one beer, and said, 'That's for mine, I've no intention of paying for his!' He glanced at broken-tooth, who was in a state of some despair, but with the money for one drink in his hand, he stood out of the way and I made rapidly for the door, the noise of a continued altercation behind me, pulled the hood of my waterproof jacket up (you never know when it's going to rain, do you?) and disappeared rapidly down the nearest alleyway, and out on to the brightly lit thoroughfare of Mohammed V, with only one thought in my head: whew!

You would think at this stage I might have said to myself, 'narrow escape, home to bed!', but then you would not know me all that well. Nonetheless, I am heading in that direction when I come across bright neon lights, and the sound of authentic Moroccan music coming from a brightly lit doorway next to the Café de Paris. It also has large men, obviously bouncers, by the door, which in many countries would be off-putting but in Morocco tends to be a clear sign that they serve alcohol within. And if Yani is hanging around outside the Excelsior, anywhere else is a better place to be.

What I did not expect was to be escaping from a sordid and unwanted encounter straight into a large-ladies' full-clothed belly-dancing club. The underground venue next to the Café de Paris is what in Casa they refer to as Cabaret Oriental, which basically means karaoke for fat ladies with big busts, with an attendant company of juggling dwarves and an inebriated audience including their mothers, daughters and an improbable number of grizzle-haired men who look like Fabio Capello or Gene Hackman. Nearly everybody is smoking and everybody, including the large ladies, is drinking. Bottles of wine and bottles of Flag are circulating rapidly, carried round by waiters on heavily laden trays, with packets of cigarettes and *sheeshah* hubble-bubble pipes. The air is full of blue smoke, loud conversation and laughter. Clearly everybody is having a good time. There are a few skinny, openly gay men dancing together on the edge of the stage,

watched benignly by gentle giants with fists like sledgeham-
mers who might be bouncers or might just be big blokes out
for a good time watching women dancers their own age and
dimensions. Two of the fat ladies are shaking their copiously
covered *embonpoints* at one another while one of the dwarves
runs between them looking up in mock awe. Fuck 'Rick's'
jumps into my mind; whatever the upmarket Disney theme
pub might pretend to be, or the big international hotel discos
catering for businessmen and pimps, *this* is real Casablanca
nightlife, even if it does feel a bit like a cross between the over-
40s night at a Newcastle-on-Tyne working men's club and an
episode of *Game of Thrones*.

The music is eclectic too, veering between traditional
Arab and nostalgic rock classics, not unsuitable for the bulk
of the age group present. Two tracks in particular make me
feel curiously proud of my generation, and more specifically
that unloved but resilient heartland of modern England:
South London. They are in turn 'Sultans of Swing' with its
wondrously street-savvy poetically evocative depiction of
kids 'dressed in their best brown baggies and their platform
soles', followed in quick succession by 'Another Brick in the
Wall' with that powerful chorus of Lewisham children (now
middle-aged adults) who felt naughty as they sang 'We don't
need no thought control'. Songs from another world, another
place, another time.

6

Croquet with Our Man in Morocco

MY TRAIN ROLLS INTO RABAT AGDAL, the capital's southern suburban station, dead on time. It is a short, hourly shuttle
service reminiscent of that between New York and Washington DC; there as here, linking the nation's commercial capital
with its political one.

On the outskirts of Casa, more *bidonvilles* line the tracks,
the polythene sheeting of their makeshift roofs all but concealed behind three-metre-high concrete walls, as if they
were gated communities, but the satellite dishes give the lie
to the attempt to conceal their existence. As the line curves
along the coast to the coastal commuter town of Mohamma-
dia and beyond, the seaward view offers a vision of Moroccan
society's past, present and maybe future. Tanker terminals
and power stations line the coast along with a sprawl of
modern apartment complexes and the occasional shopping
mall, while in between them wander herds of goats, guarded
by their Obi Wan Kenobi figures, the hoods of their woollen
jellabas pulled up though it is still over 20 degrees. A horseman gallops as if across the savannah towards a shanty town
of tents and lean-to shacks only identifiable as living accommodation by the inevitable cluster of satellite dishes. Next to
them, the occasional cow wanders and a few women pull a
cart by hand. Here and there vast stretches of rubble can be
seen where a *bidonville* has been razed, the policy here as it is

in the cities: do not repair or restore what cannot be fixed – raze and redevelop.

It is a less than appealing vision of the future: faceless white blocks with no amenities save the obligatory mosque, no corner bar in which to exchange banter or gossip with a drink, if only tea or coffee, to loosen the tongue, just the battery cages for the workers. It is not surprising that some of Casa's poorest prefer to remain in their *bidonvilles*. But this sprawling, faceless urban development is not confined to Morocco; it is a gloomily growing global phenomenon as the buzz words 'housing' and 'accommodation' replace such outworn ancient terms as 'village' and 'community'. In so many cases, the only difference is the quality of the cages.

I emerge from Rabat Aqdal station, which serves the smart residential suburb and diplomatic quarter to the south of the city centre, to see the grinning face of an old friend who is to be my host for the next two days, and who, for reasons of modesty and discretion, will be referred to in these pages simply as Our Man in Morocco, or Omim for short (in this case, I hasten to add, not a pseudonym for the ambassador).

I bundle into his smart French people-carrier and am given a whirlwind tour of the broad streets and boulevards that immediately mark out Rabat as a much more European city than even Casablanca, where the metropolitan aspirations to modernity are repeatedly blunted by the intake of an impoverished conservative rural labour force. If Casablanca could be Marseille, Rabat could (almost) be Lyon.

The Omims live in a government-owned 1930s French art deco detached house in a part of town almost exclusively populated by the diplomats and foreign business folk. Just around the corner is the capital's polo ground. Mrs Omim gives English lessons to the wife of the Romanian ambassador. It reminds me vaguely of my own days in Moscow in the last decade of the Soviet Union when foreigners lived an existence substantially sheltered from the natives – we journalists fought to escape the environment, and were much disliked by the state for doing so – and socialised to a large extent amongst each other. There are differences of course: here the state sets no barriers to contact between Moroccans and foreigners (the Omims have many local friends, but also local 'staff' – maid/cook and gardener – which for most Britons today tends to be a luxury only enjoyed in expat environments), and there is freedom of speech and movement. And then there is the weather: Moscow has four months of freezing winter, a one-month blitzkrieg spring, two months of blazing summer, with thunderstorms, then six weeks or so of 'golden autumn' before the long grey decline into the annual ice age again. Rabat has a brief, chilly for its latitude, winter, a short spring and autumn, and lots and lots of summer. But there is something about that semi-official expat community that has a global common denominator. Each quasi-diplomatic community is more like every other in any other capital than it is to the native environment.

There is also, of course, the way expats – with the dishonourable exception of the roués who flourished in the unrestrained atmosphere of cosmopolitan Tangier in its 'international zone' days – carry slightly more of 'home' with them than most travellers. The Omims, for example, currently have 'half of New College rugger team' plus girlfriends staying with them, though they are currently down on the coast at Essaouira, windsurfing for a few days. And then to while away the hour or so before lunch, Omim suggests we play a game of croquet on the lawn. This was something I had definitely not expected to be doing in Morocco.

Now croquet is a fine game, and it is far from the genteel pastime imagined by most folk who know of it primarily from reading PG Wodehouse. It is relatively non-strenuous, but it does have massive potential for spite and vengefulness – something Bertie Wooster manages on several occasions to convey bitterly to his manservant Jeeves. It is also a game in which, more than most, the condition of the pitch can play a vital role. I learned to play on a lawn as smooth as a billiard table in front of Oxford's Magdalen College's early 18th-century 'New Buildings', a lawn in fact deliberately manicured and barred to pedestrian access for this specific purpose. Most games I have played since, however, have been on domestic lawns, neither as smooth nor as well mown, which often makes for entertaining variations. Such as when a well-aimed ball fails to hit another because an unforeseen encounter with a tree root causes it to leapfrog over the target, meaning that instead of earning a 'roquet' – the chance to knock another player's ball to a less advantageous position – it leaves itself in prime position to be effectively double-roqueted itself, which can leave it halfway down the garden path, which in 'coarse croquet', by far the more common and more entertaining version played among friends and family, is the equivalent of a gold ball being sent half a league into the rough or stuck in a sand bunker.

It turns out Omim's front lawn, despite the advantage of having a domestic gardener, is at least as challenging as the worst rural English garden equivalent. First of all, the grass may look like grass, but it is not grass as we know it: certainly not the soft, downy stuff that English horticultural perfectionists shave to within an inch of its life, or armies of specialist mowers force into perfect cross-grain chequerboard patterns on the Centre Court at Wimbledon. This is coarse, thick-bladed grass, more like AstroTurf than the real stuff, grass that if it were facial hair would need a cutthroat razor rather than a Remington, grass that, rather than tickling the toes, gently pokes its blades rudely and insistently between them. It is subtropical grass, grass you expect to – and actually might – find snakes in.

Except that it is not snakes that we are worried about, or rather that Mrs Omim is worried about. And believe me, she is seriously worried. It is another reptilian life form altogether:

tortoises. In an element that only adds to the slightly surreal edge to my experience of Rabat so far, I find myself – before beginning the game of croquet – joining in a tortoise hunt. Not a real hunt, you understand, more of a sort of semi-domestic equivalent of the modern 'take photos not lives' safari, which is a fair analogy, for these are by no means domestic critters. The tortoise is as much a part of Morocco's distinctive native wildlife as the ubiquitous storks. And we are in whatever the tortoise equivalent of 'lambing season' is, which means treading very carefully on the coarse, dry grass, our eyes scanning amid the stalks. In the back garden, where the tortoises are endemic, shoes are banned for fear of standing on one. Back in Europe we might think accidentally treading on a tortoise a very unlikely eventuality and one that would almost certainly do more damage to the human toe than said tortoise. But that is because we usually encounter them when they are – even in tortoise terms – relatively advanced in years; well, adolescents at least. Here, what we are looking for is the tortoise equivalent of babes-in-arms, except for the fairly obvious point that not having arms, tortoise mummies are unable to protect their tiniest offspring who are required to fend for themselves virtually from day one. There are several in the back garden, Mrs Omim informs me, and it is there that at last we – almost literally – stumble upon one: a tiny dark brown object about the size of a two-pound coin that could easily be mistaken for a pebble were it not for the tiny lizard-like legs that suddenly appear around the edges as it decides to scuttle for the safety of the hedgerow.

I find myself unexpectedly charmed. This is the second time in a week that Morocco has transformed my attitudes towards some of the creatures we mollycoddle in the UK. First it was the no-nonsense feral felines, now it is the miniature, surprisingly self-sufficient, surprisingly mobile version of a 'pet', that is about as interesting and companionable as a lump of rock and worthy of attention only when some toddler tries to treat one like a toy car, manually making it race around the kitchen, or when what passes for spring finally appears and we venture into the garden to see if Terry or Tommy (or whatever) has finally deigned to surface from his six-month kip, or just quietly died of boredom in the drizzle.

The lack of native wildlife roaming the garden means we can proceed with the croquet competition, which takes – as ever – signally longer than anticipated and in which, despite making an accidental or deliberately polite howler, forcing him to go back to the start and allowing me an undeserved advantage. Omim finally trounces me (if only to get the bloody game over so we can have lunch).

The afternoon is set aside for an informed guide to the Moroccan capital, which, despite its status, is only the fifth largest city in the kingdom and relatively off the tourist beat, not least perhaps because it instinctively feels more European and less 'exotic' than most of its competitors for attention. Omim has spent many years in different parts of the Arab world, including Egypt and Iraq, where he had the less than pleasant experience of being one of Saddam Hussein's 'human shield' hostages. He was also the star historian of my year at Oxford so he is a better than average, well-informed guide to historic Rabat. Even though its role has waxed and waned over the centuries, and has only relatively recently (the last century) been restored to the status of capital, Rabat has a history as remarkable as any of its rivals and far, far older than most.

Our first stop is the oldest remains of habitation on a site that goes back some 3,000 years, at least. The ruins of Chellah squat on a hill above the River Bou Regreg on what is effectively the edge of Rabat, because the river separates it from what is referred to as its twin city, which if not for the river, would be the suburbs. Salé, as Rabat's other half is known, is a city in its own right, and is older than Rabat, if only because, despite being on the other bank of the river, it is the historic descendant of Chellah, of which its modern name is a largely French corruption. That in turn comes from the Romans' corruption of Chellah to Sala, and most of the ruins still visible today are those of Sala Colonia, which is what they called it when they colonised Morocco (which they knew as Mauretania – another way of saying 'land of the Moors', the different interpretations of which are still affecting modern African history – notably in Western Sahara).

'The first known inhabitants,' Omim informs me, 'were the Phoenicians, travelling west from what is now Lebanon, fleeing the westward expansion of the Persians, contemporaries of those who founded the more famous but even more ill-fated Carthage.' Since 2012, Chellah has been a UNESCO World Heritage site (as is most of Rabat) so we are required to pay a token admission charge to enter. Partially overgrown – a consequence of benign rather than incompetent neglect, it being felt that the romantic is of equal importance to the archeological here – it feels like an exotic abandoned garden, possibly artificial, the sort that might have been deliberately emulated in 18th-century England or France. The walls and pillars are of ancient Roman, thin, flat, red brick, and there are remains of baths, a forum and an arch, as well as indications that it was once an important port but suffered from the river silting up, something that is happening to modern-day Rabat as well.

It was probably the natural decline of the port that caused the remaining inhabitants after the Arab conquest to migrate in 1154 to the new city now called Salé on the other bank and further downstream. The Almohad dynasty from the south who became sultans in the 12th century established Rabat (literally fortified place) as a launching point for their campaigns to take control of the Iberian peninsula (from rival Arab dynasties, who he felt were losing their grip). Their successors (notably the Merenids) took literally the fact that ancient Chellah had become effectively a ghost town, and turned it into a necropolis; many of the remains still visible are of their tombs. Indeed, the photo shared by almost all tourists visiting Chellah has got nothing to do with the truly ancient city at all: it is of the minaret of a 12th-century mosque which is the permanent nesting place of the luckiest (or most important in the pecking order – sorry, bad joke intended) of the dozens of pairs of storks resident on the site; the others make do with filling the branches of the surrounding trees.

But Omim is drawing my attention to a less picturesque but altogether more curious sight: a few women squatting down by a bricked-in pool, possibly the remains of a Roman bath-house. We wander down to look and he nods for me to pay attention to what the women are doing. Unwilling to appear overly nosy, I try to watch in as inconspicuous a manner as possible until I realise what they really are doing, which takes a few minutes to sink in: at first glance they appear to be moving little white pebbles in the water, until suddenly one of them is gobbled up from below. 'They are feeding boiled eggs to the eels,' Omim explains, improbably enough. I am still digesting this, as it were, as we make our way back up the steps. I give him a quizzical look. 'Moroccans are as devout Muslims as anyone,' he says, pre-emptively, 'but they have their superstitions. The women believe that feeding eggs to the eels will ensure fertility. I think it has to be something to do with the visual connotations.'

Back at the top of Chellah hill, we make the short drive to the high plateau that is the site of Rabat's most enduring and most widely recognised landmarks. It was the most important of the early mediaeval Almohad sultans who made Rabat what it is today, even if it didn't become what he intended for most of the intervening centuries. Yacoub al-Mansour (Yacoub the Victorious) moved the capital here and built the walls that still surround the old city today. 'Then,' Omim tells me in an authoritative voice, 'he extended them in a vast land grab that even today encloses much of the greatly expanded modern city. The irony is that during the rest of his life and most of history since, this vast area intended for his palace and harem remained largely empty. It was not until 1956 that a king moved back.

＊

The dominating feature of Rabat's historical heritage is still Yacoub al-Mansour's greatest achievement, and it sits up here on the hill, far from the medina clustered around the shoreline, a global symbol of Rabat, echoed in more complete form far to the south and further still to the north at what were once the limits of the sultans' kingdom. It is still surrounded by the ancient wall, albeit with crumbled gaps, and guarded by royal horse soldiers in full ceremonial dress of red uniforms and red-and-green pillbox caps with flowing white capes mounted on greys or palfreys, more than elegant enough to give the British Horse Guards a run for their money. The Moroccan affection towards their monarchy is as enduring as that of the British, given a few awkward blips here and there – occasionally violent, even relatively recently, although, we shouldn't be too judgemental; only the English and French cut off the heads of their sovereigns in public – and interestingly has similar religious ties: Mohammed VI is Commander of the Faithful in much the same way as Queen Elizabeth II is Supreme Governor of the Church of England. Moroccans may be orthodox Sunni Muslims in most respects but not without a few minor variations, perhaps the most notable of which is the one I mentioned earlier, that the dates of the beginning and end of Ramadan are determined by when the moon rises and sets over Rabat rather than Mecca.

It has to be remembered that at the time of Yacoub Al-Mansour, the concept of Morocco ever being under Christian, let alone Spanish, domination was inconceivable; it would have seemed like turning the world on its head. The empire he ruled over included most of what we call Spain as merely its northernmost province. His father had died fighting on the frontier with what is now Portugal, and he himself got the al-Mansour soubriquet, because of his decisive defeat of an uppity Christian force at Alarcos in Castile, a defeat that set the Spanish *reconquista* back a generation. His successor, Caliph Mohammed en Nasir, would take the Almohad Moroccan rulers to the height of their powers by adding the Balearic islands to the empire, which might have had a serious impact on Ibiza's status as 'party island' if it had lasted.

In the mould of rulers who see their best chance of a lasting impression on history as expressed in architecture, he is responsible for some of the greatest Islamic structures in the west of the Old World. The great Koutubia mosque in Marrakech, the Giralda tower in Seville, now the bell tower of the cathedral, and the Hassan tower in Rabat are all siblings, similar in appearance and derived from the same inspiration. The main difference is that the tower in Rabat remains to this day unfinished. Originally intended to reach 60 metres, which would have placed it amongst the tallest minarets in the world, it was abandoned at 44 metres, at the hour of the sultan's death.

The mosque it towered above was also of enormous scale, intended to hold over 20,000 worshippers, which is still evident from the vast array of pillars that once supported its roof. Unfortunately, guesswork must suffice given that they are all that remain, the rest having been destroyed by a huge earthquake in 1755. There is a certain Ozymandias feel to standing amidst the ruins of an unfinished masterpiece. But then Shelley's poem has never been on the reading list of most autocrats, who tend to prefer the line, 'Look at my works, ye mighty, and despair', to the 'all around is sand' payoff.

Over the centuries from the days of Yacoub al-Mansour, Morocco expanded greatly to the south (including much of what is now the modern country of Mauretania), but gradually lost all its territories in Europe, to the extent that after the final Castillian victory of 1492, Morocco was flooded with asylum-seeking refugees, both Muslim and Jewish, who had been expelled by newly victorious and intolerant Christians. Many of Morocco's ancient *mellahs* (Jewish quarters) go back to that period.

In the wake of Yacoub's family, the Saadian sultans, commemorated by their magnificent tombs in Marrakech, were the last dynasty before the present one to make a lasting effect on Morocco by holding off the Ottomans, making theirs the only country not to fall under the sway of the Turkish sultans. Lasting barely half a century, the Saadians' reign is most remembered for the Battle of the Three Kings in which the legitimate Moroccan sultan Mohammed al-Mutawakkil, his ally the boy king of Portugal Don Sebastian, and his pro-Ottoman rival Abdul Malik all died in a spectacularly useless day of carnage in 1578, when the entire Portuguese army was wiped out. More than 16,000 died, in approximately equal numbers on either side; all three kings were also killed and Portugal was inherited by Philip II of Spain, while Morocco was taken over by the son of the dead pretender, who did rather well until on his death his three sons ripped apart the kingdom. It wasn't until the latter half of the 17th century that a new sultan of a unified country emerged in the person of Moulay Rachid, a young warrior in command of a Bedouin Arab army, who brought peace – of a rather bloody nature, including killing his own older brother Mohammed. In terms of founding a dynasty, however, rather like the near-contemporary Hanoverians in England, he did rather well. His descendants, the Alaouites, are still the rulers of Morocco today.

Rashid's brother Moulay Ismail (whose legacy I will encounter again in Meknes) went on to be the most famous warrior in Moroccan history, beating back the Turks. Much of their later history might preferably be forgotten by the current incumbents. It includes a long decline in the 19th century ending in humiliating concessions and eventually subjection to Europeans, including the Spanish whose ancestors they had once ruled. One of the best and most entertaining sources is Walter Harris, a British adventurer, freelance diplomat and part-time journalist, who lived and travelled extensively in Morocco at the dawn of the last century and was an eyewitness to the changes in attitude, the equivocation with the Europeans and the humiliations that followed. Harris was a vain and boastful character but linguistically talented; he spoke fluent Moroccan Arabic, as well as French and Spanish. He was brave, one of the last of the great imperial British adventurers who saw the world as a 'ripping yarn', and were determined to play – and narrate – their own place in it. His role in imperial history was subsequently glossed over. He received greater honours from the French government than from the British, not least because his openly homosexual lifestyle with a penchant for younger boys – was frowned upon a lot more by the British than the French or Moroccan establishment, notably in famously louche Tangier, where he settled at the age of 19 and was buried in the Anglican churchyard on his death in 1933.

The son of an insurance broker, educated at Harrow and Cambridge, young Harris had travelled widely by the age of 18 and in 1887, at what today seems the remarkably tender age of 19, he managed to get attached to a diplomatic mission to Morocco. He immediately fell in love with the exotic lifestyle and acquired a property in Tangier. On that first visit he still had native British aloofness from the natives and described with horror how the British ambassador and other 'representatives of the Great Powers of Europe' were received by the descendants of Mohammed: '…a blast of trumpets and the great green gates of the palace are hurled open, and a hurried throng of Court attendants, in white robes and crimson-peaked fezes, emerges. A band of shrill music – pipes and drums – bursts into noise. Banners and wand-bearers and spear-bearers follow, and black grooms leading horses, saddled and caparisoned in gay silks and gold embroideries which prance and neigh at the dust and noise. The Sultan, a stately figure in white, on a white horse in green-and-gold livery. Over his head is borne the great flat parasol of State, of crimson velvet and gold, while at his side attendants wave long white scarves to keep the flies off his sacred person.' The sultan would receive the ambassador's credentials 'wrapped in silk' which even still he handled 'holding the folds of his cloak between his sacred fingers and the infidel documents!' Harris would later play a minor role in persuading the next sultan to allow European representatives a less subservient welcome, though by the end of his life, seeing how they abused their privileges to turn the tables on the Moroccan monarch, he might have regretted it.

If the Europeans resented their need to kneel before the sultan, that grand ceremonial was nothing to how he was received on his travels around the kingdom. Harris accompanied the then boy sultan Moulay Abdul Aziz on the autumn 1902 court progress between the southern capital, Marrakech, and the northern capital, Fez. He describes their greeting in the lands of one of the tribal lords: 'With a hoarse cry of welcome the tribesmen dig their spurs into the flanks of their barbs and gallop pell-mell hither and thither, now singly, now in line, firing their guns the while, until the horses are brought to a sudden standstill in a cloud of smoke and dust.* There are beggars and representatives of all the dervish sects, from cymbal-beating negroes from the Sudan to the Hamacha of Meknes, who cut open their heads with hatchets. There are snake charmers and acrobats and men with performing apes; groups of white-robed scholars from local mosques, bearing white flags; veiled Arab women, uttering

---

*A spectacle still emulated occasionally for tourists over a century later.

shrill trembling cries of welcome and offering bowls of milk; lepers with their faces swathed and wearing great straw hats, bearing wooden bowls to collect alms in, for none may touch them – a thousand scenes of human life with all its pleasures and all its tragedies.'

Harris was also witness to the immaturity of the young sultan, Abdul Aziz, and how his sheltered life as a sultan would allow a young man to become intoxicated by European gimmickry, in thrall to ruthless salesmen who knew they could sell him anything at an exaggerated price so that they might reap the commission. Harris describes the moment when the young sultan, having been conned by salesmen eager to fleece this naïve 'oriental' ruler of gold in exchange for the trappings of 'modern' European royalty, took delivery of a 'state coach', built to the most lavish – and even for that era ridiculous – standards of the British imperial monarchy.

Harris recalls its arrival in packing cases slung between two camels: '…the sultan was playing bicycle-polo with some of his European suite, which included at this period an architect, a conjurer, a watchmaker, an American portrait-painter, two photographers, a German lion-tamer, a French soda-water manufacturer, a chauffeur, a firework expert and a Scottish piper.

This most expensive carriage is completely useless, Harris comments, because 'Morocco has no roads'. His account of the coach's one and only short journey in the wake of a sudden rainstorm, soldiers and slaves harnessed to pull it on account of the fact that none of the royal horses had even been in harness, is too good not to share: 'The soldiers and slaves sweated and puffed as the wheel sank deeper and deeper into the swampy ground.' It was followed by the whole royal menagerie 'led by an emu whose courage had already been proved by an unprovoked attack upon the Scottish piper, and by having danced a *pas-seul* on the prostrate form of the expert in fireworks a few days previously. Close behind the emu followed a wapiti – with the mange – and then, in turn, the zebras, the Hindu cattle, the apes, gazelles and lastly, the timid lamas, with their great luminous eyes and outstretched necks.

'It rained that night, and the next day the little lake of water in which the State coach stood was purple from the dye of the harness and beautiful hammer-cloth of scarlet and gold flapped limp and ruined in the wind. Inside there was a pool of water on the green-brocaded seat.'

I have never read a more poignant depiction of the decline of a monarchy from romanticism to ridicule. Moulay Abdul Aziz's addiction to European toys brought him into disrepute and in the end made it easier for the Europeans to take over his country. They divided it up at the 1906 conference at Algeciras in Spain, with no reference to the sultan: Britain demanded a guarantee of neutrality for the Straits of Gibraltar, Spain was allocated a few chunks of northern Morocco to be taken over at will, while the French were granted control of the rest, even if they had not yet quite worked out what to do with it. Tangier was to be given the status of an 'international city', partly as a sop to the Germans who were otherwise left out except for being handed bits of the Congo, and also to placate the British who wanted a foothold on both sides of the entrance to the Mediterranean, essential for the quick Suez route to their most prized imperial 'possession', India.

The French soon found 'an excuse' to exert the power granted them by their fellow Europeans over the Moroccan people. The spur was, as ever, misunderstanding of local sentiment in the fact that a little railway built to carry stone for the construction of the new port in Casablanca ran too close to a Muslim cemetery for the comfort of a people who believe that any damage to the buried bodies of their friends and relatives will result in an imperfect corporeal resurrection at the day of judgement (Christians used to have similar beliefs which was why cremation took so long to be sanctioned by the church), and the locals set upon the French and Italian workers, killing several. Paris was officially outraged, but probably delighted. A French warship almost immediately appeared off the coast and bombarded the city as 'punishment' before landing a force of troops 'for the protection of their citizens'. Unfortunately, given the unstable state of the country, a few local hill tribesmen saw this as an opportunity to take advantage of the shellfire and general chaos to get a bit of the action themselves. In the ensuing chaos the Jewish population suffered most in an orgy of mayhem and looting. An eyewitness a few days after this 'peace-keeping' intervention noted that while the Europeans clustered within their consulates had survived, the city presented 'a confusion of dead people and horses while the contents of almost every house seemed to have been hurled into the streets and destroyed ... out of dark cellars, Moors and Jews, hidden since the first day of the bombardment, many of them wounded, were creeping, pale and terrified. Some had to be dug out of the ruins of their abodes.'

By 1908, with widespread belief that the sultan had become no more than a puppet in the hands of his European côterie, his young brother Moulay Hafid, encouraged by conservative advisers, rose against him and forced him to abdicate. But the new sultan, as much a traditionalist, Islamic scholar and poet as his elder brother had been a liberal, pro-European, ditherer, proved no more successful in governing his kingdom, which continued its descent into anarchy as the tribes and their leaders asserted their independence. The most notable rebel was a bandit from the Rif Mountains, a cruel but wily chieftain called Rasuli who for a time held the irrepressible Walter Harris as his prisoner, fearing for his life, but in the end became a friend. At one stage Rasuli briefly managed to con both the sultan and his rival pretender to the throne into making him, for a while, governor of the northern provinces, which he treated as a private fiefdom to be milked for all it was worth.

Meanwhile the monarch was as distant and distracted as ever, and now, like his older brother, falling victim to the wizardry of the modern European world: one of his last obsessions was to have a mechanical throne built that could be positioned in the same way as a dentist's chair. The man demanded payment in advance, claiming he had still not been paid for one of his even more unusual services: procuring a lion for the court from a German zoo, a task considered no more unusual by the sultan than the fact he had decreed it the duty of the court's Scottish bagpipe player to feed his tame kangaroo.

In 1912, in the midst of this warlord-led anarchy, the sultan appealed for help to the French, whose troops were already in Casablanca. Paris forced the sultan to accept that his country was now a 'French protectorate', in return for abdication, a pension and an easy life, while his younger brother assumed the title, as a French puppet. On his departure Moulay Hafid burned the symbols of monarchy including the famous red parasol once held over the sultan's head as European emissaries bowed low. A rebellion was suppressed ruthlessly and the capital moved to Rabat where it has remained ever since. Tribal revolts from the south had their arguments effectively dismissed by French machine guns and howitzers. Morocco entered the 20th century proper with a bloody nose, in chains. Over the coming decades the real ruler of Morocco was the French governor, most famous of whom was the first General Hubert Lyautey, whose chief claim to historical memory was that unlike the brutal transformation of Algeria into an African replica of France, he preserved Morocco's ancient cities so beloved of modern tourists and built the European-style *villes nouvelles* that today sit alongside them, giving most of Morocco's major towns, and perhaps the entire country, the benign schizophrenia that, a century later, serves it rather well.

With hindsight, the current power and popularity of the Alaouite dynasty, which seemed to snuff out its own future a century ago, is extraordinary, improbable and the product of some clever footwork. All of the foregoing is background to why the white marble, green-roofed building facing Omim and me as we stand on the Yacoub al-Mansour esplanade with his great unfinished minaret behind us, is one of the most venerated shrines in Morocco. I would call it semi-secular but as the king is (and was) Commander of the Faithful, the lines are anything but clear. This is the Mausoleum of Mohammed V, the last sultan of old Morocco and the first king of modern Morocco, whose decision to abandon the ancient title in favour of the European equivalent was an attempt to claim a form of modernity (which many modern European republicans would question), but also a statement that if a sultan had become a vassal, a king would not repeat the mistake.

The Second World War, seen as a moral crusade in Europe, was a sideshow for North Africans to whom it merely served to prove that their colonial masters were far from all-powerful and only won because of distant America and Russia. Initially, it had been Erwin Rommel's Afrika Korps who seemed like the liberators.

By the end of the war, in Morocco, which had been under all but impotent Vichy France administration until US troops landed to challenge the Axis forces in North Africa, a relative liberalism had sprung up amongst the intellectuals of the cities, in particular Rabat, Casablanca and to a lesser extent the ancient capital, Fez. A new, pro-independence political party Istiqlâl was growing. Sultan Mohammed V, assumed to be a French puppet, stunned his critics with a 1947 speech in 'international' Tangier calling directly for independence. He followed up with an open letter in 1952, just at the time when French Algeria, not so much a colony as a supposedly integrated part of France, was beginning to erupt. The French forced him into exile, but as Algeria exploded into outright warfare, they eventually cut their losses and in 1955 invited him to talks in Paris. A year later Morocco regained its independence.

Mohammed V had overnight rescued his throne, instituted a nominally free parliament (though retaining control of the Ministries of the Interior and Defence – the army and police), and declared himself a thoroughly modern constitutional monarch. He immediately became a popular hero, which is why his mausoleum here in Rabat is a national shrine. A royal guard, resplendent in the red, green and white ceremonial dress, stands to attention at each door of the mausoleum. We enter respectfully and peer down at the marble sarcophagus, with flags either side of it. In the far corner, next to an open copy of the Koran and a much smaller sarcophagus, is a seat where, Omim informs me, there is normally an imam reading quietly from the holy book. But either he is off duty today or we have managed to catch his lunch break. The smaller sarcophagus, Omim again steps in to tell me, is that of King Mohammed V's son and successor, Hassan II: a clear indication that in death alone, the monarch whose ego and character were larger than life, showed a seemly modesty and deference to his father.

Mohammed V did not have long to enjoy his glory. In 1960, barely four years after independence, one of the greatest tragedies to befall Morocco struck: an earthquake which devastated the city of Agadir, then the country's most southerly city and its embryonic cash-cow resort for foreign tourists. Over 100,000 people died, the economy was blighted and the nation went into mourning, compounded a year later when the king himself died.

The succession of his son, Hassan II, was accompanied by promises of further reform intended to please the left-leaning Istiqlâl and a growing population with declining national income. Few were carried out. The backlash against the king was violent; an attack by army cadets on a palace dinner party in 1971 killed most of his guests but not Hassan himself. The following year a more drastic coup was attempted with air force jets strafing the king's private plane. Only the quick-mindedness of a remarkably loyal pilot saved Hassan: after the first round of gunfire had penetrated the fuselage he radioed to the attacking fighters, 'Allah u-akhbar, the tyrant is dead,' at which point they broke off the attack. The royal jet, with the king very much alive on board, returned to Rabat where it was met by the interior minister, whose state of distress was less due to the attack on the monarch, but the discovery that the king was still alive. Feigning shocked loyalty, he immediately summoned up an armed, armour-plated convoy to whisk His Majesty to the royal palace, only for it to be ambushed by bazookas en route and the royal limousine destroyed. The wily Hassan, however, had declared a need for an urgent 'comfort break', failed to enter the limousine, and instead climbed out through a bathroom window to the street where he found a postman with a van, whom he persuaded to take him safely to the gates of the palace. Apocryphally the man did not even know who his hasty passenger was until he left the van telling him, 'You have this day rendered a great service to your king.'

Links today between Morocco and the former colonial master remain surprisingly strong. France is the country's biggest business partner, suppliers of most technology, including the trams in Casablanca and the high-speed trains planned for the *grande vitesse* Casablanca–Tangier train line now under, albeit delayed, construction. French is not only an official language alongside Arabic and the Berber tongues, but is effectively the language of the court and administration. Yet from the historical point of view, for most Moroccans the colonial period was a brief embarrassing blip in a millennia-old history. It is not hard to imagine that the sultans – and in particular the Alaouites – stand in an uninterrupted line of succession. That is never more clear than when Omim turns his French people-carrier not far from the Yacoub Al-Mansour plateau and we drive through a great gate in an ancient red-brick wall, and down a long wide boulevard, lined on both sides with splendid well-maintained buildings in what might be called 'late neo-classical, modernism European royal-governmental' style. To do so we have to pass a guard-house and are only allowed through because we have diplomatic number plates.

'This,' Omim tells me, 'is all part of the royal palace,' built within the vast space enclosed by Al-Mansour nearly a thousand years ago and left empty for centuries. 'You'll note, though,' he added, nodding to the left, 'that it includes the Ministries of the Interior and Defence.' His modern Majesty still has his hand directly on the key controls of power. And business, it would appear. Marjane, the hypermarket chain which owns the Morocco Mall, is just one of a vast chain of enterprises that are held in a portfolio by the Société Nationale d'Investissement, which is controlled by the royal family and since 2010 has also included the private group Omnium North Africa, both of which were then delisted from the Casablanca stock exchange. As diplomats in Rabat have it, the king doesn't just rule the country; he owns most of it.

If this seems less than totally democratic, that is because it is; yet much of modern Morocco's success story is due to the royal hand mediating the fluctuations of popular whim. For many years the more militantly Islamic parties were kept out of government. Sniffing the wind of change that blew away regimes – and peace and prosperity – in much of the rest of the Arab world, Mohammed VI not only called an early election but did not stand in the way of the moderate Islamic Justice and Development party which won most seats – though no voting figures were ever officially released – thus forming the government.

'It's a clever game, but it seems to work,' Omim says with a knowing smile. 'One of the most important things is that the palace works with the religious authorities, but makes a big deal of the king's role as Commander of the Faithful. Every Thursday, for example, the Ministry of Tradion, controlled by the palace, faxes out to every mosque in the country the topic for that week's sermon.' It is as if Queen Elizabeth II were to send an email to every C of E vicar and rector on a Saturday morning, telling them what to concentrate on when they address their congregations the following morning. I suspect some of them might welcome it. But then there are a lot fewer people trickling into CofE churches on a Sunday morning than there are Moroccans packed into mosques on a Friday lunchtime. It is a deal that seems to work, though not without the occasional grumble. During my visit, one imam has been successfully prosecuted – with a minor penalty – for not adhering to a royal edict that the sermon on a particular Friday was to address the topic of road safety. Unusual, perhaps, but not exactly silly, considering most Moroccans' freeform attitude towards driving, and a lot less controversial than jihad.

✳

By now the rugger team and girlfriends are on their way back from Essaouira and Mrs Omim is conjuring up the wherewithal for a barbecue and croquet tournament on the lawn. Amongst a sizeable proportion of the population of Rabat, including virtually all the expats, this entails not a trawl through the butchery quarter of the souks, but a trip to Carrefour, a local branch of the French supermarket chain which along with Marjane, the homegrown chain owned by His Majesty, dominates Moroccan middle-class *ville nouvelle* shopping.

Apart from a wider variety of spices, all pre-packed rather than piled in conical mountains as in the souks, there is little to distinguish it – or the clientele – from that in a French city. While Mrs Omim heads for the meat counter to buy chicken wings, burgers and spicy *merguez* lamb sausages (the token gesture towards local cuisine), I take the opportunity to investigate the alcohol department, which is surprisingly large. There is a glass wall around it, but it is, after all, glass, and a separate till at which you are supposed to pay so that the evils of alcohol do not pass the same scanner as goods more sanctioned by religion. But it is rarely attended and most shoppers – and I mean most; the booze shelves are busy – just throw the hooch in with the rest of their shopping. This Carrefour's meat counter even has pork chops!

There are cases of beer, from the local Casablanca, Stork and Flag to more familiar brands including the inevitable Heineken – but also an entire two rows dedicated to Moroccan wines alone, twice as much space as allocated to those of France or Spain, and not surprising perhaps given the price of imported wine. It would be hard to buy a half decent bottle of French wine here for less than 250 dirhams (about £20), and even the local stuff on average comes in at around 120 dirhams (£10), although there are both a few cheaper and many dearer varieties. In fact, it is the sheer breadth of styles and number of vineyards represented that is surprising, looking at the reds alone: from the ubiquitous Cuvée du Président to Bonassia Cabernet Sauvignon, La Petite Fer, Amazir, Kasbah, Ksar, Toulal Prestige, Domaine du Sahari, and even Rabbi Jacob Kosher Wine. The two royal supermarket chains Marjane and Acima announced in 2013 that many of their shops would gradually stop selling alcohol. The bosses at Carrefour can only be smiling. The vast bulk of Moroccan wine production is consumed by Moroccans, and mainly the affluent middle class.

We load up and while Mrs Omim heads back to the house to get the barbie up and running, the man himself and I head down to the medina. The previous day, after our tour of Rabat's monuments we had walked through the Kasbah, the former fort now home to immaculately tended gardens, and had mint tea – bizarrely he still likes the stuff; perhaps it is addictive; the sugar content is certainly high enough – in an idyllic little, blue-and-white painted café overlooking the Atlantic waves crashing on the rocks beneath.

But now we are pushing and jostling our way through the souks at their busiest time, past butchers brandishing machetes and slicing chunks off great sides of goat or cow, as the flies buzz around them, past men with tortoises of all sizes, including some with decorated shells, crowded into cages for those too lazy to catch their own. Depressingly, there is a growing danger that at least in the clothing and children's areas, there is a risk of the more 'civilised' towns of Morocco seeing their market places go the way of some of Britain's oldest. The ancient charter market – what usually led to a community acquiring 'town' status in mediaeval Europe – in Banbury to name but one, has over the years declined from a place of exchange for quality local goods to a cheap sales place for tat imported from the mass manufacturing factories of Asia. I can see this trend happening here too: the plastic toys and dolls are almost certainly 'made in China'. There are too many stalls advertising 'Tout à Dh10', the Moroccan equivalent of Poundland. Mr Omim remarks that at least the plethora of trainers and pants just an alleyway or two from the leather goods and silverware, marks it out as real and not just for the tourists. It's then he makes his sage comment: 'It's not a real souk unless it sells men's underwear.'

But it's not underwear he is here to buy, and it's not from the mass-manufactured area of the souk either. Conscious that he will be leaving Morocco this summer, Omim has been keen to make the most of the remarkable and good-value bespoke artisan workmanship still – for the moment at least – to be found. We are going to his tailor. As a farewell present to himself, and a take-home present for his brother, Omim is having some waistcoats made, and this is the final fitting. And very splendid waistcoats they are too, at least one of which will look perfectly dashing on the croquet lawn – bright red, with vertical white stripes. He tries them on while the tailor tugs this way and that, to make sure the fit is just right, bringing out the full-length mirror and promising that any adjustments necessary can be made.

I find myself almost envious; the last time I had clothing made to measure was in an Indian tailor's shop in still colonial Hong Kong, and I felt just a little guilty at the (almost certainly accurate) suspicion that the polite, impeccably clad Indian gentleman measuring me for a silk suit, would, as soon as I left, be faxing the measurements to a sweat shop over the border in mainland China where a group of underpaid children might be turning out his wares. At least here in Morocco there is no such suspicion. Adult workmanship is very much in evidence in every souk, from late-night cutthroat shaving shops, to filigree-silver workers to the lads who heeled my shoes with fire and brimstone in Marrakech.

There is something alluringly charming about the whole business: the customer treated politely, his physique accommodated without comment, alterations undertaken to precise measurements, and at all times the relationship is that of equals: customer and craftsman. I am reminded of one of Walter Harris's lines: 'The Moor has nearly always the perfect manners of a gentleman, no matter what his position, and the sentiment of the country is essentially democratic.' I assume he was right then, and it is certainly true today.

Nor are the prices cheap, in terms of merchandise purchased: despite the tradition of haggling and the general European or North American assumption that Morocco is a semi-Third World country, the price of many goods is little below what you would pay in southern Europe. But the difference is the level of service. I could buy a good waistcoat from a decent shop in London for less than Omim is paying in the souk of Rabat, but not one made to fit, by hand, with all necessary alterations included in the price. If any of this is being eroded – and I fear it is – it is not by price or availability; it is by mass production, television and fashion. In a country where a pair of hand-made leather *babouche* slip-ons can be bought for under 10 pounds on any corner, a growing majority of young Moroccans pay at least four or five times as much for a pair of synthetic trainers, which are eventually passed down the social ladder so that you see old men in wool jellabas with a pair of holed and scruffy Adidas hand-me-downs on their feet.

For us it is back to the barbie and croquet, the rugger lads and lasses, and for me an early morning train inland to Meknes, third of the royal cities of Morocco on my route. But on the way back, ever the historian, Omim insists on a detour, in search of a local landmark he has heard of for years and always puts off until tomorrow to seek out. Now, with waistcoats packed under his arm, he is aware that his departure is only months away and my presence is an excuse to hunt down one of the mythical historical grails of the Moroccan capital.

Somewhere along the road – in the forecourt of a Japanese car dealership – there is, allegedly, a hunk of stone that is the last remnant in Morocco of the *limes*, the frontier wall denoting the most southwesterly point of the Roman Empire. This was the limit of jurisdiction of the province that the Romans named Mauretania Tingitana, after Tingis, the ancient Berber word for swamp, site of the settlement that would grow to become Tangiers (that final 's', which is non-existent in the French and optional in English, is a relic of the original name). This stone marked the point of no return, the line beyond which elephants and camels roamed and wild untameable tribes ruled; it was for centuries, to all practical ends and means, the End of the World.

Romans in general had a thing about North African elephants, since one North African in particular – Hannibal – improbably brought a team of them over the Alps and used them to decimate the Roman armies. Several centuries later, the noted historian and naturalist Pliny the elder, who spent some time in the province of 'Africa' as a procurator, wrote of them at some length (though he mistakenly believed Indian elephants to be larger). Apart from their warlike uses he had rather a good opinion of them, claiming that when they crossed rivers they 'first send over the smallest for fear that the weight of the larger ones may increase the depth of the channel'. Pliny recorded an instance of an elephant, many years later, recognising a man who had once been its keeper. He also suggested that 'when an elephant happens to meet a man in the desert, who is merely wandering about, the animal, it is said, shows himself both merciful and kind, and even points out the way.'

We could have done with one of Pliny's friendly tour guide elephants now. The legendary stone marking the end of the Roman world is proving aggravatingly hard to find. We spend a bizarre half hour driving at snail speed past each of the salesrooms of Toyota, Nissan, Isuzu, Honda, Mitsubishi and – thrown in for good measure in case our intelligence was less than precise – Hyundai and Kia, carefully examining every protruding lump of stone, rock and concrete. But by the end of our tour we have unearthed little save an impressed understanding of the extent to which the Asian car industry has penetrated the Moroccan market. Omim is more disappointed than I am. As a historian this is one of those little nuggets he has held dear and after several years living here without bothering to check it out, he is reluctant to let such a fine tale be reduced to the status of urban myth. I suggest that perhaps the stone is in fact *inside* one of the said dealerships, possibly even carefully protected within a showcase. Clearly this had not occurred to him (and frankly I think it is improbable to the extent of being pure hokum) but it cheered him up a bit and I can imagine several Japanese dealerships getting a visit from a stately English gentleman in a red-and-white striped waistcoat over the coming months.

7

Vin Extraordinaire

FOR SEVERAL WEEKS NOW, even before I returned to Morocco for this trip, I have been trying to get hold of the makers of Volubilia Gris, the excellent wine I first tasted on a hotel rooftop in Essaouira: a delicate, elegantly subtle wine that in a genuine eyes-closed tasting could pass as a fine flavoured, distinctive and exotic white, but in reality has the palest tint of pink tinged with an almost indistinguishable orange – like the first hint of dawn over the Atlas Mountains.

But it has not been easy. Christophe Gribelin is not a man who lives seated at his computer, regularly checking his emails, nor does he seem to be a man who carries a smartphone in his pocket, or indeed pays much attention to telephones of any sort. Finally, just as I am getting ready to leave Rabat for Meknes, I get hold of his secretary who says Christophe will be delighted to give me a tour of the vineyard, and arranges a time for mid-morning, just after I arrive in Meknes. The vineyard, she says, is a short cab ride from town and Christophe will email me a map.

If getting hold of Christophe Gribelin wasn't easy, finding him is a lot harder, even with the neat little schematic map he had emailed me, *très à la française*, all straight lines, which despite the centuries-long presence of the Romans in these parts does not much correspond with actual Moroccan roads; these may be straight for long sections and then suddenly detour wildly in a curve, bend or semicircle as if a new round-about – estimated completion date 2050 – was somehow fore-seen in the original plans. Or more probably just a random modification inserted by the road builders to confuse any evil-minded jinn who might be following them.

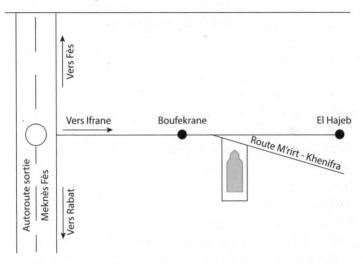

With the help of a combination of Google and Apple maps, I get the general gist, which was to head south from Meknes – the exact opposite direction to Volubilis, the ancient Roman city for which his wines are named – in the general direction of an apparently large village called El Hajeb which I assumed was the same as the El Hejeb marked on the maps. (It's that old transliteration problem again.)

Before reaching El Hejeb/Hajeb shortly after a smaller village called Boufekrane (or Boufakran), apparently we were to take a right turn and the Domaine de la Zouïna would be just along the road on the right, possibly marked by the sign of a big yellow arabesque door. All fine in theory.

The first step was to find someone to take me there, which meant the usual negotiation with the huddle of *grand taxi* drivers clustered in the shade of an olive tree on a dusty corner. Before I could get to them, as tends to be the way when an obvious foreigner appears, the most forward of them had got to me. *Taxi m'sieur.* Reluctantly, I nodded. A taxi was what I was looking for; it was just that I was not looking forward to the inevitable hassle of working out what I was going to pay for it. I may have had *petits taxis* sorted by now, but *grands taxis* are another matter, as the distance you might want to travel, and the number of people you might want to share with are always unknown quantities. My problem was that I didn't have a specific destination, at least not one that any of them recognised. Domaine de la Zouïna produced zero response. Not that I expected it to. But El Hejeb/Hajeb (I slurred the vowel) did get a response.

When did I want to go? How long was I prepared to wait before we set off (a question of waiting until we had collected enough other people, up to a theoretical maximum of five, who might also be taken with the desire to visit El Hejeb)? And how long would he have to wait before coming back. The answers were, of course, both simple and complicated at the same time. I wanted to go now. The idea of sitting around in the back of an old Mercedes until – if ever – we had collected a quorum to travel in the right direction was not appealing. Then, there was the minor problem that I did not actually want to go to El Hejeb itself, but somewhere just off the road to El Hejeb, beyond Boufekrane, along the road that turned off to the right and led to M'rirt/Khenifra. My rendering of M'rirt/Khenifra, however, provoked no response other than puzzlement. But then I had no idea if I was pronouncing it properly (the first part in particular), and as I only had instructions in Latin script, there was not much point in trying to get them to read it.

'No problem, no problem,' was the standard response, but only, it turned out, if I was willing to fork out 150 dirhams, which is the price I had seen advertised in the small hotel I booked into for a round trip to the ancient city of Volubilis, including waiting time. All I wanted here was to be driven barely six kilometres, and possibly not require the driver to wait at all (I had no idea how long the visit would last and secretly hoped my hosts would bring me back). He was adamant. I did the supposedly right thing. I began to walk away, admittedly not at all sure where I would walk to, other than to another *grand taxi* stand, a hot and dusty tramp for some 10 minutes or more and possibly the same response when I got there. To my horror, the bluff failed. He did the same thing too, perhaps reading my mind; he shrugged his shoulders and sauntered back to the shade of the olive tree, to resume nattering to his mates.

I dithered, as if changing my mind not about the price but about which direction I was heading, and within minutes another Ahmed had grabbed my arm and was leading me to his taxi, also a Mercedes, though even older than some of the others. I am no expert, but travelling around Cuba gives you an eye for decrepit old cars, and I would have put his at about vintage 1965. He squinted briefly at the map, I mentioned El Hejeb, and he nodded, asked how long he would have to wait, to which I replied I didn't know but we would discuss that when we got there. By now it was obvious that I was going alone; my estimate of a waiting time for fellow travellers on this route had expanded to infinity. He said 120. I said 60. He said 120. I said 80. He shrugged his shoulders, sighed and said 100. We shook hands. Given that with a full cab going to a more popular destination, he might have earned more, it seemed fair enough and at least I would be on the way.

Inside, the cab indeed bore more resemblance to some of the venerable motors I had travelled in in Cuba. It had the advantage of being a few years younger – the last American Buicks and Cadillacs to enter Cuba did so before 1959 – and over the decades Mercedes-owners had access to spare parts (unlike the embargoed Cubans). Although perhaps not all spare parts, not to mention local customisations: there was, for example, the mini-prayer mat on top of the dashboard

– at the muezzin's call, swerve towards Mecca and come to an abrupt halt, and adopt the brace position with hands on dash. Most impressive in terms of improvisation was that, at some point over the last 40 years or so, internal door grips for ageing Mercedes had either become unavailable or over-priced. In their place, therefore, on all but the driver's door, which retained its chrome and plastic original, the door grips were made of wood: elegant examples of Arabic carpentry, curved and pointed with the broad sweep of a minaret, and held in place with a few large-headed screws. Not just expedient, but elegant. I asked Ahmed about them, but he shrugged and said they'd been there when he bought it, just three years ago. I tried to imagine the used-car salesman's patter: 'Lovely motor, mate, just 16 careful owners.'

Little more than 10 minutes down the road we had left Meknes behind and were passing through Boufekrane, which was surprisingly larger than I had anticipated: not so much a village of a few hundred souls, but a small town of at least several thousand, sprawling on either side of the wide, well-kept main road, which, when it passed through the town centre, became practically a boulevard lined with tall palms, little cafés and a few fruit and veg stores. So far, so good.

That was when the trouble started. A few minutes' drive south of Boufekrane there was a large roundabout with a turning to the right. It was clearly a roundabout, though, rather than a fork, and the road to the right did not indicate either M'rirt or Khenifra. The driver, whom I had since learned to call Ahmed, looked at me, I looked at him and we both shook our heads. Wisely, it turned out. A few kilometres further there was another option, this time definitely a fork to the right, the main road straight ahead still indicating El Hejab (the spelling had changed). But the fork to the right mentioned neither M'rirt or Khenifra. We stopped and Ahmed called out in Arabic to a man working in a field to the side. 'Domaine de la Zouïna,' I ventured, to blank stares. *'C'est une maison?*' Ahmed asked me, looking for reassurance. I assumed indeed there would be a house of some form there, on the Bordeaux *château* principle, even knowing that in France's most famous wine-growing district, one viticulturer's *château* can be another viticulturer's roadside bungalow. But I wasn't sure. '*C'est un vignoble,*' I explained, but unsurprisingly the French vocabulary of the average Moroccan taxi driver or agricultural labourer does not include a word for winery. '*Les raisins,*' I tried. Ahhh, grapes struck a chord. '*C'est une ferme?*' I thought for a second, and nodded. More or less, come to think of it. The man smiled and gestured down the road. But when we came to what was clearly *une ferme,* in fact fairly clearly *un vignoble,* the large yellow sign on the entrance said Domaine de la Tazoudi, not Domaine de la Zouïna. Disheartened we drove on, but after about a kilometre we decided we had gone wrong and turned round. It was at this point that my driver, very sensibly, asked if I had a telephone number. I had. I had Christophe's mobile, but calling it from a phone box (they still have those in Morocco) had produced no reply, and I was reluctant to use my mobile which on a UK tariff here, outside the EU, was prohibitively expensive. Ahmed produced his. And got an answer. But from a woman, not a man. Christophe's wife? Secretary? Ahmed handed it to me. I explained who I was and where we were, as far as I could work out. The woman told me we should head back towards the crossroads and it would be on the right. That was the opposite side of the road to what was on Christophe's diagram, but we followed her instructions and headed back only to discover there was nothing at all on our right, but there was one gate not far from Domaine de la Tazoudi on our left. We stopped, Ahmed spotted a few people working in the fields beyond the high fence and we pulled into the unmarked gateway, at which point a large smiling man in a baseball cap shouted something at us from the other side, opened the gate, nodded that this was indeed La Zouïna, and beckoned us in.

A man with SECURITY in English on his jacket approached, looked a bit doubtful when I mentioned 'Monsieur Gribelin', but when I added 'Christophe', he beamed and led us along a short gravel road towards a small complex of neat, yellow-painted buildings and ushered us into a parking space next to what was indeed a bungalow.

A genial-looking bloke in his mid-thirties with a broad smile, thinning hair and wearing a thick shirt and green wellies emerged from the door and came over, said '*Bonjour*' and held out his hand: 'Christophe Gribelin.' I breathed a sign of relief, doubly when he assured me there was no point in having the driver wait; he would get me back to Meknes one way or another.

It has been my experience in the south of France, often in the Bordeaux area, but significantly in the less grand but equally extensive Bergerac wine-growing regions, that what are labelled *châteaux* are a lot less grand than the name suggests. Many are little more than ordinary, often 19th-century or even 20th-century houses, sometimes no bigger than the average rural French farmhouse. One of my favourites was the tongue-twisting Château Bouyguette, owned by a scatty 70-year-old Huguenot (the Bergerac region still has the largest concentration of French protestants and indeed keeps up links with Northern Ireland where many of the refugees who fled to England in the 17th century ended up, bringing the linen industry with them). Monsieur Dubur (his name was François but it would have seemed undue informality to have used it) was a passionate hunter. A visit to collect his robust Côtes de Bergerac wine often involved a wait outside the *château* until he returned from the hunt, bandilleros of bullets strung across his ample chest, a couple of grubby but enthusiastic spaniels bounding at his heels, and whatever form of wildfowl (or anything else) he had slaughtered in a bag over his shoulder. But the point was the *château*, for Monsieur Dubur's *château* was not so much a *grand palais*, as a form of dwelling for which in English we have a very different foreign-derived appellation: a bungalow.

And so, it turned out, was Christophe Gribelin's *château*, not that, despite his family's winemaking ties to the Bordeaux region, they used the word here in Morocco: *une ferme,* as the locals put it, was rather more accurate. It was a very nice bungalow – far nicer than Monsieur Dubur's rather grubby dwelling, which he shared with the spaniels, a giant oak table and the most enormous ancient cathode ray tube television. Christophe's bright yellow-painted home sparkled in the bright North African sunlight. We went across to the door where he introduced me to his French wife, heavily pregnant with their second child: possibly the third generation of Gribelins to bring French-style winemaking back to Morocco.

It was little over a dozen years ago, in 2002, that two Frenchmen on the cusp of retirement came here on a golfing holiday, fell in love with the land and its climate and realised they had a business opportunity on their hands. Christophe's father Gérard had for the previous 30 years been director of Château de Feiuzal, a *Grand Cru Classé* wine from the Pessac Léognan district of Bordeaux, and his friend and golfing buddy Philippe Gervoson was director of Château Larrivet Haut-Brion, another classic Bordeaux claret maker. The part of the country that they fell in love with was just outside Meknes and had long had a reputation for getting the best out of the grape. Known in French as Guerrouane, the region has already won for itself the equivalent of *appellation controlée* status. They took their courage in both hands and plunged into a venture that from the very start they knew was going to be complicated.

For a start, foreigners are forbidden to buy agricultural land in Morocco. You may buy a house by the sea in Casablanca, Rabat or windy Essaouira – many have; you can, if you are braver, invest in or indeed wholly purchase an existing

Moroccan business. But not agricultural land, or a business – such as a farm – that owns it. The government has determined that Morocco's basic food supply should remain firmly in Moroccan hands; the equivalent of land registry maps mark out areas designated as having a *vocation agricole*. And you can't change it. Tell that to the British property developers fast devouring our green belt.

Instead the two would-be entrepreneurs got themselves into the sort of negotiations with a local farmer south of Meknes that anyone who has shopped in the souks realises must have been a nightmare. It is hard enough to agree on a fixed price for anything in Morocco without feeling you've been through a wrestling match and come out the winner, but badly bruised and aware of an unsettling glint in the eye of your battered-looking opponent that is just enough to make you suspect, deep down, that he might have thrown the fight.

· They not only had to do a deal for the house, which they could legally buy, but also for a long-term lease on the surrounding farmland – which they could not – some of which was planted with olive trees, but most of which was highly suitable for vines. I can see it clearly as I hop into the passenger seat of Christophe's 4×4 and we plough our way over a landscape of rich, red, almost crimson soil, lying in the lee of the Atlas Mountains foothills, and with familiar rows of vines just coming into leaf. Christophe bends down and picks up a handful of the rich red soil: 'Clay and limestone,' he explains. 'Great soil for wine.'

There was a romanticism in their vision too, enough to wax lyrical about Domaine de la Zouïna lying at 'an historic intersection of civilisations: the Moors, Phoenicians, Carthaginians and Romans'. And indeed, as the floor mosaics at Volubilis confirm, even if it has at times been neglected, the history of winemaking in Morocco goes back several thousand years. The landscape itself is biblical in appearance, even up here at 800 metres above sea level: cypress trees, low distant hills, dark earth and blazing blue skies.

Gérard Gribelin and Philippe Gervoson, the latter the majority shareholder in the venture, spent months carrying out careful soil analysis, sending samples back to Bordeaux. They then had to clear the land, much of which was overgrown and going to seed. Preserving the olive trees, they laid out 63 hectares of the total 115 as formal vineyards, planted in regimented straight lines, then installed a system of drip irrigation – not allowed in most of France, but essential in the dry climate of Morocco, as it is in Australia. They planted French grapes Cabernet Sauvignon and Syrah to provide the raw materials for classic Bordeaux-style reds, but also added Tempranillo, the Spanish grape used in all Rioja, and Mourvèdre, a French grape mostly used in the Rhône valley where on its own or more usually in a blend it adds a lighter, more flowery note. For their rosés, sold mostly to the local market, which has a sweeter tooth than is common in France, they chose Caladoc and Marselan. For the white there was only one option they considered: Chardonnay.

To ensure quality they worked out an optimal planting density of 4,000 vines per hectare, to avoid water stress, and introduced a production system that involves *palissage*, a means of aerating the vines optimally. Christophe takes me over to where two Moroccan workers are carefully training the vines to climb the wire lines that will take them up to about a metre high. He bends down to help them, pulling off shoots that he considers surplus to needs. The objective, as in the best French vineyards, is to concentrate the energy of the vine into a small number of grapes rather than aim for the maximum harvest. Particularly in a country such as Morocco where wine drinking is largely confined to the middle classes, quality is more important than quantity. 'The other thing you will notice,' he tells me, though it is too early in the year for this to be apparent, 'is that we leave far more of the foliage on the vine, facing upwards exposed to the sun.' This is partly to make the most of the plants' photosynthesis, but also, he adds, 'to protect the grapes from the sun, especially in high summer when it can reach 48 degrees'. Indeed.

'We have an early harvest at the beginning of summer,' Christophe says. In the Moroccan climate that is already early enough for some of the vines to mature. The harvest itself is carried out wholly by hand, unlike many French vineyards today where automation has taken over. Christophe says they haven't found suitable machines, but there is no doubt that the relatively low cost of local labour plays a role and there are enough Moroccans grateful for some seasonal extra earnings. It is hardly a disadvantage, given that only the most expensive wines in Europe are still harvested by hand. All year round the estate employs 23 locals, but the number can rise to 100 or more at harvest time, particularly if it is a hot summer. Whereas vineyards in Europe normally harvest their grapes in September, in Morocco it is mid-August at the latest. 'If it is really hot,' Christophe explains, 'we have to have a very short harvest, just a couple of days, because the sugar content in the grapes can rise very quickly.'

Where the Gribelin-Gervoson team have spared no expense is in the introduction of state-of-the-art winemaking and bottling equipment, enabling them to do everything from harvesting and pressing the grapes, making and blending the wine, to bottling and packaging it ready for shipment. One of the items they are most proud of is the cold storage facility into which the grapes are harvested, essential because with searing temperatures outside they would quickly decay. The grapes are sorted by hand – another advantage of relatively low labour costs – and fermentation is begun at low temperatures to ensure the maximum preservation of the natural fruit flavours.

Our tour of the rest of the estate takes in the groves of olive trees which came with the land, and are now tended as carefully as the wine, to produce Volubilia Extra Virgin olive oil (*récolte à la main* – also hand-picked), as well as the great square concrete basin which serves as a reservoir for the irrigation system. Christophe is particularly keen to expound the virtue of their olive oil as well. Despite having little knowledge of the basics of an industry related to but quite different from their own, he and his fellow workers applied their usual perfectionist techniques to the fields they had taken over, reducing the numbers of trees to improve the quality, and working hard on the post-harvest pressing and production to the extent that, he proudly tells me, 'In 2006 the Italian tasting panel bestowed the title of Best Olive Oil in the World to Volubilia, above 3,000 oils including 344 Italian oils, from 26 countries in Europe, North Africa, the Eastern Mediterranean, South Africa and Latin America.' He claims it was the first time such a distinction had been awarded to an olive oil produced outside Tuscany. The olives, he adds, are a particularly Moroccan variety known as *pichouline*, and the domaine produces some 10,000 litres a year.

Back at the house Christophe introduces me to his French colleague and fellow winemaker, Guillaume, and we set about a serious tasting. The wine that first entranced me and drew me here is Volubilia Gris, literally 'grey'. It sounds uninspiring and is a wine that is almost unique to Morocco with a heritage that dates back to colonial times, and was equally popular in Algeria in the days when it was not just a colony but legally part of France: '*un petit gris avec le couscous*,' was practically an institution, Guillaume informs me. '*C'est un vin maghrébin*,' they concur. I first tasted this wine in the elegant surroundings of the roof garden of the L'Heure Bleue hotel in Essaouira. Looking out over the blue-and-white painted city at the vast extent of beach and the wind- and kite-surfers enjoying the brisk Atlantic winds that bring them there, I was relishing the view but wishing that just for once the damn winds would give it a break.

'A glass of wine, *m'sieu*?' an impeccably white-jacketed waiter suggested. It didn't take much for me to duck my head beneath the parapet, unwind the black and indigo Touareg Berber scarf I had haggled off a street pedlar to stop the sand blowing into my mouth, and agree. Immediately, the *gris* on the wine list stood out. The only *gris* I had come across before in the context of wine was the *pinot gris* grape, more widely known under its Italian cousin's name *pino grigio*. The waiter was keen to inform me that this was entirely unrelated, '*C'est un vin marocain, m'sieu.*' The name Volubilia looked interesting, even though it was a few dirhams more than any of the others. The waiter nodded approvingly. '*C'est le meilleur, m'sieu.*' The very best.

And it was. Sometimes there are drinks you come across in particular circumstances – a strangely bitter schnapps, a rough Italian grappa, a sugary-sweet liqueur, a Sicilian red over ice in a mountain village, a quirky banana-flavoured beer or, in memories of 1970s trips to Greece, a glass of cold retsina in a taverna – which tastes magical at the time, but when enthusiastically relocated out of time and place, to, say a wet afternoon in South London, seems to have been a temporary taste aberration caused by heatstroke. Volubilia Gris is not one of them. Indeed, on that blustery but sun-kissed rooftop in Essaouira, it seemed one of the most wonderful summer wines I had ever tasted: crisp, clean, rounded, not quite a white, not really a rosé, the subtle, muted flavours of the two red grape varieties – Tempranillo and Mourvèdre, no whites are involved – coming through clearly but only to the extent that in the brief period that the must is in contact with their skins, the hint of colour has leaked into what will become the wine. For one of the most striking features of this wine is its colour. Volubilia Gris is not pink like the rosés it might be compared to by the uninitiated. And it is certainly not grey! Held up to the light, it is the colour of a soft sunset at the end of an early autumn day in the northern latitudes, as if the colour were not so much in the wine as lent to it by its surroundings, a pale translucent glow, rose-petal water infused with orange zest. It is the colour I would imagine Orange Pekoe tea to be if I had never drunk a cup. And the best thing is, I found out, that even transported back to London, it brought that essence of the Moroccan summer with it, a subtle taste of the exotic enjoyed in shade and shelter from the hustle of the world outside. And the howling wind. No escaping that in England either.

I was surprised, however, to discover that Christophe and Domaine de la Zouïna also produce a rosé: a more traditional form of the genre, intensely dominated by the Syrah grapes but just a bit too sweet for me, although it is popular with the local Moroccan market.

'Many Moroccan middle-class families – and not just the men – drink wine with dinner,' Guillaume says. I already knew this from the segregated but still bustling alcohol shelves in the Carrefour in cosmopolitan Rabat, but what about out in the country, where bars were few and far between and supermarkets all but unknown? 'It is usually an *épicier* (spice merchant) outside the medina,' he explains. 'He will not have it on display, of course, but all his customers know, at least the ones who need to know. He will go into the back room and produce a bottle or two for them.'

It is for these customers, and their richer relatives, that he and Christophe produce their Epicuria range. In bottles that adhere to the sloping Burgundy model rather than the classic shouldered Bordeaux version, their particular pride is the Volubilia Epicuria Chardonnay, which is 'aimed at the local connoisseur'. I prefer the other bottle, but it is hard to dispute the seductive intensity of this wine, a lemon-gold 2010 Chardonnay aged in oak *barriques* like the most classic French whites. There is just a hint of oak in it, and a smooth, almost buttery mouthfeel, rich and rounded. It could be an Australian Chardonnay at its best, with a hint of oak but not too much. I am impressed. Christophe nods in gratification but agrees it is 'definitely a wine of the south'. Increasingly, they are following the New World habit of making single grape varieties, rather than the classic French blends. Christophe shrugs and says, 'The Moroccans understand it better.' And for all the prejudices about Muslim countries, it speaks volumes (literally) that Domaine de la Zouïna, one of the smaller, more select wineries, sells some 400,000 bottles a year to its domestic market. The bulk of their wine is distributed via Marjane, the supermarket chain owned by His Majesty King Mohammed VI.

I am also impressed by the shoulder-bottled Volubilia Blanc, but realise I have tasted these two in the wrong order. This is a dry, immensely drinkable, crisp white with what to me – a fan of the trap – has almost a hint of Viognier, although I am assured that only Cabernet Sauvignon Blanc and Chardonnay are involved. It is a relatively light, decidedly moreish wine, but under the circumstances is overshadowed by the rich velvet of its predecessor.

Volubilia Rouge, the wine this pair of claret-growing families started with in Morocco, tastes perhaps unsurprisingly like, well, claret. They produce and bottle some 90,000 bottles a year, stored in vats for 15 months. Merlot is eschewed – none of that plumminess – but the solid familiar taste of Cabernet Sauvignon with a hint of Syrah takes only a slight 'southern' feel with the influence of a little Tempranillo. Christophe's own tasting notes describe it as a 'dark wine, intense with reflections of rubies,' and 'notes of leather, tobacco and mocha', before he goes completely off the rails and adds: 'a smooth and delicate attack which leaves glimpses of round and fine tannins and offers a complexity of great lands.' I thought he might be getting carried away there, but the notes were written in English so I let him off with it.

I also meet one of the very few Moroccans who works in the winery rather than in the fields. A bluff, genial man in his early fifties, confusingly also called Chris rather than his

Arabic name, because that is what he was called in the nearly three decades he lived and worked in the wine business in France. Returning home a few years ago, he bought his own farm of 12 hectares growing peaches and other fruit. But he found it hard to resist the offer of a chance to get back into the business.

The estate kitchen have prepared a 'small meal' for us which turns out to be something of a banquet, the focal point being lamb chops cooked in the way I usually associate with Madrid – thinly sliced, fast fired and served with a few herbs, seared on the outside, pink and juicy within. And all the better for being washed down by a couple of glasses of Volubilia Rouge.

All of this leads us on to a discussion of the Moroccan wine business, its well-being and a general agreement on the rough degree of quality of the most widespread wines. Domaine de la Safari is, we agree, a decent claret-style red, while the 'réserve' version has a bit more depth and structure. Bonassia Cabernet Sauvignon is distinctive with almost a hint of smoke and pronounced tannins. Ksar Rouge is a decent Bordeaux-style red, able to cut it with a lot of the AOC mass-market French clarets, but nothing special. The Cuvée du Président wines are – like the unrelated Président French Emmental cheese and other dairy products – benchmarks in drinkability, but nothing more: 'un vin de tous les jours'.

I am also happy to endorse Christophe's enthusiasm over his olive oil. A hunk of rich crusty Moroccan bread dipped in it oozes depth of flavour and just the right level of peppery spice. It is hard to imagine doing anything with this oil other than dipping bread in it and eating it. Will he ever return to France, I ask Christophe, expecting and hoping for the answer 'No, never'. Instead he says, 'Probably.' There are aspects of life in Morocco that exasperate him: notably that every year, year-in, year-out, he has to explain anew to his workforce what they have to do with the vines, even though – he sighs – it is the same thing every year.

Lunch over, it is time for me to get back to Meknes and happily, as I had hoped, Christophe arranges a driver for me. Her name is Inez; she speaks perfect French and apart from a headscarf she gives the impression of being a thoroughly modern young woman. She is wearing skin-tight jeans and a white coat from one of the estate laboratories, and leans forward to shake my hand before clambering up into the driver's seat of one of the estate vans. She lives in one of the nearby villages, she tells me, as she puts her foot down on the accelerator and we spin off the dirt track estate road on to the tarmac. 'I prefer Fez, though,' she says, making clear that this is where she and her friends go for a night out. 'But Marrakech is even better,' she adds, eyes gleaming. 'Why?' I venture. She turns to me as if I have asked why grass is green: 'For the discos, of course!'

8

Recycling the Romans

HAVING FINALLY LOCATED – and tasted – the wines of Volubilia, it was time to see Volubilis itself, or what remains of the city that for more than 200 years was capital of Rome's most far-flung southwesterly imperial province, ruling as far as the mythical *limes* of Rabat, and still an important city centuries after they left.

The main road north from Meknes to the site of Volubilis is remarkably good by most Moroccan standards: smooth, evenly surfaced and relatively wide, which is a good thing given the number of sharp bends, oncoming trucks and the speed and carelessness of *grand taxi* drivers. I had taken the easy way of asking the hotel porter if he could order one for me, find out what the price might be and negotiate it down a bit, which was a lot easier than my experiences the day before. We settled on a price of 450 dirhams, around £35, which seemed reasonable enough for a 70-kilometre round trip and several hours of the driver's waiting time. I certainly doubted I could have done any better on the open market of the *grand taxi* stand round the corner.

The site of Volubilis came into view from some distance away – a few unmistakably classical columns rearing out of a luscious, green landscape in an obviously fertile plain lying in a shallow valley in the foothills of the Mid Atlas Mountains. Quirkily, the columns disappear as we round a corner and descend into a little approach road where the driver asks if he may park under the shade of a leafy oleander tree, leaving me a hundred metres to walk to the 'gates'. I wander off, and he settles down for a ciggie and a nap.

The reason for the gates is not just that Volubilis is a remarkable archaeological site, but that since 1998 it has been added to the list of UNESCO World Heritage sites, for a whole list of reasons that include not just the extent and quality of its Roman remains, but its role as an example of a mixing bowl of human society for hundreds of years, the one-time flourishing of Christianity in this part of North Africa, the transition to Islam, and the origins of Morocco as a state. There is a modest entrance fee to pay, and I am glad not to be hassled by a posse of would-be guides. I have done my own research on Volubilis in advance and in any case the couple hanging around seem already happily booked by three tour groups – one Japanese, one German and one American – descended from the buses parked outside. The entrance gate itself is situated at a gap in what was once the circuit of Roman walls, many of which are still visible, although you could hop over them and there is a wire fence instead to deter potential looters. In their heyday the masonry walls stretched for some 2.6 kilometres and were apparently guarded by a total of 34 towers, although there is precious little sign of them today.

As befits a World Heritage site, there is a small, discreet visitors' centre with shop and toilets, but it is tucked low beneath the brow of a small hummock near the gateway, where it shelters a row of remarkably well-preserved tombstones with easily legible inscriptions: a dedication from a mother to a dead son, a family crypt. They indicate just how far afield the inhabitants of this frontier city had come from its heyday, with references to the Roman province of Hispania and even one that, to my Latin, appears to say Bavaria, which would not be surprising (there were many ethnic German recruits in the legions) except that it would be a very early use of the term.

The unusual name Volubilis itself has caused much specu-
lation although the general consensus is that the site was the
scene of a Phoenician/Carthaginian town as early as 300BC.
The Roman got here a lot later – it wasn't until 43AD that the
emperor Claudius annexed Northwest Africa as Mauretania
Tingitana (the Moorish country south of Tingis, the old Berber
name for Tangier) – and their rebuilding of the city lasted more
than a century. Etymologists suggest that Volubilis was a Latin
corruption of the Berber word for oleander, which sounds sensible enough given that the small trees grow all over the place
here, including next to where my driver is presumably dozing
away right at this minute. We have no idea how that word might
have been written originally, given the lack of ancient Berber
script, but it is today pronounced *oulalit,* and that is more or
less what the name of the city reverted to after the Romans
eventually left. It is also, of course, a clear shot on goal for the
supporters of the 'w' school in Latin who argue that that is how
the letter 'v' (which also stood for 'u') should be pronounced
(also backing up the old joke in Sellar's and Yeatman's revered
1066 and All That whereby Julius Caesar's *veni, vidi, vici* was
misconstrued by the ancient Britons as *weeny, weedy, weaky,*
whereupon they immediately 'lost heart and gave up').

Within the remnants of Volubilis's walls – only in places
can they be called streets, as much of the stone has been
removed or is overgrown – it is easy to see the plan of the
city just by wandering the ancient tracks, despite the extent
to which it has suffered from plundering (including by royal
decree) and natural wear and tear. The last major damage
was the result of an aftershock following the earthquake that
destroyed the Portuguese capital of Lisbon in 1755, and not
only wreaked havoc as far south as Morocco but also caused
tremors to be felt in far distant Sweden, while people in Britain's Scilly Isles ran out of their houses in shock.

It is remarkable that Volubilis's largest structures survive:
the almost totally intact 'triumphal arch', built in the reign

of the emperor Caracalla near the end of the second century AD, the gateway to the town's main street; the Decumanus Maximus, which stretches all the way through the heart of the city to the much smaller curved Tingis gate, marking the beginning of the long road north to Tingis, although little now remains of the shops and kiosks that would have lined it. Even still, on a late spring day, the rubble and ground-level ruins are ablaze with colour from wild chrysanthemums, little lilac bell-shaped flowers, and tiny ground creepers with bright red petals, the whole given just a tinge of African exotica by a green lizard darting along the ochre stone of the arch. But perhaps the most significant vegetation of that which has reclaimed this site from civilisation are the olive trees sprouting from the earth seemingly at random, between the foundations of two houses, in what was once a main street, or in a market place. Most poignant is the fact that olive trees can live to a very great age, and many of these are almost certainly sprung from the seeds – the olive stones themselves – spat out by the ancient inhabitants.

For there is no overlooking the fact that the olive was a major agricultural crop and its processing was the town's largest industry. Almost the first semi-intact building I came across before reaching the triumphal arch was an olive press with an olive mill next to it, though I have to confess I only recognised it as such because the Moroccans (with the blessing of UNESCO) have reconstructed a replica nearby of how it must have looked nearly two millennia ago. Altogether a total of 58 olive oil pressing buildings have so far been unearthed and identified (at least half the city's remains are still unexcavated), some of them privately owned by the larger mansions. At the time such a luxury would have been the contemporary equivalent of having your own kitchen garden, pharmacy and electricity plant, given that apart from the sheer delight of eating your own olives, the oil pressed from them was used in medicines and to make soap, as fuel for lighting and heating, while the husks of the pressed olives could be fed to livestock, or burned to fuel hot baths.

Even to this day, the job of turning raw olives into something usable is hard work and a long process; back then they crushed them between millstones until they were nothing more than a thick paste, then used a stone press to squeeze out the oil into a decantation basin – to which they occasionally added a little water to make the lighter oil float to the surface so they could scoop it out with ladles, to be sold in the city's shops or exported.

One of the other most important exports for which Volubilis was famed was even more exotic: wild beasts for the gladiators of the imperial arenas and above all the Colosseum in Rome, where crowds had a voracious appetite for seeing the ferocious monsters of Africa turned out to do battle with each other, fight armed slaves or munch on a few Christians or other lunatic dissenters. Barbary lions were a particular favourite, if only for old times' sake, the native lions of Europe having been hunted to extinction. But almost anything would do, notably Barbary leopards and bears, which had to be sourced from the Atlas Mountains, where a few still survive today.

But you could always guarantee a good crowd ready to turn out to see the monster that Romans since the time of Hannibal had nightmares about: the elephant. Pliny the elder, who as we have seen was particularly fond of elephants, cited their skill in attending to their main weapons of warfare: 'These animals take the greatest care of their teeth; they pay especial attention to the point of one of them, that it may not be found blunt when wanted for combat. When they are surrounded by the hunters, they place those in front which have the smallest teeth, that the enemy may think that the spoil is not worth the combat; and afterwards, when they are weary of resistance, they break off their teeth.'

They would not have had the chance to do that in an arena. The contest that Pliny would most have liked to see in an arena but failed to – not least because one of the creatures involved was (or so we believe today) mythical – involved an Indian elephant, which he believed to be larger than the African variety. Indeed the skeletal remains of the extinct indigenous North African elephant showed it to be much smaller than the sub-Saharan African elephant we know today. According to Pliny, anyway, the Indian variety's nemesis was 'the dragon, which is perpetually at war with the elephant, and is itself of so enormous a size, as easily to envelop the elephants with its folds, and encircle them in its coils. The contest is equally fatal to both; the elephant, vanquished, falls to the earth, and by its weight, crushes the dragon which is entwined around.'

Bizarrely it is not difficult to imagine a herd of elephants wandering this high plain though it would probably require some modern rethinking of the agriculture. But it was almost certainly the appetite for blood sport – humans having the potential to be a lot more ferocious than any wild beast – that drove the North African elephant to extinction within a few decades of the Roman conquest.

British chronicler Walter Harris reports that even a century ago, the lords of Morocco had a fascination for the animal, which, turning history on its head, now had to be imported from European zoos. The last pre-colonial sultan kept two, and when he moved to Tangier after abdicating the intention was to take them with him. As Harris narrates, 'While the two elephants were being brought from Fez to Tangier at the time of the abdication, one of them escaped on the road, and being an unknown beast to the villagers of the countryside, it met with many adventures.' I bet.

The other great thing Volubilis appears to have been famous for is interior decoration, given the surprisingly large number of surviving interior floor mosaics. None of them are actually interior any more and as a result the once bright colours have largely – save for a few less-than-perfect attempts at restoration – faded to shades of ochre, as if they had all been photographed in sepia. The quality of the artwork is not always the best – indeed most are inferior to the *zellige* Moroccan tile work developed over the centuries from the Middle Ages and still, as demonstrated in the Hassan II mosque in Casa, practised today. But unless you are totally addicted to geometric patterns – Moroccan *zellige*, like all Islamic art, is forbidden from depicting living creatures – there is something refreshingly gauche about the floor frescos in this provincial capital far from resplendent Rome.

Several of the ruins that were once grand houses are today known largely for their flooring. The 'House of the Athlete', for example, has a mosaic of a boy seated backwards on a racing steed; 'The House of Orpheus' a mosaic of the mythical musician; 'The House of Dolphins' a whole school of the sea mammals placed in various directions rather like an ancestor of the paisley pattern. My favourite, though, is the great mosaic tapestry dedicated to the Labours of Hercules, which details the hero's travails in almost children's comic format, like a jokey graphic novel in cracked tiles. There is something quite magical and disconcerting at the same time about standing under the hot African sun looking at floor decoration laid in someone's home nearly two millennia ago, particularly as the characters and myths depicted are so familiar, so much a part of European culture, and seemingly alien, like the Latin tombstone inscriptions, in this African, Arabic land.

At its peak around AD 200 Volubilis would have had about 20,000 inhabitants, making it a tiny provincial town compared to the million-strong capital of the empire, but a very sizeable city in North African terms at the time. Its long, slow decline began towards the end of the third century when, ordered by the Emperor Diocletian, Roman troops withdrew, retreating to the northern coast of Mauretania Tingitana, just about the same time as they pulled out of their most northerly province, Britannia. As in Britain, however, the city's inhabitants remained, and continued to live a Roman lifestyle, even

adopting the new imperial religion of Christianity in the following century, according to inscriptions on tombs uncovered. There is clear evidence of Latin still being spoken in
Volubilis as late as the seventh and even eighth centuries,
although by then the city had shrunk and erected a new
earthwork defence within the old Roman walls. The reason
was undoubtedly the wave of invaders, and in particular the
storm from the east as the Arabs, driven by Mohammed's call
to spread the word of Allah, surged through North Africa. By
then most of the inhabitants would have been descendants
of those who had been there before the Romans arrived, and
whose own descendants are still a significant part of Morocco's population today. They survived and intermingled with
the Romans, all the while retaining their own languages and
culture; they would do the same with the Arabs.

For Moroccans today, the far more important settlement
is the one that rears up on the hillside just above Volubilis, a
couple of kilometres back on the road to Meknes. It looks to
me a rather unexceptional large Moroccan village, but Ali,
my driver, refreshed from his snooze in the shade of the oleander bushes, cannot believe I don't want to make the detour,
and before I know it we have turned off the main road and are
heading up steep streets, crowded with both pedestrians and
donkeys, with smoke from grillades wafting through the air.
This, Ali tells me proudly, is the village of Moulay Idriss.

I recognise the name, not least from some of the history
lessons that Omim gave me, but just who he was has momentarily slipped my mind. Which turns out to be a cardinal
sin, in the eyes of Ali who wastes no time in enlightening
me: 'How can you not know? Moulay Idriss was the great-
grandson of Mohammed, peace be upon him.' (The obligatory phrase makes me realise he means the man himself, not
one of the several thousand extant Moroccans named after
him.)

'Aha,' I nod reverently.

But actually I am revealing my ignorance, because he reminds me – and I really shouldn't have forgotten, it just seemed a bit out of context here so close to all these remains of the ancient Roman empire – that Moulay Idriss was the founder of Morocco. His grandmother, Ali tells me, was the prophet's daughter Fatima, while his grandfather was his cousin and first follower, Ali. He smiles, and taps his chest. I'm a bit edgy about this as I know that it was that particular Ali's death that led to the great Muslim civil war – if a war between rival religious factions can be called 'civil', which, in this case, given that the religion and civilisation were rapidly merging at the time, it probably can – between Sunnis and Shias, a row that is ongoing today. I think this might not be a great conversation.

Anyway, apparently back in 787 or thereabouts (by the Christian calendar) Idriss – Moulay is a title given to the descendants of Ali in Morocco – was on the run from one of the battles that would forever make the Shias feel they had lost the religious war, and he turned up in Volubilis, which was still a thriving town, even if its name had been corrupted to Walila and it was ruled by the local Berber tribe. He married the daughter of the tribal king and turned out to be a pretty decent warrior and leader, bringing together most of what is today northern Morocco (and a fair chunk of what is now Algeria) under his rule. He founded this little hillside village as a more easily fortifiable centre than low-lying Volubilis – and, after his string of victories, went on to found the city of Fez (my next destination), which would remain Morocco's capital (in the north at least) for most of the next millennium. He was largely helped by other warriors on the run from defeat by the Sunnis, so that in addition to consolidating Islam among the Berber and Arab population, it was quite clearly the Shia variety, as a result of which the Abbasid Sunni Caliph, claiming to rule all Islam from Baghdad, had him poisoned in 791 in the hope that the new kingdom would collapse. His son, Idriss II, proved up to the task and it didn't. It was only a few centuries later that a new dynasty definitively switched Morocco to the Sunni side. In fact, in 2008 a major row blew up with Iran (the major Shia nation) when Tehran was accused of illegally proselytising in Morocco. I am relieved I didn't have that conversation with Ali.

The conversation we do have turns out to be very different, not least because apart from the windy, steep, and rather pretty, cobbled streets, there is not a great deal to see in Moulay Idriss, given that the chief attraction, one which draws tens of thousands of Moroccans every year, is the mausoleum of the great man himself; his body was brought back and buried here. But like nearly all religious buildings in Morocco, apart from the Hassan II mosque, it is completely off limits to Christians and even surrounded by a wooden fence so you can't see it without making a trek up into the surrounding mountains to get a glimpse from above. What Ali wants to talk about in any case is not the mausoleum but the donkeys! Apparently the local government in Moulay Idriss have decided, partly because of the steep slope the village is built on and for the sake of the environment – and presumably at the instigation of the local donkey-keepers – to ban *petits taxis*. Most of the village is pedestrian only. We are allowed to drive up into the centre because he is a *grand taxi* from Meknes and that is the way most tourists and visitors arrive, and they get a lot of visitors, although for obvious reasons few non-Muslim tourists. 'Imagine being a rubbish collector here,' he says, stretching my imagination. 'You'd have to hire a donkey or two to get up and down the steps.' I make a spontaneous decision never to apply for a job as a rubbish collector in Moulay Idriss.

Back in Meknes, it is time to discover what happened to most of Volubilis's fine stone and marble, which requires little more effort than wandering around the palace district of the medina. The fact that Meknes is cited as one of the 'four royal cities' of Morocco goes back to the 17th century and its sole spell as capital of the country under just one ruler, but one who happened to be long-lived, a great warrior, sadist and lover, with several hundred sons and an unknown number of daughters. He gloried in a remarkable enthusiasm for displaying thousands of severed heads of conquered enemies around his prime architectural achievements, of which there were many, for he just happened, also, to be a great builder.

Moulay Ismail was the younger brother of Moulay Rachid, the founder of the present royal dynasty who died in an admirably peaceful, if mildly entertaining, manner by falling from his horse when he was caught by a low branch during a madcap late-night ride around his palace gardens in Marrakech. His younger brother's reign was immediately threatened, as so frequently on the handover of the reins of power (a particularly suitable phrase in this case), by a series of rebellions which he promptly defeated by raising a superbly trained and signally devoted army, which was one of the best examples of reverse racism in Moroccan history. Ismail's mother and his favourite wife were both black, and he created a crack regiment by recruiting ex-slaves from the caravans coming up to Marrackech from the sub-Sahara. After consolidating his position he would make them a major part of his military machine, providing them with black wives, encouraging them to breed, and taking their sons from the age of 10 and placing them into military academies, until at age 18, they in turn were recruited into the army and given domestically-trained wives from the palace kitchens. By the end of his long reign this racially elite army would be 150,000 strong, half of them stationed in his new capital, Meknes.

By then Morocco would be at its greatest territorial extent, including a chunk of what is now western Algeria, and all of the modern Western Sahara, thereby setting the precedent for his descendants' controversial and still disputed 'reconquest' of the territory in 1975. He also forced the Spanish out of most of their coastal enclaves, and starved the English out of Tangier, which had been given to them by the Portuguese as part of the dowry of Charles II's wife, Catherine of Braganza. His other coup – comparable to England's Elizabeth I authorising English captains to effectively act as pirates against Spanish galleons – was licensing the Muslim corsairs along his coast to prey on all Christian shipping, providing them with ships and a safe haven in exchange for 60 per cent of all profits to subsidise his building projects in Meknes.

I was beginning to realise just how vast Moulay Ismail's projects had been by the time I staggered up the steep alleys – inaccessible other than by foot or donkey – of the medina, which I was discovering is in effect just a series of parallel streets on the slope up to the immense and forbidding palace walls. At the top is the Place el-Hedim, before the massive Bab el-Mansour gate, an extraordinary grand entrance – supported on either side by two classical columns removed from Volubilis – studded with *zelige* mosaic and dating from the beginning of the 18th century, which makes it contemporary with Versailles. This is not just coincidence. Moulay Ismail and Louis XIV, France's *roi soleil*, were two absolute monarchs of vast lands whose dynasties, though neither knew it, were coming to an end. Each knew of the other, corresponded, and hoped to outstrip the other in the grandeur of his palace.

The main difference is that it is today impossible to see inside Moulay Ismail's as it remains a royal palace, even though Mohammed VI rarely comes here and its walls are crumbling. Built by prisoners of war and Christian slaves taken by his licensed corsairs, the *makhzen*, the royal palace was of vast dimensions. The Moroccan sultans virtually built entire private cities. Like Gormenghast in Mervyn Peake's trilogy, the palaces *were* the cities, while the medina outside the wall was seen by the rulers as hovels for tradesmen.

It brings to mind the historian Tom Holland's description of the palace of the Byzantine caesars in Constantinople in the Middle Ages: 'The sharp angles of Constantine's original palace had long since been swallowed up by extensions, so immense and sprawling in scale that for every new one being built, another would be decaying and forgotten.

'There were gardens and judicial tribunals, pavilions and reception halls, banqueting chambers, secretariats and even an indoor riding school ... deep underground there stretched sepulchral storerooms, kitchens and massive cisterns.'

*

Because of its continuing royal status – and the fact that the Dar el-Kebir palace was all but levelled in the 1755 earthquake – there is a huge tranche of historic Meknes that is simply inaccessible. The Bab el-Mansour gate is reserved for the king.

After a few minutes spent dutifully standing and staring at it in appropriate awe, I need to get out of the heat. The open gate to the right, used by traffic, leads into the shady part of the ancient palace monumental complex that is actually accessible, and importantly through a little gate on the left to the mausoleum of the great tyrant himself. In its yellow-painted courtyards a few old women in headscarves sit on a bench in the shade, holding out their hands hopefully for a few dirhams. There is a legend, apparently, that just visiting the mausoleum brings *baraka*, good luck. In which case living on its doorstep ought to be a blessing.

The antechamber to Moulay Ismail's mausoleum itself is blessedly cool, reinforced by the stupendous mosaic tile floor on my bare feet. The anteroom is considered almost as sacred as the adjoining mausoleum, the doorway of which can be approached but not crossed by unbelievers, as it is considered a mosque. There is a grandeur and taste to the whole ensemble, but I can't help remembering that most of this stuff was plundered either from the Roman ruins, or from the El Badi palace and the tombs of his immediate predecessors back in

Marrakech. Not to mention that the long avenue I have come from was regularly used by Moulay Ismail for one of his favourite sports: riding in a chariot pulled by women slaves or eunuchs while he randomly hacked off the heads of prisoners or even his own servants assembled there. This was a man who in his own right is believed to have slaughtered 30,000 people. One of his lesser but curiously more lasting fetishes was the banning of black shoes. Having seen their popularity amongst his Spanish enemies, he considered them a symbol of Christianity, and outlawed them for all but, bizarrely, his Jewish subjects – presumably being a bit vague about those who were neither Christian nor Muslim. He decreed instead that the colour for Moroccan men should be canary yellow – the same colour as the paintwork in the courtyard of his mausoleum – a tradition that survives in leather *babouches* to this day, which is why male tourists receive a smile when they buy red ones, traditionally reserved for women.

Strolling back down the same, long, straight, walled avenue today leads to the only parts of the one-time royal complex that are inhabited. Turning left leads me into a vast, intimidating labyrinth of dark, domed chambers, twisting and turning like the alleys between the riads of Marrakech, but huge and intimidating instead of narrow and claustrophobic. Guidebooks often describe these as the sultan's stables, but common sense supports the more modern opinion that they were vast storerooms for mountains of grain, though some might also have been used as prisons.

There is a sense of relief on escaping from Moulay Ismail's vast, neglected legacy back down into the parallel terraces of the lower medina. I stop for something to eat, and hopefully a beer at the Collier de la Colombe, partly because the 'Dove Collar' of its name is attractive, but mainly because it has an open terrace with a view down over the *ville nouvelle*. It turns out not to be the best of choices. The place is undergoing renovation work, with polystyrene tiles from the roof on the floor and only a reduced menu available. They have no beer but they do have some *gris* wine, albeit not the Volubilia from down the road. Interestingly, however, the waiter, at once both enthusiastic – I am one of only three guests – and apologetic, tells me that the reason most of Morocco's vineyards are in the Meknes area is less to do with the soil than the fact that the French made the city their military base during the years of the protectorate. And the officers needed something decent to drink. I wish I had asked Christophe about that one. The meal – the only one he recommended from a choice of four – is a dish of couscous topped with slow-roasted lamb, raisins and almonds, and to my surprise it is quite delicious.

Nightlife in Meknes is quiet, in the medina all but nonexistent. I take a stroll round the *ville nouvelle* and discover a few art nouveau gems. Meknes has a cinema, called Camera, all straight lines and curves, white – or, this being Morocco, just off-white – with horizontal red stripes. Sadly they are not showing *She is Diabetic, Hypertensive and Refuses to Die III*. Its obvious contemporary is the Vox bar next door, which must have been spectacular in its 1930s heyday: all high bar stools, vertical cylindrical ceiling lights, with French officers smoking Gauloises and drinking cocktails or *un petit gris*. Today it is still not a bad bar, just one that looks as if time stopped here around 1962, with a jukebox above the bar and bottles of Heineken and Flag instead of Pernod and Ricard. Crackly speakers churn out, at just acceptable volume, crackly Arabic pop, and there is the obligatory photo of His Majesty (may God be with him), in a broad pinstripe jacket with a racy tie and slicked-back hair giving him the air of a smiling Soho nightclub owner.

After a couple of Flags, I bid him and Meknes goodnight and grab a *petit taxi* (they are blue here) for the customary *dix dirhams,* and head for bed.

9

Howzat then! Souk and See

THE COMMONPLACE THING to say about Fez is that there is nothing quite like it in the Arab world. In reality, there is nothing quite like it in the whole world. Nowhere else has a mediaeval city been so perfectly preserved: perfect not just in the sense that its architecture has survived, but in the fact that it still functions and exists in very much the same way it did half a century ago.

Unlike European walled cities such as Carcassonne in France or Rothenburg ob der Tauber in Germany, which feel like pretty tourist museum towns, Fez with its vast encompassing defensive walls surrounding the whole of the medina is labyrinthine, dirty, grimy and, in places, full of shit. It strikes me strongly that, in size and the way its streets seem to have grown together rather than been laid out, it might resemble what the City of London – with its Bread Street, Cannon Street, Leathermarket, Fish Street and Pudding Lane – might have looked like in the early Middle Ages, before the Great Fire.

Okay, there is electricity – but not everywhere, oil lamps are still common – and yes, there is gas, but it has to be delivered in cylinders, on carts pulled by donkeys, or precariously strapped to their backs as they are led down treacherous cobbles by a man with a lit cigarette in his mouth. Marrakech's medina is a thriving, functioning city, unchanged in layout since the Middle Ages, but the medina of Fez is unchanged in layout, industry, cuisine and in the arrogant self-confidence of its inhabitants, who for all the ups and downs in its history consider their city never to have lost its true role as capital in the thousand years of its existence. It is still considered the cultural heart of Morocco, the intellectual centre of the country with its oldest university, and its inhabitants played a leading role in the struggle against French colonialism that led to independence.

There is a certain irony, therefore, that the man who probably did most to ensure that it remains the most intact and unchanged of all Arab cities was a Frenchman. Hubert Lyautey not only saved Morocco from the forced Europeanisation imposed on Algeria, he fell in love with the native culture and so determined that the people, their way of life and their architecture should not be tainted by colonialism. He may have been the man who used the murder of European workers in Casablanca to send in the troops, which in the end led to the establishment of the protectorate, but that was primarily to do with the jockeying for colonial expansion of the European powers that would end in the First World War. His motto in Morocco was to 'change nothing that need not be changed, do nothing that will cause offence'. Not only did he see the establishment of the *villes nouvelles* as a way of providing residential and commercial facilities for the colonists that were separate from the natives, he even issued an edict that no homes could be rebuilt in the medinas with windows facing on to the street, a law that suited the domestic modesty and privacy beliefs of Islam, but put off any Europeans from moving into and transforming the customs of the old cities.

The influence is most specifically obvious in Fez in the distance between the old and new towns, the latter several kilometres away on the other side of the valley of the River Sebou. Getting between the two is, for foreigners, a taxi ride, because for all its fame and splendour, Fez is less of a tourist destination than Marrakech and although the road linking the two would make a pretty walk amongst the greenery, its relative isolation has made it the scene of muggings, even in daylight. The inhabitants of Fez – known as *Fassis* – are famed for what they might term a 'fierce independence of spirit'. The less kind might call it 'attitude' towards 'incomers', which means just about everybody else on the planet. Not exactly along the lines of the 'nobody likes us, we don't care' chant of Millwall football club supports, but not exactly 'we welcome you and the changes you want to make to our lifestyle' either. For example, Fez's ancient medina is actually two: Fez el-Jedid was built in 1276, some 200 years after its other half Fez el-Bali, by a new dynasty – the Merenids – who surrounded it with high walls, primarily to keep them safe from their new subjects. Over the centuries the two grew together, though it was not until the 19th century that their walls were joined. The much-smaller Fez el-Jedid, with the Jewish *mellah* attached at one side, still feels like a ceremonial addition to the older city; for instance it includes the royal palace, which, as in every other city, is closed to the public in case His Majesty might pop in.

The main point of entrance to Fez el-Bali is the bustling Bab Boujeloud, a great multicoloured tiled gateway surrounded by cafés and restaurants. From Bab Boujeloud the 'main street' – really a crowded but reasonably broad alley – leads into the heart of the medina. Then you're on your own. The American writer Paul Bowles, a die-hard denizen of Tangier in its louche *cité internationale* days, advised visitors to 'get lost in the crowd'. In reality it's hard to do anything else.

But I have a mission: to visit an ordinary hammam, and those in Fez are reputed to be among the oldest and best in the country. It is too simplistic a Western – American and European – attitude that ancient Arab cities might not be the cleanest. There is good reason for it, but it doesn't mean that their inhabitants aren't. Cleanliness is one of the most important rules in Islam. You'd never find a church with a place outside to wash your feet, even if Jesus Christ did make a bit of a thing about it. The hammam recommended to me by Mohammed, the Fassi chef who helped me make my *tanjia* in Marrakech, is on the main alley; in his words, 'halfway between the *medersa* and the Kairouine mosque'. This is a typical Fez instruction, which assumes you know where everything is. Improbably enough, armed with a map that looks like a maze book for hyper-intelligent 10-year-olds, this works, chiefly because I am held up by a large group of tourists queuing to enter the *medersa*. There is a queue, and I join it, because the Bou Inania *medersa* – the name for an Islamic college which we in the 'West' know, with more clouded connotations in its Pakistani form, as a *madrasah*.

The Bou Inania is reputed to be by far the most beautiful *medersa* in Morocco, though it is of course hard to pass judgement as an infidel since we aren't allowed in any of the others. The 14th-century sultan who built the *medersa* allegedly threw the accounts for the building of it into a river rather than take heed of the immense cost, declaring that 'you can't put a price on beauty'. The layout is the same as any other; an open space enclosed on four sides with study rooms and open communal dormitories, but it is the sheer scale and intricacy of the decoration captured within the marble walls and thrown into relief by the bright sunlight flooding in that makes the Bou Inania so remarkable. That and the fine detail of the carving on the cedar wood around three of the four sides. It is as if the Islamic ban on the depiction of living creatures, no matter how foolish it may seem to us today in a world awash with graphic imagery, may have contributed to the swirling intricacy of Arabic script. But would the ability to read what looks like pure decoration make it better or detract from it? I have seen spray-tagged graffiti on the walls of underpasses in London that look like works of art until you read what they say.

The problem with the sheer exoticness of North Africa – and a lot of the Islamic world in general – is that it occasionally inspires overly romantic idealism in Westerners. Lawrence of Arabia didn't so much 'go native' as fall in love with the idea of Arabia. Even here, admittedly in the midst of a radiant example of Islamic artistry, I heard one fey young man, a British tourist judging by his accent, remark in an awestruck voice to an older man, 'You know, I heard something really beautiful the other day: the last call to prayer of the day should come when your shadow is as long as the height of a man.' I felt like turning around and telling him that they didn't set the time because of the length of their shadow, or rather they did, but only because they had no other way of telling the time.

They did, however, have clocks – highly intricate ones if we can believe the extraordinary contraption on the wall opposite the *medersa* entrance: a great ensemble of wooden projections from the wall, which was partly dismantled for restoration some years ago, but has not yet been replaced because nobody is precisely sure how it is supposed to work. This is the clock that gave its name to Café Clock, the original Fez branch of which is down an alleyway beneath it.

Having located the *medersa*, it is easier to watch out for the hammam, which I locate behind a typical Moorish arched doorway, white walls within. No sooner have I stuck my head round the door than a street lad rushes in after me to say, *'M'sieu, m'sieu, hammam hammam,'* as if he thinks I am expecting a mosque (where my presence really would be both unrequired and unwanted) or about to be horrified to find it full of naked men. So it is very much to his surprise when he realises it really is the hammam I'm looking for. But inside it is not at all as I expected: just a little room with green-and-white tiles, a pale-skinned elderly chap with a sunken chest wrapped in a towel sitting on the plastic seating around the walls, and another bloke, swarthy, skinny, of indeterminate age, wearing a hat, fully clothed and fully bearded, who looks

up with a mixture of disbelieving curiosity and mild annoyance on the little that is visible of his face.

I begin, uncertainly, hanging a few things on the row of
hooks above the plastic seating, already more than a little
worried about the lack of security – I mean, I have an iPhone
and two credit cards in my trouser pockets. The pale-skinned
man smiles kindly at me. I explain, with some embarrassment, that it is my first time and I'm not quite sure of the
routine. In fact I have no idea at all if this is it, or just an anteroom. He looks at me as if I may have learning difficulties,
and replies as if it were the most obvious thing in the world,
which it actually is: '*Déshabillez-vous!*'

Obvious, isn't it? I mean it's a bathhouse. Except that he's
the only one in any state of undress. I've noticed another
bloke now on a sort of mezzanine level who is fully clothed.
He wakens from a snooze, jumps to his feet and makes a big
show of pointing to a blue on white enamel sign on the wall, in
Arabic, which, of course, I can't understand. He also points to
a sign next to it, this time red on white enamel, with a translation into French beneath it: *Fumer interdit*. Well, that's okay
with me; smoking in the bath has never been something I'd
advocate, especially when it's a communal bath. Except that so
far it doesn't look much like a bath. '*C'est chaud*?' I ask the sole
obvious francophone. Not too hot, he tells me. By now, trousers with their precious cargo hanging from a peg on the wall,
I'm down to my underpants and not too sure about whether
removing them is the thing to do – it certainly is in Finnish
saunas, and even more definitely in Russian *banyas*, where,
examining the uniforms hanging up in the changing room,
you realise that in the stepped steam room, where crouching
on the steps as you mount to the hotter levels is obligatory, you
are staring at the massed buttocks of the higher ranks of the
Red Army. Not a pretty sight.

But I have been told that even amongst men alone, there
is a greater concern for modesty in the Muslim world, and I

am not the man to shock the status quo, at least certainly not under these circumstances. There may be – undoubtedly is – an age limit up to which displaying one's torso, and if needs be, tackle, may be a subject of boastful, masculine pride, if you have the right build and basic ingredients, but it almost certainly comes to a slithering halt somewhere after the age of 50.

Happily, it is at just that moment that my pale, hollow-chested interlocutor lets his towel slip to reveal a pair of bright purple semi-boxer shorts. I breathe a sigh of relief; I can keep my Sloggis on, after all. At virtually the same moment, as if to reinforce the message, a man in his mid-fifties, whose rippling, if grey-haired, torso all but gives the lie to my above assertion, enters from a door at the end of the chamber carrying two very large plastic buckets. His nether regions are covered by a pair of what may be swim shorts or just possibly satin boxers. My francophone friend explains that I should pick up my bucket and walk. And that if I want a massage, I should come back to the bloke who has just entered the room and he will perform the service.

I open the door and walk through tentatively, not least because I am walking on a beige tiled floor totally awash with warm water, and feel that I could at any moment lose my footing. The room is hot, very hot, but somehow not oppressive, and there is none of that hot, dry, almost burning smell of toasted pine that you encounter in a classic Scandinavian-style sauna, probably because the humidity has to be 100 per cent (at least) and there is no wood anywhere to be seen, just large smooth green-and-beige tiles rising up the walls to the vaulted ceiling, and big russet and off-white tiles on the sopping floor. Curiously, and again unlike a sauna, or indeed any other 'steam' bath I have encountered, there is no sensation of sweating – the opening of the pores in a hot, dry environment. And yet my pores are unquestionably open and I am certain that I must be sweating because my entire body is already covered with moisture, but then in an environment of total humidity, so is everything else – walls, floor, ceiling – and I realise that the effect is not so much a steam bath but an actual bath except that the entire hammam room fulfils the function of the tub.

There are more of the big buckets, in either green or black plastic, littered around. In the first of two such rooms a skinny man in late middle age is sprawled out on the floor rubbing himself with a rough one-handed scrubbing mitt. In the next room there are two younger men, both in dark shorts or underpants, one of whom is squatting on the floor actively using a similar mitt to terrorise his glistening wet skin. He gestures towards the buckets and two raised pools set into the wall on either side of the tiled chamber, indicating that I should fill a green one from one side and a black one from the other. I do so and discover to my surprise that the water is warm, but not uncomfortably so. I repeat the process with the other and start slopping it over myself only to discover that the contents of this 'well' are hot, almost to the point of scalding. The water in the other bucket is obviously meant to be the 'cold' one.

I think of the other side of the wall behind the hot 'well' where the furnace will be regularly stoked, and where, some-where in the ashes piled up alongside it there may well be an earthenware pot containing somebody's lunch! I mix a 'cocktail' of the two, a bit like filling a bath without a mixer tap, and follow the example of the others and pour the water over myself, pants and all, and begin rubbing myself down, without the benefit of the mitt, which, I realise later, I should have bought at one of the souk stalls next to the hammam. I might also have benefited from the purchase of some of the glutinous piles of shiny brown goop that I have seen at similar souk stalls, and now understand to be soap, in a form of thick sticky paste somewhere in between a solid bar and the liquid stuff we buy in dispensers. I realise this because the man at the far end of the room, as well as I can distinguish in the low light coming from the opaque window panes set high up in the walls, is massaging it indiscriminately into hair and body, producing a rich lather which he then rinses off by emptying another bucket over his head, and holding open his Y-fronts for the cleansing qualities to make their way down to that part of his anatomy too. The suds go almost unnoticed as they pass down the concealed drainage along with the slow but constant flood of hot water.

I have since been told by a Western woman living in Morocco that she used a public hammam only once because – in a surprising contrast to the relatively modest attitudes of the men, and in stark contrast to what, to Western eyes, seems undue prudishness about female modesty – the women are all completely naked and they 'indulged in a lot of rather more intimate cleaning than I was comfortable with'. What really sealed her decision not to revisit was the realisation that one of the women squatting on the floor just a few metres away ostentatiously soaping her nether regions, was the same woman she regularly passed squatting in a similar position begging inside the entrance to the medina. Given that she regularly passed her by, affecting to pretend she didn't even see her, it seemed unsuitable to make eye contact under such uncomfortably intimate circumstances.

Equipped with neither soap nor scrubbing mitt, I feel I have done a less than wholly satisfactory job at the cleaning ritual, although there is no doubt that I certainly already feel cleaner. But it is time to finish the job. I gesture towards the masseur who suddenly strikes me as an improbably stern and athletic-looking version of Victor Meldrew in boxer shorts. He nods at me to indicate I should sit on the floor, head up, legs stretched out in front of me. He then squats behind me and takes first one arm, then the other and twists each in turn into a rough equivalent of a half-Nelson. Not violently, you understand, but determinedly, so that I can felt the strain on my muscles

– which doesn't take much these days, I can tell you. He then tells me to lie down on my back while he lies opposite, his feet pushing my arms as he stretches my legs and starts work with a rough mitt, scrubbing robustly. He switches sides and repeats the process. I am relieved to find the mitt not quite as abrasive as I had expected, more the texture of a plastic bath scourer than the wire wool I had feared.

This, of course, may be because he is conscious of having a 'soft' European to work on rather than a hardy local. At any rate there is no obvious sign of him peeling away layers of skin. I had been worried by tales of hammam masseurs proudly displaying layers of scraped-off skin, in the manner of the ancient Roman slaves who used sharpened rulers to peel the dead skin away and display it to their now baby-bottomed masters as evidence of a job well done. The modern European tourist would be more inclined to see it as an unfortunate waste of a hard-earned suntan.

Now I have been turned over to lie on my stomach and legs and arms are given the same stretching and scouring treatment, though with relatively little pummelling, until the masseur indicates with little more than a grunt that he considers his job done and I should go back to pouring buckets of water over my head until I am satisfactorily rinsed. Ever so slightly more uncertain of my footing, I do as he suggests

By the end of little more than half an hour in the hammam, I feel squeaky clean and light-headed, and I wander down the street outside in a bit of a daze, until I realise that the small entrance to my right leads directly into the most important mosque in Morocco. Founded in the middle of the ninth century by a woman (!), the Kairouine mosque, confusingly, has nothing to do with Cairo, which just happens to be the location of the Al-Azhar, its main rival to the claim as the greatest centre of Islamic learning. It was simply a reference to her home city by the founder, who was a refugee from Kariouan, then the name of today's Tunis. The Kairouine was the largest mosque in Morocco until King Hassan II built his pharaonic structure in Casablanca. But unless you are a Muslim it is hard ever to see very much of it, beyond a glimpse, so thoroughly, so organically has the medina grown up around it on every side.

It is still the custom that no other mosque in Fez can proclaim the evening call to prayer until after the Kairouine has done so. The mosque complex that is effectively the heart of old Fez, despite being all but invisible at ground level, claims to be the oldest continuously functioning university in the world. This has been disputed by some secular Western scholars who would like to claim the university as a mediaeval European invention, dismissing the Kairouine as a *medersa* that focuses primarily on Islamic religious education to the detriment of other subjects. But that wholly ignores the fact that European universities, including those that claim to be the oldest, such as Paris, Oxford, Bologna and Salamanca, were founded specifically as institutions for the study and teaching of Christianity, and the study of other subjects such as law was based on the Bible as much as sharia is based on the Koran. But then one man's religion has always been another man's hogwash.

One of the most famous scholars to have lived in Fez and studied at the Kairouine was the 12th-century traveller and mapmaker Muhammad Al-Idrisi who was born in Ceuta, when what is now one of Spain's two enclaves in Morocco was still Moroccan and Muslim. He later went on to spend many years in Córdoba (when Spain itself was both Moroccan and Muslim), but also travelled to Anatolia (now Turkey) and even ventured as far north as a cold, distant country called England. But he would spend most of his later life in Sicily working for the island's Norman rulers, where he created his most remarkable and enduring work, a ground-breaking map in which he merged his own experiences with the knowledge of Arab traders and explorers with the world view of the Norman French.

The result is the most complete early image of what was then the known world, from North Africa to the North Sea including the British Isles (which Irish nationals who prefer the name Western European Islands, may be pleased to know he labelled *Irlanda al-Kabirah* – Great Ireland), and extending east into much of Asia, including India and China. Even to a modern traveller's mind it looks remarkably accurate – for something produced in 1154 – and the only things that detract from the sheer magnificence is that to be properly understood by modern eyes, it needs to be turned upside down, and the fact that, owing to the name of the Norman ruler for whom he created it, it has gone down in history as the *Tabula Rogeriana,* a name not much improved in the original Arabic: *Kitab Rujar.*

One of the best vantage points for an overview of old Fez is one of the nicest places – if you don't mind paying over the odds for the privilege – to drink a cold beer and watch the sun go down at a local landmark that has only a token relationship to the almost perfectly preserved mediaeval city spread out below it, and a lot more to do with the modern world and international French hotel culture.

Built on the site of a former vizier's palace on the edge of the old medina, the Sofitel Palais Jamaï is a classic French top-end luxury hotel with red carpet running up to the door and token homage to its historic setting expressed via little more than a faux-Oriental theme to its archways and window shapes. This carefully calculated veneer of a little, but not too much, local colour is augmented by a row of tall palms towering above the swimming pool, around which the usual selection of overfed, underdressed, pale-skinned Europeans lie exposing decidedly un-Islamic quantities of flesh to the hot North African sun.

The terrace above, with its comfortable chairs and welcome sunshades, offers the perfect place for an ice-cold Casablanca, although even at an extortionate 60 dirhams a bottle it can prove a challenge to get the waiters, wise native *Fassis* pre-ferring the air-conditioned darkness of the indoor lounge to the sun-drenched terrace, to emerge and provide it. They pay little more attention than the slowly simmering tourists do to the speakers atop the Kairouine mosque in the sprawling mediaeval warren announcing in the familiar rising drone the call to evening prayer.

✴

One of the advantages, or disadvantages, of the labyrin-thine honeycomb that is Fez is that you literally never know what is around the next corner, apart from another corner. I refuse to buy a red, tassel-topped fez even here in Fez (yes, the famous Tommy Cooper trademark originated here in the 18th century and was originally called a *Fassi farbouche,* even though it went on to be associated with the Ottoman empire to which Morocco never belonged); I can't get past the idea that people would keep coming up to me in the street saying 'Howza bout that then?' I can't help wondering if the late Tommy's reputation extended even here: the only people I have seen wearing a fez are restaurant waiters. And not many of them, either.

But the biggest shock is to walk around the corner that leads to the Chouwara tanneries. I would like to say that I could hardly believe my eyes, but it was my nose that was most assaulted by the stench that accompanies the ancient, little-altered process of tanning and dying hides. Vast pits of white stuff, which is actually pigeon dung, are spread out before vats of bright, brilliant and stinking hues, originally from turmeric, poppy, antimony and mint, in which workers wearing little more than shorts tread the hides, softening them and soaking them in colours, in a process largely unchanged for the past 400 years. In fact, the only major change that has come about is the replacement of some of the natural colourings with modern dyes, a process that makes the job cheaper; cheaper, that is, if you don't take the health of your workforce into account. Just fifteen minutes standing there gaping, at first with open mouth and then rapidly closing it and holding my nose as the overall atmosphere gets to me, and I am seriously considering a second trip to the hammam (not least because my hotel, the so-called Grand on the edge of the *villa nouvelle* has a sign in the foyer announcing that hot water is available from 8 a.m. to 10 a.m. only).

Instead I recoil back into the alleyways only to realise within minutes that I have lost track of Talaa Kabira, the main through route, which is easy to do if you stray because despite being a relatively safe and easy route through the labyrinth, it changes names repeatedly and veers off at angles which defy attempts to keep on it. Before long I find myself squeezing past donkeys laden with ten-litre water containers, or large, full, orange gas containers, being whipped along twisting alleyways. Eventually, after 40 minutes walking and the bleak realisation that I have passed the same stall three times, I emerge on to something resembling a square, and with traffic, suggesting I am out of Fez el-Bali, and hopefully somehow back at Bab Boujeloud.

I am not. This is the tongue-twisting Place Er r'cif, the end of a long spur of actual road that penetrates into the medina, allowing buses and taxis access and thus preventing total congestion at Bab Boujeloud. This is where what passes for Fez's bus station is located, and in early evening, it is both welcome and unwelcome to emerge on to it: an escape from the lightless back alleys of the mediaeval warren but at the same time an exhaust-choked, sweltering, in-your-face intrusion of the 21st century.

The saving grace is that at one end of it rises the great stone bulk of the Palais de Fez, a hotel, restaurant and carpet warehouse built into part of the city walls. I climb the four floors of ancient stairs that are the only way up from this part of the medina to its spectacular terrace. Prices are not cheap, but not all the clients are tourists – this is one of the more renowned places to taste the famous *Fassi* cuisine. I choose – because it is there – the set menu and order a bottle of wine for myself. Self-indulgent, but after a long couple of days in the hottest, most enchanting and infuriating city I have ever visited, I feel like the girl in the face cream advert: I'm worth it.

The meal is a delight even if there is enough for four! The first course alone is a meze of 15 different traditional salads from basic, but beautifully spiced, tomato, fennel and cucumber to *zalouk*, cold roast aubergine paste, steamed artichokes, steamed courgettes in *ras-el-hanout*, spinach with preserved lemon or simply green beans with garlic and chilli. In particular, the caramelised aubergine slices with spiced sugar are to die for. I'm stuffed before I'm anywhere near the main course.

But then the main course is a particular *Fassi* special: pastilla, sometimes written as *b'stilla*, one of the odder dishes I've ever tasted, which goes against every tradition in the European cookbook but is delicious nonetheless. There are variations, but this is the traditional Fez special made with pigeon, toasted and ground almonds mixed with cinnamon and sugar, the whole thing coated in *werga* pastry, a thinner version of filo, and served as a round pie dusted with icing sugar. The combination of sweet and savoury is jarring, yet superb, and makes me wonder if somehow there is a link to our festive mince pies, which were also once made with meat. Unquestionably one of the more innovative, unexpected and exotic dishes I have ever tasted. A bit like Fez itself.

10

Slow Train to Oujda

OUJDA IS NOT QUITE the end of the line, though it is as far west as you can go in Morocco. This pleasant little frontier town on the Algerian border, closed for decades now, is the one part of Morocco that was once part of the Ottoman empire. The Turks got this far, but no further, holding it for 100 years from the 18th century until the 19th when the French occupied it.

From here the trains go north to the relatively isolated port city of Nodor, from which it is possible to reach Melilla, one of the two ancient Spanish enclaves still clinging to the Moroccan coast. Once upon a time they also trundled slowly – very slowly – to the south, to mining country, past isolated concentration camps where Vichy French guards, at one stage, housed Moroccan Jews in concentration camps on behalf of their Nazi mentors.

The six-hour train journey that links Oujda to Fez and the imperial Moroccan heartland turns out to be one of the more interesting experiences in terms of what it shows up about modern Moroccan life. To the North are the Rif Mountains, strongholds of Berber conservatism and Islamic orthodoxy. The train line, as so often, is a carrier of more modern, liberal attitudes. By the time I arrive at Fez Ville Nouvelle station, it has already been waiting for an hour before commencing its long cross-country trek.

For the first few hundred miles the land on either side remains as remarkably verdant and fertile as I have seen, with fields of wheat and corn, olive groves and vegetable crops. Only gradually, as we head eastwards, does it begin to grow more dry and dusty, the farming reduced to isolated herds of goats or sheep. It's even drier and more empty as we approach Taza, just beyond the Oued Mountains, the northerly tip of the Atlas: large rocky outcrops tailing away along the horizon.

The seats are broad and comfortable. All the other passengers are Moroccan, but they are relatively quiet, save for a group of 40-something men, dressed European-style with sunglasses, seated together and chattering in Arabic about what I can only guess from dropped names to be the Champions League prospects of Chelsea versus Réal Madrid.

Moroccans, as I have noted before, are surprisingly restrained on train journeys, and do most of their talking, if at all, on their mobiles. The main source of audio entertainment, if I can call it that, is the immense number and variety of ring tones, varying from Arabic hiphop to grating electronic and the usual tediously insufferable variations of the Nokia theme. Disconcertingly, the phone in the purse of the 50-something woman in headscarf, sunglasses and thick green jellaba with her feet in woolly socks on the seat in front of her, is clearly programmed with a series of tones according to who is calling, most surprising of which is the opening bars to Oasis's 'Half a World Away', instantly recognisable as the theme tune to *The Royle Family*.

But when we reach Taouirt, the old crossroads of the caravan routes between Algeria and the Moroccan coast, a group of young men, late teens to early twenties, board and spend the next hour or two chattering about football, inevitably, but also about girlfriends and school. The most interesting thing to me, however, is that their conversation is totally in French with barely a word of Arabic.

This is the clearest link yet to an article in *Le Temps*, a biweekly news magazine I coincidentally picked up at Fez station to read on the journey; Rabat-based columnist Loubna Bernichi was defending her decision to send her children to a bilingual school – by which she means French and Arabic. But to my intense surprise, it is not the French she doubts the wisdom of; it is the Arabic.

'Nowadays, when parents are paying fortunes to send their offspring to schools run by foreign embassies, nobody in my circle understands why I am throwing my child to the wolves, leaving him with an uncertain future. What's the point of Arabic? they ask. Why have him learn a dying language when others are learning the languages of the future, such as Chinese?' I can hardly believe, given the paranoia in Western Europe about the influx of Muslims to our countries, and endlessly hearing that Arabic is the language of the Koran and therefore the language of God, that here in what is unquestionably a Muslim country where Arabic is the language of the masses, an educated Arab is calling the language 'dead'. Or rather that she believes that is what most of her peers think.

She regrets that by discarding Arabic at secondary-school level the country has turned its back on the language and that even though the PJD (the current, moderate Islamist ruling party) has tried to reverse the trend, it is too late.

'My reply is that I want him to grow up immersed in his own culture, with the reality of the society he lives in, and of course that he will know his own religion, be able to read the Koran. But people aren't convinced and I'm not sure either, at times. I was rubbish at classical Arabic in school.'

This, of course, is the heart of the problem, and takes me back to my dinner conversation in the Dauphin in Casa; that Arabic is a written language, and the Moroccan spoken version of it is barely comprehensible to Arabic speakers from the Gulf, Syria or Egypt. But what she is suggesting here is that because French is the language of business, diplomacy and government there is a danger of a new generation not only discarding written Arabic, but also losing touch with even *darja*, the popular vernacular.

'I know lots of people who reject dialect Arabic as a means of communication. Even at home they speak to their children in the language of Molière, to improve an ability which is the key to social success ... I can't help thinking that when this child grows up, how's he going to be able to talk to a vegetable seller, butcher or spice merchant? Will he need an interpreter?

'But Moroccans are convinced that French schooling is an absolute must for membership of the elite, this francophone elite that governs Morocco!'

I glance over at the two male groups on the train, the 40-something football fans and the lads a generation younger, every bit as keen on football but who can only discuss it in French.

She then turns to the Berbers, scornful of the popular enthusiasm for their reintroduction and teaching of the Amazaghi languages – all three variants, Tamazight, Tamarift and Tashelhit, are now broadcast and taught in school.

'I haven't even mentioned the Amazighs – thirteen years after the creation of IRCAM [the royal institute for Berber culture, yet another indication of the king keeping a finger in every pie] and the adoption of Tifinagh [the 'recovered' Berber script] I still don't know anybody who can write it, or anywhere to learn it. According to a Kabyle [south Moroccan/Algerian Berber] friend, sometimes even the translations you see on posters or street signs are wrong.'

Yet in a way her arguments are circular. Morocco has a free press, with the convention that the king and royal family are rarely criticised, but the most liberal attitudes are to be found in the francophone press. The same copy of *Le Temps* has an enthusiastic report about Islamic theologian Abdelbari Zemzemi saying: 'Young girls who are not virgins have the right to conceal the fact from their future husbands!'

We might take that in Europe or America as a given, but in more conservative parts of Morocco it is still regarded as up for discussion, though that in itself is a radical departure from many Muslim countries.

The new *code de la famille*, introduced with royal sanction, means that for the first time both partners share equal rights to property and wealth (as opposed to once upon a time when the woman effectively became part of the man's property) but there are strict sub clauses which effectively mean both parties – or either – have the right to demand what we would call a 'pre-nup' so that they can agree with legal force how much, if any, of their property pre-marriage, or indeed acquired during the course of the marriage, is to be shared. There are worried agony-aunt questions in the press from men who fear a woman will snare them purely to get hold of half their property. In the past men could – and many still think they can – take and discard wives at will.

And the old attitudes die hard. The sister of a friend of Abdel in Larace, whom I shall call Yasmin, for revealing her identity would not be in her interest, was married off amidst much celebration, at the age of 21. She immediately moved in with her new husband, with whom she had conveniently been much in love, seeing as the marriage had looked like a very useful alliance, commercially and financially, for both families. But the problems started almost the moment she moved in with him. He did not have a house of his own – few Moroccans do, unless they are seriously rich, the normal practice being to build another storey on the family home, which accounts for much of what European tourists often mistake for the 'unfinished' look of so many houses. They haven't stopped building out of laziness or given up for lack of money or materials – they are just waiting for the next generation.

In Yasmin's case, however, moving in with her new husband meant fitting in with the established order of his family household. Despite the usual euphoria that surrounds any wedding, even in our own society, there are not many young brides who would relish the idea of living full-time with their mother-in-law. And in a traditional Moroccan family the hierarchy is strict: Yasmin found herself being ordered around by her husband's mother, being treated like something between a kitchen maid and a cleaner for the older women, who rejoiced in the ability to hand over all their daily chores to a young woman. Her husband, meanwhile, over the period of little more than a few weeks, transformed. Not only would he not even dream of criticising, much less contradicting, his mother, he also began to get angry with his new wife if she complained, and eventually even if she went out of the house without another member of his family accompanying her.

Yasmin's family had been relatively liberal in comparison, and would certainly not have imposed such Saudi Arabian-style strictures. Within three months she could stand it no more, ran out of the house and home to her father who was furious for about 10 minutes until he had listened to her story, then took her in and agreed she should immediately file for divorce. Filing for divorce was one thing; getting the terms agreed turned out to be another. Eighteen months later they were still arguing about a financial settlement, while Yasmin, who was young, beautiful, intelligent and sensitive – all the qualities needed in the 'West' to admit you have made a mistake and start looking for a new boyfriend – found herself considered by young men of her own age to be 'soiled goods'. Even worse, she found some of them acting as if she should be 'easy', the atavistic attitude being that 'if she's done it once, she can do it again', and that no longer being a virgin she should 'put out' for almost anyone. It is an attitude that most modern young Moroccan men would deny with almost as much vehemence as would most modern Western men (of any age). But as any girl will tell you, in any country, what men say does not always reflect what they think. And ingrained social attitudes take time – decades at least – to atrophy.

One of the most famous postcards you can buy in Morocco, particularly in Essaouira, is of a tree with several goats balancing sure-footedly on its branches, at least a metre or more off the ground. Allegedly the goats are so addicted to the nuts of the argan tree that they spontaneously leap up into its branches – and even from branch to branch – to get to them. To be fair we did, from the window of the *grand taxi,* catch sight of one such tree with two goats standing in its branches but as we slowed down with the intention of stopping to take a photo, three young goatherds immediately jumped out from bushes by the roadside clamouring for money. 'I think they put the goats up there and they don't know how to get down,' said our driver with a wry smile. I think he might have been right. More than a few apocryphal stories you hear in Morocco are just that: made up.

In fact the whole story about goats and argan nuts is open to embroidery. For a start there is a whole, and probably apocryphal, background story that would have it parallel the rare coffee known as *kopi luwak,* supposedly the world's most expensive, all because it is at its best when passed through the digestive system of a palm civet, an Indonesian tree-dwelling monkey that looks a bit like a cat, which eats it and excretes it. Yes, the world's dearest coffee ought to taste like shit. Apparently it doesn't; I wouldn't know. But the Moroccan myth-makers – believe 'em or not – have picked up on the theme, insisting that because the shell of the argan nut is softened by going through goat guts, the best way to exploit it is by delving in mountains of goat poo.

The argan oil industry boasts – a little too loudly – that most of those involved in it are 'female cooperatives'. Our driver on the road to Essaouira all but insisted we stop to 'see the process of making oil' at an all-female co-op, adding 'you might wish to help these ladies'. Almost certainly he was in on his cut, and the 'process' seemed only to begin the moment somebody inside spotted us coming up to the door, and I am 90 per cent sure that the moment we left, having bought the token minimum amount of products, the said 'ladies' went back to the lounging around that even a few of them declined to give up while their colleagues went through what was effectively a demonstration of traditional argan processing (without the goat shit). Yet the moot point in all this was – and is – that the 'female collectives' are effectively job-creation and maintenance organisations for women who have 'lost their place' in traditional society, and the main reason is often the simple fact that they got divorced.

But attitudes and society are changing. Moroccan women are feeling more emboldened and less hidebound by the attitudes of their fathers (and mothers) than ever before. Back in 1960 the average age at which women married was 17, now it is over 26. I am fascinated to find the local newspapers producing statistics revealing that in 1982, the percentage of marriages involving girls aged between 15 and 19 was 17 per cent, whereas today it is just 9 per cent. It is not just that marriages are taking place later; more Moroccans, particularly women, are having doubts about the concept of marriage at all and either remaining single or choosing divorce. As recently as 1994, the percentage of single women aged 50 in Morocco was just 0.9 per cent, whereas by 2010, the last year for which figures are available, it had soared to 6.7 per cent.

The copy of *L'Opinion* I am reading has a virulent attack, signed by 'Sanae, a young woman in revolt', on what she calls the way 'men can be democratic and polite with their friends at the café, but tyrants to their womenfolk at home'.

She laments the position of her mother, 'oppressed by her male boss at the office during the day and in the evening by her husband at home. She spends all her time telling us all is well, all her needs are met, but I hate that at the end of every meal prepared by her little white hands, my father thanks

God, but never his wife, my mother.' She adds, 'Like all the women where we live, my mother has no time for herself.' But even the angry Sanae will not dare say where she lives, beyond 'a certain town'.

L'Opinion, the most liberal of the francophone newspapers, is proud that its daily double-paged spread 'Facebook in print for the youth of Morocco for 45 years' includes jokes and sayings that increasingly touch on the changing situation and old attitudes. Here's an example of what might be considered a modern-day Moroccan proverb: 'A woman's past is like an oil well. Don't light a match to look into it, it may blow up in your face.'

The jokes cut both ways, but reveal just how much the relationship between the sexes is a bit part in the national debate: 'Two soldiers in the desert ask one another, "Why did you sign up?" The first says, "Because I'm a single man and I like the excitement of war. What about you?" The other smiles ruefully and says, "Because I'm a married man and I long for a bit of peace."'

But right below it: 'A woman finds an old lamp in a cupboard and cleans it. Immediately a genie appears and says, "You have freed me, now name your wish." She replies, "I wish you could move that mountain which blocks the view from my window." The genie says, "That's impossible, ask for something easier." She thinks for a minute and says, "Give me a perfect man." The genie replies, "Okay, now where did you want me to put that mountain?"'

There are few women, even in the West, who would not smile at that. It is indicative enough of changing attitudes that Moroccan jokes about the gender relations (what used to be called the 'war of the sexes') would get a laugh in London, Paris or New York. The following perhaps, particularly in Paris: 'There is this young wife who shortly after her marriage goes out one night and doesn't come home until the morning. Her husband is furious, but she insists it was too late to walk home so she spent the night with one of her friends. When she is not about, he rings up her 10 best friends and asks if his wife spent the night with them. Each one in turn says "no".

'The next night, he goes out and doesn't return until morning. His wife is furious and asks where he was. He tells her he spent the night with one of his male friends. When he leaves the room, she rings up his 10 best friends to ask if it was true. The first eight all confirm his story, and the last two add, "In fact he is still here, asleep."'

I have since told that one in a few British pubs and got a laugh of recognition from all the male company. And a sigh of sarcastic recognition from any women present.

11

Oujda, the Final Frontier

I AM NOT SURE why I have come to Oujda. Because it is the end of the line, the final frontier. Although it is not even that really, given that it is occasionally possible to ride a mostly disused line south on the 12-hour return trip to the small desert town of Bouarfa, on a railway line built in 1941 by Vichy France to mine ore for the Axis war effort.

In real terms, however, Oujda has been Morocco's dead end ever since the Algerian frontier to Morocco closed in 1994. Oujda has all but lost its *raison d'être*. It just doesn't know it. Once upon a time there were plans for a Maghreb super train network, the *Projet Euro-Med*, a grand design for a railway that would traverse national boundaries all the way across North Africa, and, in the more fanciful schemes, even under the Straits of Gibraltar and on to Madrid. Needless to say, the realities of politics have relegated that dream to the world of future fantasy.

Yet the rail link keeps Oujda alive and very much part of the Moroccan mainstream. When the frontier was open, its links to relatively close Oran meant that some of Algeria's vibrant *raï* music scene spilled across. For somewhere so distant from the urbane west coast of Morocco, this city retains a very European feel, resolutely francophone. There is even an Ibis hotel next to the station, where I book myself a room. It is subtitled Ibis Moussafir but it feels as if I am in some provincial city of metropolitan France – Tours, maybe, or Angoulême.

I walk along boulevards that could also be provincial France, to a medina unlike any other. For a start it is tiny, and none of the buildings are more than one storey high, but most remarkably of all, it is no warren of alleyways but is built on a grid system. The reason is that here not just the *ville nouvelle* but the 'old town' too was built by the French who occupied Oujda on two separate occasions in the 19th century, long before the protectorate, having taken it from the Ottoman Turks who had been masters here for a century. Surprisingly, I still manage to get lost, as several of the lanes have been 'modified', in other words, closed off. Moroccans and grids just don't go well together.

When I finally reach the edge of the medina, I come across an edifice as unlikely as the Ibis: a small Catholic church, which on closer inspection turns out to be the old French cathedral of Saint Louis, which still offers mass two days a week. The Commander of the Faithful, his majesty, is tolerant of Christians and other religions in Morocco, although proselytising is strictly banned. A few kilometres outside town the little village of Sidi Yahia is supposed to be where John the Baptist (*Sidi Yahia* in Arabic) is buried, though save for a festival in autumn when locals tie scraps of cloth to bushes, there is nothing to see. I give it a miss.

Security outside the cathedral is high, with large numbers of police on every corner, although there is no obvious reason. The people of Oujda seem set on no more than the typical evening promenade, buying balloons and ice cream for small children. Even so there is an edge in the air. At one corner a grey-haired man in jeans and a sweatshirt comes up to me and asks the inevitable: 'Where are you from?' I try to give him the usual brush-off, assuming he is trying to seek something or ask for money. But he puts a hand out and takes me by the arm and, flashing a badge, says: 'No, no, sir. We are police.' I am wondering frantically what offence I might have accidentally committed, when he smiles and says, 'Are you all right? Is everything okay?' I say yes, and he nods politely, and says, 'Very good, please enjoy Morocco.' He returns to conversing with his friend, a younger, heavier-set man standing next to a motorcycle. Maybe it is just that they don't get many foreigners out here, but the incident is at once reassuring and disconcerting, as it always is in a foreign country when the people most concerned for your welfare appear to be secret police. I recall the police I encountered in Marrakech and, considering the security, wonder fleetingly if the king is in town. It occurs to me that I might be taking the 'King and I' syndrome a bit too far, but then it is clear that like mediaeval European monarchs who travelled widely to let their subjects see them and know that all is under control, Mohammed VI keeps a careful eye on his subjects, and likes them in return to know that he is concerned enough to visit all parts of his kingdom regularly, yet often without ceremony.

The Café de France, with the usual tables of smoking men drinking tea on the street outside, looks a possibility for a bite of dinner. The waitress seems glad to see me, but firmly and politely tells me that if I want a glass of wine, I shall have to sit in the restaurant upstairs. It is not the most cheer-inducing atmosphere: a large room with blue lighting, one other solitary diner – a middle-aged corpulent man smoking a cigar – and with a television on in one corner.

I order the pan-fried sea bass, almost immediately afterwards realising that it is probably a mistake at this distance from the coast. It arrives, dry and tasteless, with a dollop of couscous on the side. But then nobody recommended Oujda to me for its cuisine. After a while I become aware that the television programme I have been largely ignoring has, for Morocco, an unusually high number of 'action women' in skimpy bikinis or short skirts and push-up bras. It is only when the credits roll that I realise it is an ancient 70s episode of *Charlie's Angels*.

Already Oujda is winding down for the evening when I spot the couple of doormen outside the Hotel Ryad (not exactly a riad, but an ageing French sort of travelling salesman's bed-for-the-night place). But that is usually a sign that there is a bar where I can have a night cap. It is on the fourth floor, and looks more like a restaurant, with tables laid, a few people eating, and just a couple of drinkers at a long aluminium, French-style bar.

The waiter smiles and suggests, inevitably, a bottle of Flag, and pours some nuts into a little dish. His name is Ahmed, and he seems a friendly bloke, willing to have a chat. I ask him if the restaurant ever gets busier than this. He looks at his watch, smiles broadly and says. 'Just wait. It is not really a restaurant.' And indeed, within the next half hour or so, more and more people drift in until the place is jammed, every table taken and the bar crowded. Which is when the music starts up, and the fat ladies appear and I realise I have stumbled into Oujda's equivalent of the Casablanca Cabaret Oriental.

*

Breakfast the next morning is a dire disappointment and I realise that choosing the Ibis for a spot of European 'luxury' was a mistake. The orange juice is French, which means it comes out of a bottle rather than the freshly squeezed stuff that is all I have drunk in the way of juice for the past few weeks. Worse: I have to fetch my own coffee from a Nescafé machine. I emulate the Moroccan guests by ignoring the buttons that offer 'espresso, capuccino, long, etc.' all of which dispense a small shot of coffee followed by a long gush of water or milk into your cup on the drainer below. The thing to do, the Moroccans know, is to keep your cup in your hand, not on the drainer, push any button at random, then quickly insert your cup to get the shot of coffee, remove it before the dilution material pours out, then repeat.

By now I think I have got the measure of Oujda, and spend the day rather aimlessly wandering the streets. There comes that point in travelling when the country that initially seemed so alien has become the backdrop to your life and you stop noticing things. It is a sure sign that it is time to move on. A North African frontier town that would previously have seemed exotic has become humdrum. I have acclimatised. Too much. I find myself spending the day, like most Moroccan men, with time to spare: wandering the backstreets, checking out the mobile phone offer, stopping here and there for a coffee, or a mint tea. The souk in the medina seems like a normal shopping street, which it is, in comparison to the organic chaos of Fez or Marrakech, even though there is still a distinct jewellery quarter, with intricate hand-made silver brooches and earrings, a fruit market with ruby oranges, high piles of ripe tomatoes that would fail any of the uniformity tests of our supermarkets, and baskets of fresh strawberries, which here, in late April are at the height of their season.

Again, like many Moroccan males of a certain age, I wander into a bar and order a cold Stork beer, only to find that what Oujda's restaurants still lack in culinary expertise, its bars make up for plentifully. By the time I have downed my third beer – it is a hot day, I have time to kill and an overnight train journey ahead – I have already had one of the better lunches of my trip: *harira,* lentil soup, a spiced potato salad, a tomato and cucumber salad, and lamb couscous. All these come in minute portions, no bigger than a saucer – including the soup – but on a hot day with a cold beer in a shady bar, they make for more than adequate sustenance. In fact, it would seem most of the men drinking in the Concorde where the medina meets the busy main street are here as much to eat as to drink. And smoke, of course, although the Concorde features one of the more interesting, unusual, if particularly selective No Smoking signs I have seen: *Interdit de fumer le hachiche. Kif* is off.

✳

Railway buffs may be disappointed that I have not given more details of rolling stock and on-board experience of Moroccan trains. That is because I am pleased to report, if rather disappointed from a writer's point of view, that they are remarkably humdrum: not the swish *TGV* experience of France or Spain, or even the *ICE* in Germany, but if you are used to travelling on British (or indeed American) trains, there is really not much difference. They are, as a rule, remarkably similar to the standard of most British rolling stock, and their timekeeping, cleanliness and quality of service little different too. All in all, a far cry from the dilapidated chaos of Cuba. As it turns out, the leaving of Oujda is unquestionably the most pleasant experience I have had on Morocco's until now serviceable but unremarkable railways.

On my train journeys around the US I mostly slept in my seat, except for an endless sojourn through the wasteland that is Texas. Traversing Cuba, like everybody else, I slept where and when I could: on trains, in waiting rooms, when and wherever there was a chance of doing so without missing a train that didn't abide by a timetable (all of them). In Russia I have slept in *myagkii* (soft) class, in Soviet days when that was all foreigners were allowed to book, bizarrely to prevent us infecting the natives with dangerous ideas of democracy: cosy little two-berth compartments with a fierce lady *dezhurnaya* at the end of each one to keep out strangers and provide a constant flow from her in-coach *samovar* of glasses of hot tea in little pewter holders engraved with the Soviet star, hammer and sickle. Since the counter revolution (or whatever) I have also travelled from Moscow to Vilnius in the *obshchii vagon,* the hard-benched communal car, which most of the male inhabitants deserted mid-trip to go and watch the 'special' movies in what was effectively a hard-core porn cinema on rails. Despite the lack of security and obvious risk of theft, everyone looked out for everyone else, and conversation led to a father and son, with whom I shared the same hard bench to snooze on, inviting me to come to Karaganda one day and join them on a paddle-steamer bear-hunting expedition, an offer that to this day I regret never having been able to take up.

In this case, I confess to being a wimp. My timetable called for me to catch the last train out of Oujda back in the general direction of Tangier. There were two alternatives: one to take the seated accommodation only, which left at 20.00 but required changing trains at Sidi Kacem (the Crewe of Morocco?) at 2.57 in the morning, before arriving at Tangier around dawn. The other, much more inviting option, was to take the later 21.10 to Casa Voyageurs, via Rabat, where I would, in theory, arrive at the relatively more civilised hour of 6.15, and have little over 20 minutes to wait for a connecting train north, having had at least the advantage of a decent night's sleep, which, again in theory, was what ONCF promised! I would be travelling on the 'Train Hotel', Morocco's equivalent of the Trans-Euro-Nuits, with the option of six-berth couchettes, four-berth cabins, doubles or singles. Now, given Morocco's conservatism when it comes to gender separation, I decided to go for the ultimate in luxury – I mean how luxurious could a Moroccan train be? – and opted for the first-class single.

A hotel train in Morocco: you had to be joking? No? I was even so concerned about getting a ticket – in case the train itself was full, never mind the comfy cabins – that I went to the effort of booking it in Rabat five days early. The price: an extortionate, by local standards, 650 dirhams (£50), about the same as a second-class off-peak single from London to Liverpool.

When I arrived at Oujda station, having taken the precaution of buying a bottle of water from the kiosk – and pinching a wine glass from the Hotel Ibis so that I would be able to glug from the half-bottle of wine concealed deep in my rucksack (though I would still have no alternative when it came to opening it but to force the cork in with the handle of my razor), I was directed to a smart chef-de-train, who assured me he could keep my ticket for the duration of the journey and wake me on arrival in Rabat, and he told me to take carriage 1, compartment 2. Still unsure of what awaited me, I walked down a corridor of closed doors, and mine opened into a little wonderland of rail delight! Only a country that believed in the separation of the sexes could have dreamed up such a little cell of individual mobile comfort: to the right of the door, a narrow but adequate single bed with clean sheets and red velvet counterpane; to the left, a forward-facing seat, a space for luggage, and a sink fully equipped with a pre-chilled half-litre bottle of mineral water; today's newspapers in French and Arabic, a little plastic vanity bag containing razor, toothbrush, toothpaste, cologne soap, sewing kit and shoehorn. And to the side, a power point. Okay, so the walls may be woodgrain Formica, but when I touch them, they are genuine wood veneer, and compared to what I had been expecting ... a veritable riad on wheels!

Of course, there is no running water, at least not when you expect there to be – not on demand, and not in the corridor toilet either; even though it makes a sound of running water there is no particularly evident H_2O. And that is not helped by the inclusion of a little bottle – in the vanity kit – of what is proudly labelled 'toilet water, which somehow never sounds the same as the original French *eau de toilette*.

A 5.30 wake-up call is softened by the smiling conductor delivering a breakfast that is at least as good as anything served in the Oujda Ibis, with orange juice – a bottle is acceptable on a train – a warm croissant and hot fresh coffee poured from a pot. I change trains at Rabat for the early morning connection to Tangier.

By now, the first stage of Morocco's first high-speed rail link, modelled closely on France's *TGV* network but as controversial in budgetary terms as Britain's still unstarted HS2 from London to Birmingham, should be up and running. When I was last in Tangier, with Abdel, nine months earlier, we could clearly see the groundwork being laid for the track. When it is finished, it will cut the journey time from Tangier to Casablanca from three hours and thirty minutes to two hours, all in line with the grand plans for the development of Casa Port. But the first stretch, due to open in 2013, has now been postponed to 2016, so it is at a sedate pace, giving plenty of time to observe Tangier's gently sloping hillside medina, that we crawl into the once sleazy port that for centuries has been hailed as the Gateway to Africa.

12

Tangerine Dreams

TANGIER IS THE PART OF MOROCCO that almost wasn't, which lends a quixotic note to the hordes of tourists who flock over from the Spanish *costas* every year for a much-trumpeted 'taste of Africa'.

Over the millennia, the city that first entered history as *Tingis,* the Latin corruption of the Berber word for swamp, has been grabbed in turn by every power that ever aspired to have control over the entrance to the Mediterranean – which means most of them. In recent centuries it has been Portuguese, Spanish and British, while both Germany and France had aspirations here. This was where the last sultan of pre-independence Morocco was exiled after the country was partitioned by France and Spain in 1912. But there was no way Britain, then the prime global maritime power, was willing to cede access to its rivals, and from 1923 until independence in 1956 – apart from a brief Francoist occupation when France was on its knees from 1940 to 1945 – it was an 'international city'.

During the Second World War, German, French, Russian, American and British spies would hang out together at the Café de France, swapping secrets and women. And more than occasionally, boys. Tangier's 'international' status theoretically meant it was subject to a special code of law; in effect the law cared only about treaty status and great power influence over the straits. Local customs and morals atrophied, to the delight of the more louche, artistic, and in the eyes of their more straitlaced Western contemporaries, blithe spirits of Europe and America.

Homosexuality – for so long taboo and illegal in Europe to the extent that great men were jailed (Oscar Wilde in the 1890s) or threatened with chemical castration (as was inflicted on computer genius Alan Turing in the 1950s), but now so accepted that to even show surprise at two men kissing in the street is considered uncivilised – was, like the consumption of *kif,* one of those things that Moroccan law simply preferred to ignore.

It was also a refuge for paedophiles, particularly though not exclusively homosexual. The old adage, and one frequently cited in Europe and America as an insult to 'effeminate' Arabs – 'across the river there is a boy with a bottom like a peach but alas I cannot swim' – applied particularly in Tangier, and was not even considered unusual. It was just another hangover from antiquity, perhaps even going back to the days of the Roman empire, when for a general to take a boy for a lover was accepted but a grown man frowned upon. It was to Tangier that Evelyn Waugh's hopelessly romantic and subliminally gay aristocratic antihero Sebastian Flyte retreated with his teddy bear, Algernon, to die of alcoholism.

But it was not just a 'perverts' haven', as some Europeans claimed at the time. It was genuinely an inspiration to artists seeking a relatively safe taste of the exotica Africa had to offer: Eugène Delacroix, Henri Matisse, Camille Saint-Saëns, William Burroughs, and last, and possibly most enduringly, the American writer and composer Paul Bowles whose novel *The Sheltering Sky* and translations of Moroccan native authors made him one of the great apologists for the kingdom of the sultans. He moved here in 1947 and lived in a modest Tangier apartment until his death in 1999.

Effectively, modern Islam only arrived in Tangier in 1956 when it joined the new Kingdom of Morocco. Tangier has retained some of its reputation, mostly undeservedly, to the extent that it has gone from being one of the world's great fleshpots to a relatively relaxed modern city with arguably a less *risqué* reputation for sleaze than its Spanish counterpart, Malaga. The ancient port of Tingis is now being turned into a yachting marina, while the new container port east of the old city – *Tanger-Med* – is being developed to rival the other great ports of the sea at the centre of the old world: Alexandria and Marseille.

Yet the old veneer lingers. Tangier has more open-to-the-street bars than any other city in Morocco. I find myself drawn to seek out some of the supposed haunts of the roués who once upon a time gave Tangier its unsought reputation. One of the most famed is Dean's Bar, named after the enigmatic character who ran it during the 1940s and 1950s. Nobody to this day is absolutely certain of his real name or nationality, and inevitably he has been repeatedly identified as the role model for Humphrey Bogart's Rick in *Casablanca*, though that is almost certainly post-factum wishful thinking. All that is certain is that he spoke English with a perfect Oxford university accent, was the soul of discretion and ran a bar that was all things to all men, and quite a few women. Among the rumours surrounding his identity are that he was a half-Egyptian Englishman raised in London's Notting Hill, and that his father was a West Indian who had had an affair with a Ramsgate seaside boarding-house landlady. He sold drugs, dressed occasionally in women's clothing but his real trade was in people. Amongst his clientele were Errol Flynn, Samuel Beckett, Jean Genet, Ian Fleming and Ava Gardner. If you wanted to leave a safe message for anyone in Tangier, you left it at Dean's. Likewise, if you wanted a little girl or a little boy, you let Dean know and it was done. He died in 1963 and has a headstone that proclaims simply, 'Dean. Missed by all and sundry.' By the 1970s, the tail end of the hippie wave that washed over Morocco in the direction of Marrakech,

Dean's Bar was a second-rate celebrity hangout, then closed and reopened, with almost all vestiges of its notorious past removed.

I know from the tourist maps where it is supposed to have been located, but in the end I stumble across it totally by accident after a morning investigating the souk in search of that classic piece of Moroccan kitsch – a leather pouffe, no Tangier double-entendres intended – for a friend back in England. My quest is successful, even in terms of price. By now, like taxi fares, I have got the hang of bargaining. The *'J'habite à Casa'* – I live in Casa – line helps. When presented with an initial price, I offer 30 per cent, face a return serve of 80 per cent, up my ante to 40 per cent, and eventually as I walk out the door am handed the said pouffe for 50 per cent of the original asking price, coupled with a stern look from the shop proprietor and the gratifying words, *'Tu est dur.'* I like to think so.

Leaving the souk at the top of the hill, in dire need of a seat, what should greet my eye but a beer sign, that rare sight in any Moroccan town, with the exception of Casa; in this case, it's for Mützig 33, which inevitably isn't on sale inside. Or anywhere else in Morocco as far as I can see. I stagger through the door, blind from exchanging brilliant sunlight for darkness save for the glimmer of the inevitable television, and find I have accidentally wandered into 'Dean's Bar, founded 1937', according to the sign on the door.

No Disneyfied recreation of long-gone glory days of sleaze, sex and drugs, Dean's Bar today is a typical Tangier boozer, which is to say a lot more inviting than those in many other, more conservative Moroccan cities: for a start it keeps the door open, even in the daytime, so a passer-by can actually see the consumption of alcohol taking place. And indeed, as elsewhere, most of the alcohol is being consumed by other Moroccans, exclusively male in this case, although there is a large, mixed-sex group of young Spaniards in one corner taking advantage of better, cheaper and more plentiful quantities of their native pub grub than available back home: tapas.

I plonk my pouffe and other bags in a corner – the bar is rammed – sit down, and order a Stork, always a sign of the cognoscenti, choosing the bigger 0.33cl quantity over the 0.25cl bottle of the more well-known Flag/Spéciale. It arrives within seconds, rapidly accompanied by a small dish of four grilled anchovies, with a slice of lemon. Delicious. The inevitable television in the corner is showing the inevitable Spanish football match, but before I even have time on this occasion to notice the score and teams – usually by how many Réal Madrid are beating their hapless opposition – the barman has seized the remote control and is flicking, not through the channels, but through the satellites. From the huge list that appears – Al Jazeera, Eurotel, Ariadne, etc. – he eventually plumps for FR3. The display advises him that the satellite is being moved – something that wasn't even imaginable in dear old Deano's spooking days – and within seconds the telly has switched from footie to *le cyclisme,* which may or may not be the *Tour de France*: a barrage of fit young men in Lycra hurtling through some provincial French village.

By now, I have got round to ordering a second Stork, and with it comes a little saucer of paella, and a very good little paella it is, not just as I had first imagined, a bland vegetarian version, but a richly flavoured saffron-and-stock medley of rice, peas, peppers and chicken. A tiny quantity, but apart from lacking the expensive seafood, undoubtedly one of the better paellas I have ever eaten. And this for nothing, in a tiny, albeit famous, corner bar, and one which despite its faded fame charges no more for its beer than any other of the same level, and certainly a hell of a lot more relaxed than almost anywhere in Marrakech.

Beer three is accompanied by a dish of spiced chickpeas in sauce, with the tiniest amount of lamb, which is more for flavour than protein content, but it does its job admirably well. And while I am just thinking that my three beers (less than two English pints, it should be remembered) might do for now, a further plate of grilled anchovies comes out, and and I feel obliged to order a fourth in thanks. Or that is my excuse. The footie is back on, Italian rather than Spanish this time, and Milan's *Internazionale* are winning 3–0. There are worse ways of spending a Sunday afternoon.

The other great legend among Tangier's bars, also not what it used to be, is Caid's Bar, the extremely salubrious watering hole of the most stylish and expensive hotel in Tangier, El Minzah. It is named after Caid McLean, a Scottish soldier who wandered far from home in the 19th century and became a general in the army of Sultan Moulay Hassan. A portrait of him in full Moroccan military fig, all but identical to that worn by the Royal Household guards to this day, hangs on the wall of the bar, largely unregarded by foreign drinkers, most of whom think 'Caid' is some sort of unusual Celtic Christian name, whereas in fact – normally transliterated as Kaïd – it is a Moroccan title, roughly translated as 'general' or 'feudal lord'.

A huge man who had begun his military career in the 69th (South Lincolnshire) Regiment of Foot, he literally threw his weight about among his subordinates, and he remained a true Scot and keen bagpipe player. He fought in British colonial conflicts in Bermuda and Canada before being posted to Gibraltar, where he became friendly with the British consul-general in Tangier, Sir John Drummond Hay, who, after McLean nearly wrecked his career and reputation by having an affair with a senior officer's wife, covered up the scandal and persuaded him he would be better off resigning his commission, crossing the straits and joining the sultan's army. He did, and despite retaining his Scots identity – to the extent of regularly playing the bagpipes – he adopted local costume and customs and was even sent back to Britain as an emissary of the Moroccan court, upon which he received a KCMG, effectively confirming that he had all along been a British agent.

After the death of Hassan I, he continued to serve his ill-fated son and heir Moulay Abdul Aziz and, sent on an expedition to deal with the rebel Ahmed al-Raisuli, he was captured by the bandit chief and held prisoner for seven months, to be released only on the payment of a substantial ransom of some £20,000. That was the third and (by a hair) most risky of three occasions on which McLean's career was nearly curtailed, the first being his Gibraltar affair, and the second, potentially more dangerous, when, as a keen amateur medic, whose actual competence was restricted to a knowledge of the contents of his first-aid box and a book of instructions, he was asked to provide both an antiseptic for an injured palace servant and an indigestion cure for some young women in the sultan's harem.

He sent potassium permanganate tablets for the former, and tonic water for the latter. Unfortunately the recipients confused them, and the ladies swallowed the tablets, causing them to break into fever and vomit up what appeared to be blood. It took some hasty explanation from McLean and a lucky recovery by the ladies for him not to suffer having some body part struck off as a result. 'The Caid' eventually married a suitable Scottish lady, Eleanor Dulce Maclachlan, but his real love, like that of his contemporary Walter Harris who met him on several occasions, was Morocco and he died within months of returning to Britain in 1920.

Given its history, it is no surprise that Tangier is mostly *ville nouvelle*. But its medina has its charm, once you get past the fringe of souvenir shops for the 'taste of Africa' tourists. I wander through the fish market, in awe at the quantity and quality of fresh red mullet, squid, octopus, sea bass and bream, all glistening and shining – much of it still writhing – and stop off at a little coffee shop Abdel's cousin introduced me to, where I buy a half-kilo bag of freshly roasted and ground espresso. Unlike most of the sprawling medinas of the interior, the European influence on Tangier means that the 'old town', which somehow seems more appropriate terminology, is less of a warren and more of a mediaeval-style *cité*, with the two squares on its edge integrating it with the rest of Tangier. The lower, the *Petit Socco* is a sloping hillside piazza lined with cafés, a favourite with ageing Englishmen in chinos, pink shirts and panama hats who walk hand in hand, fondly imagining themselves still in the universe of Sebastian Flyte.

I have just found my place, on the edge of the shade, so I can choose to have a little sunshine if I want it – an option considered unthinkable by sensible Moroccans who hog the seats as deep as possible under the canopy, lined up against the café walls like vampires on a day trip – when a shoeshine boy comes up, begging for work.

Once upon a time, my instinct would have been to shoo him away with exasperation, not least for being disturbed by someone little better than a beggar. On my first trip to the Arab world several decades ago, a visit to Tunisia in my early twenties, I spent hours on end virtually every day shooing away a pestilential small boy who persisted in following me and my girlfriend around crying '*Schuh pützen, Schuh pützen*', having for some reason or other – probably our blonde hair – decided we were German. Trying to explain to him, in French or English, that we were not, was as much a waste of time as trying to persuade him that we did not want to have our shoes polished, not least because, to the best of my recall, we were wearing trainers.

This time, however, I have no such compunction; I nod politely to the young man – a lad in his early twenties – and put my feet out. I am wearing brown leather Birkenstocks, the only shoes that allow me to tramp hot dusty cities all day long without being crippled (and even then), and he sets to work. I owe my new-found conversion to having my shoes shined in public to my Moroccan friend Abdel, who, while we were sitting in a similar situation outside a café, convinced me to give it a go, having made the indisputable observation, 'Your shoes look like shit!' I reluctantly agreed, and after a couple of minutes, my tired, scuffed, scratched leather uppers no longer made me look as if I was on my uppers. When the lad had finished I asked Abdel awkwardly how much I should give him; the difficult bit, you see, is that they never mention a price, almost as if it is a public service they are performing. 'Give him whatever you like,' said Abdel unhelpfully. I thought for a moment and pulled out a 20-dirham note. Abdel shook his head imperceptibly but sternly, so I rooted a little more in my pocket and handed over a ten-dirham coin. The lad did his best not to look disappointed as the note slipped back into my pocket, took the coin and smiled happily. 'That was more than enough,' Abdel said approvingly.

This time I am conscious that I don't even have ten dirhams in coins in my pocket, and asking a shoeshine boy for change is hardly the done thing, but after a bit of rooting, I come up with 9.50, coming across one of the coins that for foreigners in Morocco may as well not exist, but for many locals is the stuff of life: a riyal. There are 100 of them in a dirham. This is a 50-riyal piece, worth slightly less than an English five pence, but when you put it into that context you see what an unreal life Western tourists in Morocco lead: five pence may be for many Britons small change indeed, but although we try to avoid them in change, we do not wantonly throw them away, and there more than a few (million) of our fellow citizens who literally count the pennies to make ends meet. How much more so then in a country where the living wage is a fraction of that in Europe?

By now the work is almost done, though the lad kneeling at my feet asks me, with minor embarrassment, to take off one shoe, noting that as the Birkenstocks are open-sided and I am not wearing socks, he has inadvertently got the tiniest smidgeon of brown Kiwi polish on the side of one of my feet. I wave the matter away, rubbing it off and handing him the shoe, which he proceeds to burnish to a mirror-finish glow, a remarkable transformation from the grubby scuffed items I had been wearing a few minutes ago. *'La playa!'* (Spanish for beach) he says, shaking his head, and indeed it was probably my afternoon stroll along the sands the day before that probably did most of the damage. I hand him the 9.50 and he smiles, puts his hand on his heart and says *'Merci'*, in best Tangerine international-speak, before hurrying off in search of another client.

I look down at my beaming Birkenstocks and wonder why the practice is not more widespread. I have just given my efficient young Moroccan what amounts to little over 80 pence, which to him is probably the equivalent of between two and three times that sum. If he could do half a dozen an hour he would be earning a lot more than the British minimum wage.

With my shoes newly sparkling I head down to Tangier's broad, sandy beach, lined with the disco clubs that will be hopping after dark. At this time of day, however, with the sun slowly slipping towards the horizon, it is still an oasis of familial calm: parents with children playing in the sand and paddling in the shallows. In the distance, cantering towards me along the shoreline, is a lone horseman, a solitary rider on the sands, a celebration of sheer *joie de vivre*. It is an image that will stay with me, of Tangier, but also of Morocco.

13

The Pillars of Hercules

THE TRIP FROM TANGIER to the border with Ceuta, or at least the nearest Moroccan town to it, some 35 kilometres to the west beyond the vast and rapidly expanding container port that is Tangier-Med, takes just about an hour, given the average speed of Moroccan buses. That is, if you get on the right bus. Deposited by my swift, efficient and cheap *petit taxi,* fast becoming my world-favourite means of urban public transport, just across the road from the semi-structured chaos that is Tangier's *Gare Routière,* I made my way inside to try to find information on the next bus to the town the hotel porter had phonetically spelt out to me as Fnidek. He had assured me that there were lots of them, and there were: so deregulated is the Tangier-area intercity transport system that there are any number of bus companies, all with their own little offices inside the terminal, each displaying a multiplicity of destinations in Arabic and French. I started looking for Fnidek and decided that Fni Daq was probably close enough to be the same place (hoping that phonetics and geography were allies here), but the buses seemed to be few and far between, the next in over 90 minutes' time.

The next window, however, also had buses to somewhere called Fenideq, which I was taking a punt on probably being the same. This company didn't seem to have that many either, but the next was sooner, less than an hour away. I stuck my head through the door and said something that hopefully somebody would understand to be where I wanted to go. (There couldn't be that many places so similarly named, could there?)

'Ah,' the guy behind the desk shouted, 'Fnidek,' (or whatever), 'si, ahora, ahora,' (Spanish for, 'now, now'). It is a feature of northern Morocco, particularly outside 'international' Tangier, that while French is the official second language, in practice it is Spanish, and even bus companies will have *viajes* rather than *voyages* painted on their signs. He pointed me towards the bloke by the door, or to be more precise, pointed the bloke by the door towards me; he duly came, grabbed me by the arm and led me out to where a bus was already revving up its engines, demanded 22 dirhams and ushered me onboard, luggage and all. So far, so good, yet again. Not least because there were only a few of us on board, and the driver seemed raring to go, although the ticket salesman told me it was leaving at 11.15, in just over 10 minutes' time. That ten minutes turned out to be more than enough for the entire bus to fill, to the extent that I was embarrassed at having to pile my rucksack on to my knee, when – had I known it was going to be rammed – I could have put it in the luggage hold like everybody else.

But only a few minutes late, we set out past the sprawling industrial outskirts of Tangier and into the rolling lush agricultural landscape that historically made the Maghreb, these strips of land and mountain between sea and desert, so coveted. Time went by. I was struck yet again by how quiet Moroccans are on all forms of public transport. Londoners are famously taciturn on the Tube, regarding it as almost a breach of manners to exchange any form of conversation, and anyone nattering to somebody else is an obvious tourist; it isn't the same on cross-country trains where the supposedly notoriously repressed English will rabbit on like lunatics, but not the Moroccans. I don't know what it is – shyness, respect, manners, worries about what to talk about and who might be listening (I seriously doubt the last but having spent years of my life living on the wrong side of the Iron Curtain, I never rule out the secret police, and there is no doubt that Morocco has them, although I seriously doubt they are listening for outspoken dissent on the buses). Nor was anybody reading. I find it disturbing enough in Britain today how few people on transport read, as opposed to just playing with their smartphones, but here nobody at all was reading a book, newspaper or even a Kindle, and nobody was really looking at their phones either, though there were more than enough incoming calls over the next hour or so.

Wait a minute! Next hour or so? It took that long for it to dawn on me. As mindlessly as any of my fellow passengers – and I dare say a good deal more mindlessly, as they clearly knew where they were going – I had been reading a bit, glancing out the window a bit, taking in with interest the view of the distant Rif Mountains and noticing that as we wound up into the foothills, it was getting mistier and colder. There were also a lot more police by the roadsides, carrying out the random checks – thankfully not on us – that are a feature of Moroccan life, particularly when you head east from Tangier into *kif* country, the mountain cannabis-growing farms. Except that I had expected us to be going along the coast. After nearly two hours we pull into a big city, which I quickly realise has to be Tetouan, the second city of North Morocco, and considerably further inland than I had intended to be. For most of my fellow passengers this was the end of the line, such that I even began to wonder if were going to Fnidek/Feni Deq/Fnidaq at all.

Sitting there in the stationary and by now three-quarters empty bus looking out at this large and growing city stretching up on all sides into the mists that descended from the mountains, I managed to get my concern across to one of the few other passengers remaining on board, an elderly lady in a turquoise jellaba with matching headscarf. To my relief, she nodded, saying, again in a sort of Spanish '*delante, delante*' – further on. Which, when finally I took a proper look at the map, seemed to make sense. Obviously what the bloke back in Tangier had done was the old trick of getting bums on seats: yes, his bus was going where I wanted to go, and it was leaving now; no need to mention that it wasn't going the direct route and that if getting there soon was my intention I would have done better putting my bum on the floor of Tangier bus station to wait for the next – faster – one!

But then I wasn't particularly in a rush. I had no idea if the border to Ceuta closed at night – I somehow doubted it – but it would have taken an extreme dose of bad luck for me to be delayed *that* much! Aptly, an extreme dose of bad luck was precisely what was now visited upon us. That or royal grace. When we finally set off again, for the next 20 minutes we barely moved more than as many metres, held up by a vast tailback of cement lorries, other buses and endless overfilled cars, all, of course, continuously parping like madmen. I was beginning to suspect a serious accident ahead when I became gradually aware of the enormous number of policemen on roadside duty, here and there backed up by men in khaki, obviously army personnel. It didn't look like an insurrection – although from the noise of their horns blaring it didn't sound that far off one – and the sight of a small control tower just up ahead to our right, gave me a hint. It could only be one thing: yet again his Majesty and I were to coincide. This suspicion – which in fact I have never been able to back up conclusively – was reinforced when the numbers of police and army doubled around the outskirts of the airfield, and then, when traffic finally began flowing again, we passed a large compound on the outskirts of town, with not just police and military at the gates, but also ceremonial troops in the unmistakable toy-soldier outfits of red with green capes. His Maj was *definitely* inbound, although judging from their relatively relaxed demeanour – and the fact we were moving – not just yet.

Tetouan is one of those cities – like so many others – that has from time to time felt less sure of its role in the kingdom. The ancient Berber city having been sacked by Romans in the first century, the Tetouan of today was largely begun by a combination of exiles – Jews and Muslims working happily together – when the Spanish dual monarchy of Ferdinand and Isabella, *los reyes católicos* (the Catholic monarchs) completed the *reconquista* of Spain for the Christians. They celebrated by sending Columbus off to discover America, and booted all residual Muslims and Jews out of the Iberian peninsula forever. A few centuries later, the Spanish added insult to injury by briefly invading when they thought Tetouan could be a base for an assault on their Ceuta fortress, and then finally making what they thought was an end to it by a fully fledged takeover in 1913, expanding and substantially rebuilding the city to be the capital of their North African Protectorate.

But Tetouan's main claim to a place in the hall of fame (or notoriety) in European history came in 1936 when a young army general based there got fed up with the wishy-washy socialist liberals running the country from Madrid, and declared he was launching a *coup d'état*. There are no statues of Generalissimo Francisco Franco in Tetouan today, yet those who like to see history as a series of swings and roundabouts – particularly true in the relationship between Morocco and the Iberian peninsula – will nod knowingly at the fact that Spain's bloody suppression of rebellion in its North African possessions directly resulted in the fascist victory in the civil war, thanks to the army of Rif tribesmen Franco was able to bring with him from Tetouan.

It was also Tetouan where the English fleet lay off – and it was English in 1704, not yet British; the Act of Union with Scotland came three years later – during the war of the Spanish Succession, when Admiral John Rooke, in theory acting on behalf of the Habsburg Holy Roman Emperor Leopold I, saw his chance to seize the largely undefended little outpost on the Rock of Gibraltar.

Not far beyond Tetouan the bus winds down along the coast through a series of holiday villages remarkably like Brighton and the English south coast, only with better weather. There are already symptoms of an urban, Spanish *costa*-style sprawl, with villas and hotel complexes swallowing up the coastline, while golf courses spread like a bad rash across the hinterland. Fnideq itself (let us settle on one spelling) is the last in the line, a pretty pastel blue-and-white seaside town, not as cutesy as its partners further south along the more obviously designated riviera, but all the more genuine for that, with a bustling souk that is clearly genuine (it does sell men's underwear), and a few beachfront cafés. Hungry and tired after a bus journey longer than anticipated, I dip into one that stretches along the seafront for a last Moroccan meal before crossing the frontier into the strange enclave that is Europe in Africa.

It turns out to be an inspired choice, full of Moroccan families with not so much a menu as a cold cabinet full of the freshest fish. I pick some mullet, squid and prawns and within minutes the chef has thrown them on the grill, sprinkled with salt, dusted with spice, and served with salad. Delicious, even if all there is to wash them down with is a glass of water.

Just before I leave, with an uncertain frontier crossing ahead of me, I need to find the toilets, but am reluctant to leave all my baggage, containing cameras, phones and money, just sitting there next to the door. I mention it to the waiter who looks at me at first uncomprehendingly, then almost angrily shakes his head. Just the idea that anyone would interfere with, let alone steal from, my possessions is almost an insult to the honour of his country. He puts his hand on his heart and points me to the bathroom. I feel like a schoolboy sent by teacher to the naughty corner. I had forgotten a line I had read in one of the translations of the old fables told by the storytellers in Jemaa el-Fnaa: no man is a thief, unless that is a profession.

It matches with a line from that intrepid Edwardian adventurer Walter Harris: 'In all life and on all my journeys I have made a point of trusting every one, and seldom, if ever, have I been disappointed. I have put natives taken from the wild mountain districts into positions of confidence. I have given them every facility to rob, but I have trusted to their honour and they have not failed me.'

*

The border with Ceuta, just a kilometre and a half north of Fnideq, is a classic scene of chaos: dozens of cars parked, if that is the right word – which it isn't; scattered more like – all around the approach to the multi-lane frontier, while pedestrians, including me and the six other passengers squirted out from our sagging Mercedes, are immediately seen as prey for the dirham-grabbing hustlers who descend on us like ravening vultures. They stagger – literally; most are glazed-eyed either from *kif* or alcohol – up, both hands outstretched, the one full of photocopied A6-sized paper versions of the Moroccan landing card, the one you are required to fill out on arrival in the country and (in theory, because I could find no sign of it being enforced) on departure. I shoved a five-dirham coin into the hand of one of these bleary-eyed touts (I had been warned that it can save substantial time queuing up for them), who reciprocated by pushing two scrappy pieces of paper into my hand (BOGOF offer at Ceuta frontier, don't miss out!). Sadly that did not stop his fellows trying to push exactly the same deal, remarkably undeterred by the fact that I clearly already had one (two, actually), nor the continuing hassle as I approached the pedestrian entrance to what I was to discover was not so much the frontier as the frontier corridor.

In all, the pedestrian corridor is nearly a kilometre long, with a concrete wall on one side, a high fence on the other – through which you can see the cars being unloaded and searched, along with their passengers – and barbed wire curled over the top. In sheer determination to get away from the bustle, I headed straight down it, without bothering with what seemed like the formality of showing anything at the little, low-windowed concrete box at the beginning. I had barely gone 50 metres when one of the touts who had, against all expectation, pursued me, called me back, urgently telling me I had missed Moroccan passport control. This, to be fair, halted me in my tracks. Despite unremitting distrust of the swivel-eyed touts, I had no wish to get on the wrong side of the Moroccan frontier police, or indeed reach the end of the long walk ahead of me only to be told I had to go back to the beginning. I turned around, reluctantly, and followed the retreating tout, by now being called at, with some urgency by his mates, for having apparently broached some unwritten rule by following me into the corridor, to find I was indeed expected to show my passport and the completed photocopied form, to a Moroccan emigration officer who duly rubber-stamped it. Managing – perhaps unkindly – to avoid the tout who had alerted me to my mistake but did not dare to venture down the corridor a second time, I set off on the half-kilometre trek to what was obviously the median point, where a laid-back (literally) Moroccan policeman in a reclining chair glanced briefly at my passport and waved me on for a further half a kilometre to where a sturdy Spanish policeman did the same and waved me through to a booth which separated EU and non-EU citizens, where I was once more duly waved through into Europe. In Africa.

My clear intention, now that I was in 'Europe', had been to jump in a cab and dump my luggage in the hotel before settling down to a nice cold Saint Miguel or Cruzcampo in the sun at an outside bar (rare luxury!), but this was not to be so easily fulfilled. For a start there was an obvious lack of cabs to jump into, the last having just been grabbed by a large Moroccan family, and it didn't look as if there would be any more arriving any time soon. The reason for that was a traffic jam of cars and buses stretching in the opposite direction for as far as the eye could see. The only upside to this depressing scenario was that there were several buses ready to depart from the border. I jumped on to the first, inquiring *'centro ciudad'* which elicited a nod, paid my €0.80 fare and we were off, a mere half dozen of us, including one stern-faced Moroccan woman in a headscarf who scowled at me the whole time as if I had no right to be on the same bus.

After 20 minutes or so of winding up hilly backstreets, remarkably similar to the working-class quarters of any small Spanish city except for the numerous red-yellow-red Spanish flags hanging from balconies along with the washing, in a defiant statement of nationality here on the cusp, eventually we wind down again into the compact town centre. I throw my bags into the hotel and head to the main square, only to find that every bar is closed. I had forgotten: I am in Spain in mid-afternoon. It's *siesta* time. The only place I can find open is a corner café on the main street with two blokes sitting outside drinking milky coffee and, God help me, mint bloody tea.

The waiter comes out promptly to ask with a beaming smile if he can help me. I order a cold beer, no matter what, and he shakes his head as if I were some naughty child and says, *'Cerveza no hay'*. I could murder him. I have walked into a bar run by Moroccans. That is why it is open, not only because they don't bother with *siesta*, but because it turns out this is *semana santa*, Holy Week. All the Spanish are indoors snoozing, because tonight they will all be out eating and drinking and watching the parade.

I spend the rest of the day grumbling, and reluctantly admiring Ceuta's impressive fortifications, and noting the large plaque that plainly states its place in the hierarchy of Spanish royal cities, as if it were not on another continent. But then I reflect that over the past two millennia the Spanish and Moroccans have each only ever seen the strait of water that separates the south-western tip of Europe from the north-western tip of Africa as a bridge rather than a divider. Ceuta in antiquity was an outpost of the Visigoths who ruled Spain, and remained a Christian stronghold until it switched sides before an advancing Arab army and became a launch pad for Tariq ibn Ziyad's attack on Gibraltar, which in turn restored the link with 'mainland' Spain as it in turn became part of the Caliphate. It is one of those twisted ironies of history that the Spanish claim to this exclave on the African coast dates its legitimacy back to the Moorish conquest of Spain. Apart from a brief spell of joint ownership by the kingdoms of Fez and Aragon, as odd a partnership as can be imagined, it has been Christian and under Iberian rule while Spain and Portugal were one country, and Spanish ever since.

It was from Ceuta that aircraft of the Fascist and Nazi regimes in Italy and Germany airlifted Franco's troops to the Spanish mainland after his declaration of rebellion against Madrid's republican government in 1936.

As evening falls, the drumbeats begin, and with dusk approaching the bizarre spectacle of Spanish Catholicism has transformed the town into a beautifully lit theatre of the absurd. No matter how many times I have been told that the Spanish Holy Week processions are all about love and faith, my Anglo-Saxon background – and particularly having been brought up as a Protestant in the North of Ireland where even the commonplace ritual of a Catholic mass was considered some sort of pagan ritual – I still find it odd and alien. The sight of a statue of the Virgin Mary, here revered as *Nuestra Señora de África,* carried shoulder-high and bowed down before the doors of the cathedral, almost makes me understand Islam's aversion to imagery.

But it is the sight of the procession leaders, many of them teenagers as well as older men, marching, swinging their incense burners, in purple robes with high pointed hoods and only holes cut for their eyes to see through that genuinely sends a chill down my spine. Our Americanised culture and the mythology – should I say demonology – of the Ku Klux Klan, whose racist rituals and lynch-mob mentality never had any impact on this side of the Atlantic, is too engrained for me to shed my shivers of apprehension. Nor is it helped the next morning when I discover, in a small square, a bronze of a man in the same sinister pointed hood leading a small child by the hand.

The ferry ride is barely a 40-minute journey, an internal trip on Spanish public transport, which lands in Algeciras. I gaze out through the spray-lashed windows at the great looming shape of Jebel al-Musa, the vast chunk of mountain that is assumed to be the southern of the two Pillars of Hercules. Although the straits are remarkably narrow – barely 14.3 kilometres (7.7 nautical miles) at the narrowest point – it is never possible from sea level to catch a glimpse of both 'pillars', the northern indisputably being the colossal bulk of the Rock of Gibraltar, given the curvature of the Earth. One of the best, relatively early, maps of the straits was made by the Ottoman cartographer Piri Reis in the early 16th century, clearly suggesting that the southern 'pillar' was Ceuta itself. But to me the legend of Hercules smashing through the original Atlas mountain, the barrier between the Mediterranean and the Atlantic and the protective wall for the mythical city of Atlantis, has to refer to some primordial cataclysmic change in sea levels, or maybe an earthquake, maybe even the myth of the Great Flood, that is reflected in the geology rather than the history books.

It is easy, and to a certain extent, legitimate for Britons to throw in Spain's face as hypocrisy the dispute over Gibraltar while it continues to hold Ceuta (and Melilla further east) on the Moroccan coast. The difference is that Spain treats its African coast possessions as integral parts of Spain, using the euro, whereas Britain and the Gibraltarians have insisted on a bizarre hybrid status. Gibraltar is in the EU – the blue-and-gold flag waves over its anomalous border posts – a British 'possession' but not part of Britain: almost the direct opposite of those other anomalous outposts, the Channel Islands. It even has its own currency – Gibraltar pounds, pegged to sterling, similar but separate. I can't imagine passing one over a bar in South London.

I have come back to Gibraltar not out of any outdated sense of national pride or imperial fervour, but because there are more regular flights back to London than from Tangier. And that is about all that can be said for it. Breakfast in the Queen's Hotel, a drab and dated block that is one of the few on the peninsula and like something out of Fawlty Towers: stale coffee, packets of orange juice.

'Would you like the cooked breakfast, sir?'

'What is it?'

'Bacon, eggs and baked beans.'

'Is there an alternative?' I ask, thinking of yesterday's double espresso, freshly squeezed orange juice, mineral water, and a ham and cheese croissant on the promenade in Ceuta.

'No.'

What arrives, served by an unshaven waiter who had to fetch a cup from another table and threw cutlery on to a dirty tray, is almost inedible; the bacon – the first pork to have passed my lips in weeks – soggy and limp, the eggs crispy at the edges from having sat in the pan too long, the baked beans: baked beans. Whatever the past or future of Gibraltar, it is a poor ambassador for the country it half claims to belong to: a relic of the worst of British seaside resorts circa 1955. With added smugglers.

Yet I cannot help but notice the dates inscribed on the great stone fortresses carved into the rock recognising the date of its conquest. From 1704 to 2014 is 310 years. That is substantially longer than the 212 years (1492–1704) when it was ruled from Madrid.

Maybe Abdel was right; we should give it back, to the Moroccans. It wouldn't half annoy the Spanish.

Epilogue

MOROCCO TODAY, the Morocco I was compelled to seek out and the people I discovered in journeys that, to be fair, only scraped the surface of one of the most entrancing countries on Earth, is a lesson to the world on how complex and how fragile human society can be. It is a civilisation that over the centuries has combined peoples, religions and cultures, and succeeded in merging them without smashing them against one another.

It is an Islamic country but without extremism or absolutism, one that history has swept into Europe and then has been washed over by Europe, a nation that has fused the ancient Amazigh-Berber peoples with the vast influx of the Arab invasions, taken in Jewish refugees along with Muslims from the vanished empire of Iberian Andalusia. Through the wars and collapse of colonialism in the 20th century to the tumult of the so-called 'clash of civilisations' and rampant extremism that have so far been the hallmark of the 21st, it has remained the perfect tightrope walker on the high wire over the chasm of disaster, into which, to a great or lesser degree, Algeria, Libya and Egypt all have fallen.

Much of the credit for this has to go to an institution a large part of the world regards as outdated and heading for extinction: monarchy. The Alaouite dynasty, which has held the throne of the sultans since the 18th century, staged the most remarkable comeback of all time when Mohammed V returned to restore his country's independence and declare himself no longer sultan but king in 1956. He and his successors have given a masterclass in managing the demands of democracy, too often backed by the so-called Western world without any consideration of what populist power can bring about, despite multiple demonstrations of disaster.

The post-independence kings of Morocco have had the power to become autocrats but have not, and in so doing have fended off the evils of unchecked revolution. They have listened to the theologians but also to the economists, to the conservative patriarchy but also to the young libertarians, to the capitalists but also to the trades unions, to the military but also to the civilian populace. They have not banned what does not need to be banned, but nor have they permitted what does not need to be permitted. To us in Europe or America, it might seem an outdated, less than perfect fusion of personal power and uncertain democracy. But those are both stages our nations have been through, and even today, it would be a foolish citizen who called any of our democracies 'perfect'. To the traveller – or just the tourist – I would say open your heart to Morocco and its people, trust them and be worthy of their trust in return.

The complex world we inhabit today is necessarily one of checks and balances. Morocco straddles a fault line between an ancient, paternalist, conservative tribalism and a new society where individualism is respected. Cities like Marrakech and Fez are proof that one need not conquer the other. There is place for both.